LITTL

NEIL CARRIER

Little Mogadishu

Eastleigh, Nairobi's Global Somali Hub

OXFORD
UNIVERSITY PRESS

OXFORD

UNIVERSITY PRESS

Oxford University Press is a department of the
University of Oxford. It furthers the University's objective
of excellence in research, scholarship, and education
by publishing worldwide.

Oxford   New York

Auckland   Cape Town   Dar es Salaam   Hong Kong   Karachi
Kuala Lumpur   Madrid   Melbourne   Mexico City   Nairobi
New Delhi   Shanghai   Taipei   Toronto

With offices in

Argentina   Austria   Brazil   Chile   Czech Republic   France   Greece
Guatemala   Hungary   Italy   Japan   Poland   Portugal   Singapore
South Korea   Switzerland   Thailand   Turkey   Ukraine   Vietnam

Oxford is a registered trade mark of Oxford University Press
in the UK and certain other countries.

Published in the United States of America by
Oxford University Press
198 Madison Avenue, New York, NY 10016

Library of Congress Cataloging-in-Publication Data is available
Neil Carrier.
Little Mogadishu: Eastleigh, Nairobi's Global Somali Hub.
ISBN: 9780190646202

Printed in India on acid-free paper

CONTENTS

PREFACE

This book seeks to understand Nairobi's remarkable Eastleigh estate and its transformation into a Somali-dominated commercial hub packed with shopping malls. It tells the story of how Eastleigh became a 'Little Mogadishu', offering urban refuge to thousands of refugees, and linking Kenya to both the worldwide Somali diaspora and to vast global networks of trade. The chapters that follow elucidate key factors underpinning the Eastleigh transformation and explain the ambivalence, and often suspicion, with which many in Kenyan society continue to view this estate and those who live there. The book also draws out the wider significance of Eastleigh by analysing the national, regional and global networks of which it is a part, showing how the story of this particular place speaks to many other urban transformations in our contemporary world.

The Eastleigh transformation, however, continues, and the speed with which history seems to take place within its environs makes offering a definitive account of the estate impossible. Eastleigh is caught within the changing political dynamics of the Horn of Africa and Kenya, and my research and writing have often involved recalibration to reflect these dynamics, especially those related to Kenya's military incursion into Somalia in 2011 and the subsequent horrors of Al Shabaab reprisals in Kenya. 2014's Operation Usalama Watch (which I discuss in chapter 7) emerged out of all these political dynamics and has had a profound effect on the estate, raising many questions about its future.

I write this preface at a time of yet more uncertainty for Kenya's Somalian refugees, a population crucial to Eastleigh's story and future development. As of July 2016, the future of the Dadaab refugee camp, a place intimately tied to Eastleigh, is especially hazy. It is threatened with imminent closure by the Kenyan government, and while this may well be a bargaining position rather than a realistic threat, the disbanding of Kenya's refugee agency (the Department of Refugee Affairs) suggests the government are serious about closing the camp, even if this means deporting its population to a still dangerous Somalia. In this uncertainty, the lives of those refugees who live in Dadaab and in Eastleigh grow yet more precarious, as does the future of Eastleigh itself, tied up as it is with these refugees.

There was temptation to include these new developments in the spirit of greater completeness. However, an author must move away from the keyboard at some point, accepting that ethnographic presents inevitably, and at times rapidly, become ethnographic pasts. And while new events may well alter this book's subject matter in some respects, in others recent developments follow all too familiar patterns from the perspective of Kenya's Somali population. Furthermore, while Eastleigh's transformation is ongoing, it builds on foundations delineated in this book: these foundations are the socio-cultural, economic and political processes that have forged its current shape and no doubt will play a role in shaping its future.

Of course, what insight this book does provide into Eastleigh's foundations is built on the contributions of many. Most important are those living and working in the estate who have shared so generously their time and stories. My debt to Mohaa is particularly great for all the business wisdom he passed on to his anthropological 'apprentice', and for making Nasiib Fashions such a welcoming refuge in the heart of this busy estate. His former business partner Siad, and others running nearby shops (including Lula), formed a wider web of friendly support without which the project would have floundered.

Other Eastleigh people and institutions have been crucial too. Sky School taught me the basics of the Somali language, while also teaching me more profound truths of human kindness and resilience through its staff (led so ably by Daud), and pupils. Sky's former teacher Dahir Hirey deserves particular thanks. Now resident in the UK, Dahir has helped greatly in translating various pieces of Somali, and in sharing his story of life post-Eastleigh and post-resettlement. All at the Eastleigh

PREFACE

office of Kituo cha Seria (especially Solomon, Sahara and Awol) deserve thanks not just for the help they gave me, but more importantly for the help they have provided so many refugees. It was a privilege too to get to know Burhan Iman, an energetic entrepreneur, and a key player behind Eastleighwood, a youth group I got to know well in my time in at the estate. Eastleighwood reveals the artistic force simmering away in a part of Nairobi more known for commerce, and I wish them all the best as they attempt to rival Hollywood, Bollywood and the rest. Over the years Blackie's kiosk has also proven a haven, one that placed me at the heart of Eastleigh's Meru contingent, while at the Grand Royal and Barakat Hotels I found great accommodation, and great contacts. I especially thank the Grand Royalists led by Abdihakim Aynte who formed an insightful focus group. Of course, I thank all other residents of Eastleigh who took the time to talk with me or respond to surveys, too many to detail here, though my young diaspora 'crew' of Nimo, Nasra and Yousef deserve a mention.

Many people have collaborated with me in conducting this research. Hassan Kochore has proven a fantastic friend over the years, and his research skills were crucial in working with the estate's Oromo. Hannah Elliott helped me much in researching the gold traders of Eastleigh, and in sharing insights drawn from her earlier research into its camel milk traders. Emma Lochery too has been a great source of inspiration, especially in our collaboration on an article where several ideas contained within this book were developed. All three of these young researchers are destined for great things. My old friend and collaborator Kimo Quaintance also brought much to the project, joining me in Eastleigh in 2011. There are few people better to enjoy the highs and lows of fieldwork with, and I thank him for all his contributions, intellectual and photographic.

Through Mohaa and Siad I met Elias Madey, another Eastleigh stalwart who has become a good friend. Elias introduced me to many people and places of great significance in the chapters that follow, and also proved a wonderful companion on a trip to Kisumu and Kakamega, where we followed networks of Eastleigh goods and practices. He was also invaluable in surveying many traders in the estate, as was another friend, and energetic contributor to the project: Kaamil. For Kimo and I, Kaamil catalysed our research, as within hours of meeting him we were meeting people across all echelons of Eastleigh society. I am also very grateful to a number of other Eastleigh residents who helped conduct surveys: Gitonga and Sophia for their work on the Meru side of things, and Kemal for his surveys of the Oromo. Gitonga deserves a particular mention for overcoming disability with grace and humour.

Beyond Eastleigh, Philimon Murungi deserves credit for helping me understand the intricacies of 'goodwill' payments, while Farah Abdulsamed has also helped greatly, and I draw on his Chatham House report in what follows. I thank too, all my friends at the British Institute in Eastern Africa and the Institut Français de Recherche en Afrique who provided help of many different types. IFRA in particular were instrumental in securing a research permit for the project, and I thank Amelie and Christian for their support. The Rift Valley Institute and its staff also aided the project by hosting a workshop in September 2014 on Eastleigh and Somalis in urban Kenya. This workshop was pivotal in many ways: I co-organised it alongside Tabea Scharrer of the Max Planck Institute, whose energy and drive have helped shape the recent direction of my own research and writing. The workshop drew together a stellar cast of researchers on the estate and Kenyan Somalis, more broadly, and allowed me to meet Mheshimiwa Yusuf Hassan, M.P. for Kamukunji, the constituency under which Eastleigh falls. This man has done much to change Eastleigh for the better, and it is a pleasure to know him. The workshop also introduced me to other important activists in the estate, such as Ahmed Mohamed of the Eastleigh Business Association, and Lul Issack, both of whom dedicate much energy to improving life there.

Numerous people have generously looked over chapters and helped me improve the ideas and material within (though any deficiencies remaining are, as the usual caveat goes, my own). Kari Dahlgren, Adam Gilbertson, Idalina Baptista, Gunvor Jonsson, as well as Hannah Elliott, Emma Lochery and others, have all dedicated time to this work. Adam also put in much work on the book's bibliography, as well as visiting the National Archives in London on my behalf. Of course, I wish to thank all at the Hurst team too for their diligent work on the manuscript and for the great front cover. I am also very grateful to Sebastian Ballard for his excellent maps.

This project would not have come about without the support of the Oxford Diasporas Programme, a programme of research led so ably by

PREFACE

Robin Cohen, alongside Nick van Hear and Olly Bakewell. The ODP administrative staff have been especially able and efficient. I thank them, and the Leverhulme Trust whose programme grant funded such a rich array of projects on diaspora. Dave Anderson has been a great ally of mine over many years, and I am grateful for his efforts in establishing the project. My home institution of Oxford also deserves much gratitude. My colleagues and students in African Studies and Anthropology have been a joy to work with over the last few years, while the University's Fell Fund was a vital source of additional funding.

My partner Amber has helped in countless ways: connecting me initially with Sky and Kituo, offering intellectual input from her migration and refugee expertise, and helping refine the book and its bibliography. And, of course, just for being there for me and our lovely Sylvie.

LIST OF IMAGES

LIST OF IMAGES

LIST OF MAPS

Map 1: Kenya

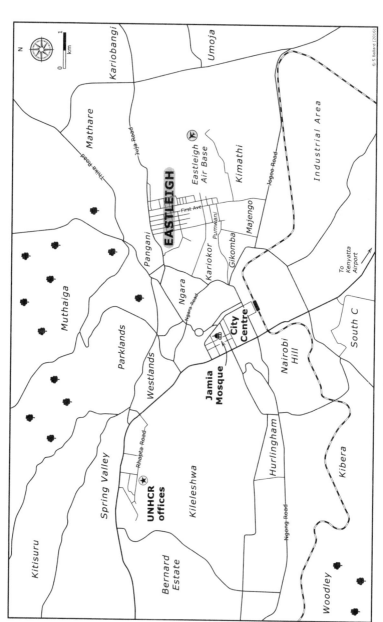

Map 2: Greater Nairobi

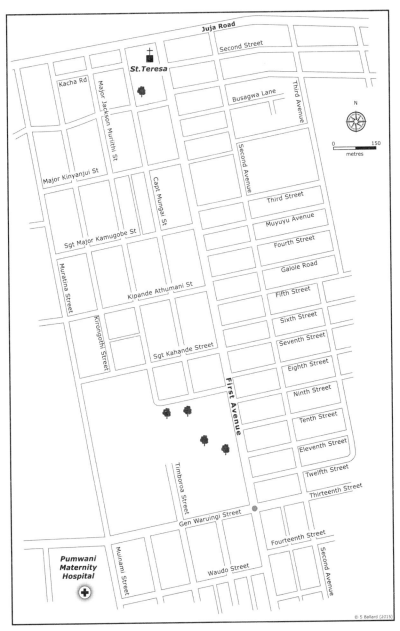

Map 3: Eastleigh

INTRODUCTION

WELCOME TO EASTLEIGH

Each morning, with a quiet prayer of *Bismillah ir-Rahman ir-Rahim*, Mohaa pulls up the shutters of Nasiib Fashions, a gentlemen's outfitters of small physical proportions crammed with a prodigious amount of clothing. Suits, shoes, T-shirts, football tops, belts and sundry other items neatly line its three walls, while a simple stool provides Mohaa with his perch for the day. Although modest in size, Nasiib Fashions is a prime representative of a commercial revolution that has developed over the last two decades; it and the thousands of shops like it—and the tens of thousands of small businesspeople like Mohaa who operate them—form the heart of a Nairobi estate so dominated by Somalis that it has gained the nickname 'Little Mogadishu'. This estate, only a few kilometres from the city centre, is officially known as Eastleigh—or Islii as Somalis[1] themselves refer to it—a place that has been transformed in the wake of the Somali civil war.

From the late 1980s onwards, hundreds of thousands of people have poured out of Somalia, most ending up in refugee camps in Kenya and Ethiopia. A significant proportion, however, came to Eastleigh, bringing economic as well as demographic change. As the real Mogadishu collapsed into conflict, Nairobi's Little Mogadishu became what it is today: a commercial hub that draws in not only refugees, but also shoppers from as far afield as Tanzania and Central Africa, and investors from the UK, USA and elsewhere. In the process, over forty shopping malls have mushroomed, all crammed full of hundreds of small retail

1

Plate 1: Mohaa at Nasiib Fashions, Eastleigh 2012

shops like Mohaa's that sell cheap textiles, clothes, electronics and other goods. Alongside these malls, multi-storey apartment blocks and hotels have also sprouted, overwhelming a once-residential landscape of single-storey buildings. Thousands now work in this estate, and many more have started businesses elsewhere in Kenya, supplied by the networks that run through it. Such is the volume of all these people, as well as traffic and new buildings, that Eastleigh's infrastructure has struggled to keep pace, its pockmarked and often sewage-filled roads gaining great notoriety. Despite infrastructural decay and a far from salubrious environment, its mass of commercial activity makes Eastleigh very valuable to Kenya, though the informal nature of much its business makes this value hard to quantify.[2] Certainly the many Kenyans who work, trade and shop there would testify to the opportunities its economy has brought.

However, despite the opportunities it has brought Kenya, this development is viewed with great ambivalence within and beyond the country: Eastleigh itself is held in considerable suspicion, and is imagined by many as a place of danger. Rumours persist in Kenya and beyond that the estate has been built on money-laundering of ill-gotten gains, and many fear that it harbours terrorists and terrorist sympathisers linked to the Somali militant group Al-Shabaab, which is in control of much of southern Somalia. Some even see it as a very alien place despite its proximity to the heart of Kenya. To them it really is a Mogadishu displaced: an estate where Somali identity and power are to the fore, and where similar dangers to those faced in Somalia are now felt on the home front. This impression of a dangerous place apart has recently been given the Hollywood treatment in the 2015 film *Eye in the Sky*, where US drone operatives target a house in an Eastleigh overrun by armed-to-the-teeth militia. For the people who live and work there, such representations matter: its population—especially its refugees— have suffered over the years at the hands of Kenya's security forces, including during the infamous Operation Usalama Watch (*usalama* means 'peace' in Kiswahili) in 2014 where many were rounded up and held in Nairobi's Kasarani Stadium, some being deported to Somalia.[3]

This reputation for danger and dangerous people has been heightened following the Kenya Defence Force's invasion of Somalia in late 2011, which had the avowed purpose of degrading the military power of Al-Shabaab and securing the Kenyan border. Sadly, rather than making Kenya more secure, at least in the short term, Operation Linda Nchi ('Operation defend the nation') has inspired attacks on Kenyan soil, 'blowback' as some commentators have labelled them.[4] These include the 2013 attack on the high-end Westgate Shopping Mall in Nairobi, the 2014 attacks on the village Mpeketoni near Lamu on the coast, and the 2015 attack on Garissa University College, where gunmen murdered many Kenyan students. Eastleigh itself has been directly affected by this insecurity, as a number of grenade attacks have occurred in the last few years—some deadly. Such insecurity means that the very name of the estate generates anxiety in some Kenyans, while British and US travel advisories urge their nationals to avoid the estate. Eastleigh has become a 'no-go' area.

Yet thousands continue to go to Eastleigh daily, mostly for the mundane purpose of earning a living, or shopping at establishments like Nasiib Fashions; others also continue to arrive seeking refuge. Furthermore, despite the advice of foreign governments, many foreign

3

nationals—British, American and others—also come to the estate. These are not Kenya's typical tourists, but Somalis from the diaspora who come to the estate to invest, as well as for holidays to catch up with family and enjoy a very Somali atmosphere lacking in their homes abroad. Thus, despite fears of insecurity and despite the advice of foreign governments, Eastleigh draws in crowds that rival London's Oxford Street at its busiest.

A Tale for our Times

This book is a historical and ethnographic portrait of this remarkable estate, that attempts to understand its commercial transformation and its societal implications for Kenya, Somalia and the wider Somali diaspora. At its heart are two core questions:

1) How has a once modest residential district of Nairobi transformed into a global, commercial hub in the wake of Somali displacement?
2) Why has this development met with such ambivalence, suspicion and even hostility?

These questions are worth answering for many reasons, but especially as how such a place is perceived and understood has a bearing on how its residents are perceived and treated. This is all the more important in the context of Eastleigh, where residents are subject to heavy-handed security operations. In this regard, clarifying the factors behind its growth is important as a number of widespread suspicions of what underlies its vibrant economy are wide of the mark, and unhelpfully add to perceptions of the estate as a place of exception where exceptional measures can be taken against its people. This is especially true of explanations linking its growth—and a general rise in Somali real-estate purchase in Kenya—to the recent flourishing of piracy in the Indian Ocean, explanations that rely more on stereotypes of Somalis than hard data. Such explanations stick, as many people accept the 'urban legend' of Eastleigh: a place of excess where anything goes and anything is sold.

This book attempts to get beyond this urban legend. Instead of invoking such sensationalised explanations as piracy, it explores more profound factors underlying its growth and its reputation. These factors are all linked strongly to the movement of people, capital and trade goods that are shaping the societies, economies and politics of our world, and to the responses of states and host populations to this movement. In telling the story of Eastleigh, one thus also tells a contemporary story of urban transformation in a world of movement and interconnectivity, one that connects to key themes in the contemporary study of migration, forms of global trade and the city, as I describe in the next two sections: one focused on the movement of people, the other on the movement of goods.

Migration, diaspora and urban transformation

Migration has been described as a defining issue of our century,[5] and few could doubt this in an age where so many try to move across borders in search of secure and better lives, while governments attempt to strengthen their borders and build fences to keep the migrants out. Policy makers the world over contemplate how to manage the dynamics of migration, and debate highly fraught questions of how much migration is too much or too little. An enormous self-perpetuating industry of policing and control has emerged in response to all this, generating not just profits and livelihoods for human traffickers, but for those charged with fighting them too.[6] Meanwhile, in academia, migration has generated a vast intellectual industry: migration studies is a booming field, while in anthropology—my own discipline—debates about transnationalism, diaspora and mobility are ubiquitous, recasting classical anthropological concerns such as kinship and identity. Around Eastleigh—a place built out of and transformed by migration—many of the most pressing themes in the migration debate coalesce.

Firstly, as a place known for its Somali refugee population, Eastleigh connects strongly to the so-called 'refugee crisis' of our era, tragically personified at the moment by the millions who have fled Syria. As a precursor 'fragile state', Somalia, and its two decades of conflict and forced migration, offers insight into the challenges of aiding refugees. Somalia's refugee exodus has led to an estimated 'missing million' of its citizens living outside its borders,[7] many in countries such as the USA and UK, but most much closer to home. Indeed, dealing with the hundreds of thousands of refugees—most 'warehoused' in the two large refugee camps of Kakuma and Dadaab—has been one of the greatest challenges of recent decades for Kenya, a neighbouring country to Somalia that, like Turkey and Jordan in the case of Syria, hosts far more refugees than the wealthier countries of 'Fortress Europe' and North America. Similar challenges of encampment and resource-strain— faced by host countries and the United Nations Refugee Agency (UNHCR)—characterise all such situations of protracted conflict.

Eastleigh's refugee population has long been a source of anxiety for the Kenyan state, especially given the government's avowed encampment policy, and given the emphasis it places on refugee repatriation as the 'durable solution' of choice in a context where integration appears unthinkable.[8] How to provide help to refugees living outside camps has also been a concern for the UNHCR, for whom Nairobi and Eastleigh have long been sites of experimentation for their urban refugee policy. However, refugee policy in this post-9/11 age is being shaped by a new emphasis on securitisation—refugee flows being seen as potential vectors for terror—and Eastleigh, as a place of suspicion through alleged links to Al-Shabaab, offers vivid insight into how the 'refugee crisis' and the 'war on terror' are blurring into each other,[9] something highly resonant in the situation of Syria where refugees are seen as potential Islamic State terrorists.

But Eastleigh also offers a different take on migration that shows how out of displacement opportunity can emerge, both for refugees and migrants and for their host communities. Indeed, the vast networks that displacement often generates can breathe new life into the places into which they are woven: hubs forged out of migration become sites of innovation, and often sites of commerce. Refugees and migrants should not be preconceived as 'burdens', and displacement can be paradoxically productive economically and socially, as Hammar elucidates in her focus on 'displacement economies'.[10] Camps such as Dadaab have become economic hubs,[11] deeply affecting the local communities around them despite the government's desire to restrict refugee interaction with wider society to a bare minimum. But it is Eastleigh that offers a concrete demonstration of the power of refugees and migrants to catalyse change, even in the urban heart of the host country.

Indeed, in all this contemporary focus on migration, urban areas of hyper-mobility such as Eastleigh loom large, as it is in cities that most migrants wish to live, and it is in cities where their presence and economic activity is most conspicuous, most debated and researched, whether London or New York, or Dakar or Libreville. Indeed, cities are increasingly the focus of migration policy debate, as witnessed by a recent International Organisation of Migration (IOM) conference and report focused on cities and 'managing mobility', a phrase suggestive of the perceived need to tighten control of this mobility, despite acknowledgement of the benefits migrants often bring.[12] Furthermore, recent scholarship suggests that there is a need to move beyond seeing the city as simply a backdrop for migrants and migration, but to study them as mutually constituted.[13]

Migration has long been a constitutive part of urbanisation processes, as the vast literature on rural–urban migration and ethnic enclaves—the 'Chinatowns' and 'Little Italys' of the world—suggests,[14] but now it is getting more attention than ever. However, this new attention is very much 'transnational', exploring not just how migrants integrate into a particular urban context—as the literature on ethnic enclaves tended to do—but also on how social and economic ties maintained to urban 'elsewheres' across the world affect both receiving and sending contexts of migration.

In African studies, such concern with the impact of migration on cities is now a burgeoning field, one whose scope goes well beyond the analysis of the rural–urban migration so focused upon by much classic work on migration in Africa.[15] This field encompasses not just Africans travelling to and settling in cities in other African countries,[16] but also those venturing outside the continent, for example to Europe and Asia.[17] There is also focus on non-Africans moving to African cities, Chinese migrants in particular becoming a significant and growing presence.[18] All these coming and goings have important effects on African cities and urbanity. Bakewell and Jonsson suggest that the challenge for current research on migration in African cities is to understand 'on the one hand, how mobility interacts with the development and change of urban space, and on the other, how the life of the city transforms people's mobility'.[19]

Eastleigh gives insight into both processes: it is a place transformed by waves of migration—not just from Somalia, but also from Ethiopia, and from within Kenya—that have brought new ideas for commerce as well as global connections, and it is a place where many onward migration dreams and plans are concocted and brought to fruition. It is a place that clearly shows how migration can lead to urban transformation, which in turn can lead to more migration, which in turn, etc. All this migration has produced an estate of great social and ethnic complexity. It is also linked into a global diasporic geography, maintaining strong connections not only to Somali cities and home regions, but also to other 'Little Mogadishus' around the world: for example, districts of Dubai, Johannesburg, Toronto and Minneapolis that have all been drawn into the same transnational social field woven through Eastleigh.

Eastleigh also elucidates the impact that migrants and their networks can have on 'development', especially as it has become a key site for investment by the Somali diaspora. Migration is now part of global thinking on development, being integrated into the Sustainable Development Goals, which have replaced the Millennium Development Goals. Diaspora has become a key concept in this regard as scholars and policy makers explore the links migrants maintain to 'home',[20] links that can have profound economic implications. Although there is concern that diasporas can have negative effects on 'homelands' by perpetuating conflict through funding belligerents, governments and international organisations are placing ever greater emphasis on the positive role they can play through investment and example. Key to recent interest has been the growing realisation of quite how much money diaspora communities remit home, sums that 'surpass by far the amounts of official development aid and foreign direct investment flows'.[21] Furthermore, migrants have come to be seen as exemplary entrepreneurs—risk takers who can rely on strong networks of mutuality and trust built out of tight community ties—and hence as critical agents of development unsullied by connections to corrupt states.[22]

This policy interest is subject to suspicion as it appears to place the burden of development upon often marginalised refugee populations, and might well be a way for richer countries to renounce obligations to poorer ones:[23] promoting remittances as a path to development does little to undermine global structures that perpetuate underdevelopment. Furthermore, as Bakewell argues, despite the focus on migration and diaspora, much of the policy debate still reveals a 'sedentary bias', one in which current migration is to be used to curtail future migration through development of 'home': the aim is thus to keep potential migrants 'in their place' rather than truly embracing migration as a force for good.[24]

Nonetheless, there is much policy being devised with the aim of encouraging diaspora populations to commit to development at home, and to funnel investments in socially productive directions. In all this, the role of the Somali diaspora as economic and political actors in the Horn of Africa has been much discussed lately,[25] especially the role they play in rebuilding a currently more stable Mogadishu, as well as in Somaliland, where diaspora returnees from the UK have turned a part of Hargeisa into 'Half London'.[26] Indeed, given the instability of southern Somalia in particular, non-Somali private business interests are hard to mobilise, while Somalis themselves are seen as willing to take on the risks.[27]

Eastleigh's large malls are testament to the power that such investment of transnational capital can have. It is a place where the social, religious and cultural underpinnings of a diaspora are salient, and a place where migrant and refugee economies and their links to urban transformation can be seen in action. Despite being in Kenya rather than Somalia, it is a place to which many Somalis in the diaspora feel attachment through shared memories and family connections, and also a place where investment opportunities are attractive. It thus offers an important case study of diaspora, migration and development that not only suggests the promise of the migration–development nexus, but also the political, geographical and temporal ambiguities that can complicate this nexus: ambiguities that revolve around questions of whose diaspora is doing the developing, and what kind of development they are instigating.[28] It also reveals how this nexus is hamstrung by the tendency to see so much of our world through a securitised prism, whereby instead of mobilising the opportunities offered by migration for the greater good, we react to them with suspicion. Rather than being hailed as agents of development, migrants and refugees are far more likely to be seen as threats to the nation-state.

Global trade in a global neighbourhood

Thus Eastleigh is an exceptionally fertile place for the study of migration, its impact and its ambiguities. However, it is not just a place transformed by the movement of people, but also by the movement of things. Indeed, Eastleigh is very much a story of commodities, often ignored by scholars of globalisation, yet critical for many the world over. These are the commodities that Somali networks have brought to Eastleigh, and the lifeblood of its commercial transformation. Goods sold in Eastleigh are often 'low end' in nature: in Nasiib Fashions one is more likely to find 'Hoog Boss' than 'Hugo Boss', reflecting the many fake labels found in the estate's shopping malls. Such goods have played an important role in transforming economies and consumption practices the world over. They are the products of what is termed 'low-end globalisation' or 'globalisation from below'.[29] Rather than the economic activity of multinational corporations and investment banks usually associated with the term, this globalisation is mostly operated by small-scale traders, often trading goods through networks supported by personalised trust rather than legal contract, and often smuggling them through customs in suitcases to evade duty. In many ways this is the 'informal economy' gone global,[30] whose trade often bypasses state regulation not just in countries that import them, but also at source in the manufacturing cities and trade hubs of Asia.

Such trade should not be underestimated, and Gordon Mathews and others show how deeply significant it is for those marginalised by higher-end forms of globalisation. For Margaret Lee, it is a crucial aspect of 'Africa's world trade'.[31] Such trade has also created low-end global trade hubs where great wealth is generated, including Hong Kong's famous Chungking Mansions, ethnographically portrayed by Gordon Mathews: this is a commercial and residential building in Hong Kong frequented by many traders from Africa (some from Kenya and some Somali), as well as India and elsewhere. It is also regarded by the wider Hong Kong population with the kind of ambivalence, suspicion and fear accorded to Eastleigh as a place of 'otherness' in the heart of the familiar.[32] Eastleigh is a very similar trade hub, linked to the likes of Chungking Mansions by mobile Somali traders and Somali freight companies, as well as by Somali agents who have settled in Chinese cities such as Yiwu and Guangzhou.[33] Its malls and retail units—originally carved out of hotel rooms—also bear much physical resemblance to such buildings as Chungking Mansions and malls elsewhere in the East. Furthermore, they connect with the wider informal economy of

Kenya and beyond, where other mobile traders bring goods from the trade hubs of the Global South to sell in mini-shops that have revolutionised the retail environment of downtown Nairobi.[34] The trade in these imported goods from such premises has made entrepreneurs of many in Kenya and beyond.

Much attention has been given to 'global cities' (in Sassen's terminology),[35] cities that transcend the national borders of the countries where they are located and form nodes in vast webs of transnational and global flows. The literature on the global city focuses more on mega-cities such as London and New York, but scholars have argued that it is important to study globalising processes in less wealthy cities too.[36] Eastleigh is one of the most globally connected parts of the global city of Nairobi. Unlike New York and London, however, it is built on low-end global products rather than high-end finance.

However, the term 'low end' does not do justice to all goods sold, nor to the estate's buildings, which are becoming more 'high end', and its business practices, many of which have become more formalised over the years as its economy has grown. Indeed, there is an increasingly sophisticated side of this trade evident in Eastleigh, as Somali displacement has prompted the creation of a global infrastructure of freight and shipping companies, and money-transfer remittances, that lubricate the paths these global goods take. Indeed, Eastleigh shows how economies catalysed by the trade in cheap consumer goods characteristic of this 'low-end globalisation' can evolve into something much more multifaceted than the term suggests.

In short, Eastleigh is a concrete manifestation of contemporary mobility and global connectivity, and demonstrates the power of migrants to transform urban landscapes and urban livelihoods. It is a vibrant and successful economy built on transnational networks that connect it both to the West and to the East. However, it is also a place where the presence of the refugees and migrants who have generated this economy creates great tension and uncomfortable debates about what should be done with them. Its story thus offers a window into the particularities of one of the world's most dynamic urban spaces, and also onto how migration and mobility are shaping the world in the twenty-first century.

Eastleigh in 3D

As all the above suggests, understanding Eastleigh requires understanding transnational processes and ties that link East Africa to communities of Somalis elsewhere in the world, and to the trade and manufacturing hubs of the East. However, also critical to Eastleigh's growth are factors much more local in scope. Indeed, to understand Eastleigh—and similar 'global neighbourhoods' and economies—requires understanding a range of converging factors, some particular to the place in question, others more universal in scope,[37] as well as the 'friction' between them, in Tsing's terminology.[38] This requires a multidimensional approach, one that can better grasp how processes of mobility, displacement and global economic change coalesce within and transform a particular place and those who live and work there. Thus, the chapters that follow tell the story of Eastleigh in 3D, exploring a Somali dimension, a global one, and one very Kenyan, dimensions intertwined in intricate ways.

First, it is a story of Somali migration and the centrality of hubs such as Eastleigh for their transnational networks. As a 'Little Mogadishu', Eastleigh has become a home in exile for many thousands of refugees, as well as a place that attracts visitors and investors from the diaspora. Eastleigh has become symbolic of the Somali experience of exile in the twentieth and twenty-first centuries, and speaks much about the evolution of Somali trade and its infrastructure in this context. It offers insight into all levels of the global Somali economy, from that of modest refugee enterprises to the high-end investments of the wealthy, as well as how Somali culture and society are imagined and reimagined transnationally. Critically, Eastleigh offers a vantage point on to the social, cultural and religious infrastructure that allows vast amounts of goods and capital to flow in a transnational economy almost wholly free from legally binding contracts: one that runs on 'trust', a key theme of chapter 5.

Second, Eastleigh is deeply linked to much wider global processes as a commercial hub for goods coming to East Africa from the Gulf region as well as Asia. The commerce that has forged the estate resembles that seen in other parts of the world, especially in the wake of the rise of China as a manufacturing giant; as mentioned above, Eastleigh has been built on the cheap manufactured goods of the East. The transformation also took place in the context of global pressure for trade liberalisation under the banner of structural adjustment and the conse-quent expansion of the informal economy, a context crucial for under-standing its story.

Third, Eastleigh is interwoven with local and national stories within Nairobi and Kenya. While forged through regional and global processes of diaspora formation and trade, the estate and its economy are also distinctly Kenyan. Eastleigh has been built on Kenyan resources and institutions, and its economy would scarcely have boomed were it not for Kenyan and wider East African demand for its goods. The story of Eastleigh is also one of Kenya's adoption of economic reforms and structural adjustment, reforms that Somalis have made great use of in Eastleigh,[39] while Kenyan politics looms large in the estate. In many ways the Eastleigh story is one of the absence of a functioning Somali state, but it is also a story of the simultaneous absence and presence of the Kenyan state. Eastleigh—like much of Kenya's 'informal econ-omy'—is not wholly divorced from the state, yet not wholly integrated either, and debates rage about how much tax is and ought to be paid by its traders.

In short, Eastleigh cannot be understood through the global or the local alone, or indeed through the national either: it requires attention to these varied scales. One could of course study these dimensions separately, but Eastleigh offers a compelling laboratory of how they interact in one place to create a hybrid environment at once Kenyan, Somali and global.

To these three dimensions should be added a fourth: temporality. There is a great historical depth to Eastleigh, from the many migrations into and out of the estate over the years, to the historical changes in the global economy that precipitated its growth as a trade hub. This *longue durée* to the story of Eastleigh is one this book probes through an approach both historical and ethnographic. As Glick Schiller and Caglar put it in a phrasing that brings these Eastleigh dimensions together: 'The role of migrants as actors within a city changes over time. Migrants respond to and contribute to each city's historical and insti-tutional legacies, even as they are part of the continuing reconstitution of global processes that are substantiated locally.'[40]

Finally, in talking abstract 'processes' and multiple dimensions, there is a danger of obscuring the individual people—their agency and their cultural practices—who animate Eastleigh's economy and who have driven forward its transformation. As Brettell emphasises, 'an anthropological approach to migration should emphasize both structure and agency; it should look at macro-social contextual issues, micro-level strategies and decision-making, and the mesolevel relational structure within which individuals operate. It needs to articulate both people and process.'[41] Through the voices of people like Mohaa—who opened this introduction—I hope to weave their agency into the story of Eastleigh and make these processes less abstract.

Displaced Development?

Eastleigh is a place of much ambiguity and ambivalence. It is a place people want to leave, yet to which others want to return; a place where the upheaval of war has brought opportunity and development; a place where great wealth is made out of low-end goods; a place of shiny malls and hotels sprouting from muddy decayed streets; a place of refuge that can be a place of danger; a place where the state is both all too absent and all too present. This ambiguity and ambivalence runs through how the Kenyan state and wider Kenyan society have viewed all its recent change: at times praising Eastleigh's development and entrepreneurship, at others condemning it as an economy built on dubious goods and capital.

Indeed, its economic growth is rarely portrayed as unalloyed good, and reservations about it focus not just on the sources of its capital, but also the type of development it has brought. Eastleigh's growth can be characterised in various ways as 'informal', and so dilemmas about its economy mirror those about the informal economy more broadly. There is great policy interest in their role in development and governance in our era of liberalisation, and many celebrate their capacity in this regard.[42] However, others see a darker side to such economic activity and the networks that support it, a side that links to social exclusion, criminality and the atrophy of the state.[43] Reservations about Eastleigh also resemble those about the growth in the trade of second-hand clothes (referred to as *mitumba* in Kiswahili) and a decline in Kenya's manufacturing industry that some link to it.[44]

Yet centres of the mitumba trade in Nairobi such as Gikomba market do not raise the same levels of suspicion as Eastleigh. Indeed, what is different in Eastleigh from the mitumba trade and the informal economy more broadly is the identity of those who operate it: Somalis and refugees. As elsewhere in the world—including South Africa, where Somalis have suffered much from xenophobia—debates about autochthony and belonging are rife in Kenya.[45] Indeed, in many ways the ambivalence towards Eastleigh and its economy is a function of ambivalence towards people often seen as out of place in Kenya, and, in the case of refugees, out of place in the city. Worldwide, the 'camp' has become seen as the space for African refugees, a place where they can be warehoused and the nation-state kept safer. Urban refugees such as those in Eastleigh subvert these notions of the place of refugees, while their economic activity and success in Eastleigh subverts notions of them as passive recipients of aid.[46]

In this regard, I coin the term *displaced development*. Without doubt the migration and mobility that have produced a global commercial hub out of a Nairobi residential estate are responsible for some of Kenya's most impressive recent economic development, and not just in Eastleigh: Somali trade and business is gaining power in other parts of the country. Yet for many, all this economic growth is displaced: this capital should instead be going to Somalia itself. Furthermore, some argue that this Somali-led development is displacing Kenyans from Eastleigh, and from their own economy. Indeed, Eastleigh is a peculiar case of diaspora- and migrant-led development, seeing that the diaspora in question is perceived as developing not their own homeland, but someone else's. This perception is held not just by those Kenyans who resent Somali presence, but also by some Somalians who feel that their investments in Eastleigh and elsewhere are not appreciated, and would be better placed in Somalia.

Such a perception, as this book will show, is not just dependent upon ambivalence to hosting such a large urban refugee population of Somalians, and their scapegoating as agents of Al-Shabaab. It is also partly built out of the ambivalence felt towards Kenya's own Somali population, those born within borders not so long ago carved out by colonialists. Kenya has a large indigenous Somali population, both in its cities and in its north-eastern regions, a population that has suffered a long history of repression and abuse in post-colonial Kenya, especially in the wake of conflict in the 1960s surrounding a movement for north-eastern Kenya to secede to Somalia. This—often hazy—distinction between Somalians and Kenyan Somalis is critical in understanding both the ambiguities of Somali identity in Kenya and the history of a Somali space such as Eastleigh. Indeed, many Somalis are very Kenyan, in terms of both legal and cultural citizenship. Furthermore, some of the original inhabitants of Nairobi—and Eastleigh—were Somalis. Kenyan Somalis—and other people of northern Kenya long marginalised in much of Kenyan history—have for many decades suffered from the feeling that they are 'not yet Kenyan', an impression that also affects Eastleigh. Countering this is a key cause for Kenyan Somalis in the estate, keen to show how Kenyan both they and Eastleigh are.

In all this, the name Little Mogadishu is not entirely helpful. It suggests a displaced Mogadishu, part of Somalia dropped into Kenya, where all the troubles facing that once-great city are to be found in the Kenyan capital. While the estate's growth does indeed owe much to the collapse of Somalia, and to the economic activity of its Somali refugees, it is in many ways a very Kenyan place, where Kenyan Somalis—and other Kenyans, including Kikuyu and Meru—are also crucial players in its economy. Indeed, the book will show that despite a nickname suggestive of a mono-ethnic place of foreigners, it is in fact a highly diverse and very Kenyan social field. Indeed, its diversity goes beyond this, to even encompass different Ethiopian ethnicities too, including the Oromo, as well as various subdivisions among its Somalis. It is a place of 'super-diversity', to use Vertovec's term designed to capture the contemporary complexities of identity wrought by different waves of migration to cities such as London.[47] Such a term can also be applied to such complex urban spaces of migration as Eastleigh in the Global South. In this regard, this book undermines its very title, showing that while 'Little Mogadishu' captures much of what goes on in the estate, it can obscure much else, especially this Kenyanness. In fact, the estate is firmly embedded in the nation-state that hosts it, even if this relationship is at times fraught.

Recent events—including Operation Usalama Watch—have led to speculation that Somalis will repatriate their investments in Eastleigh as the real Mogadishu develops, or even move to developing Somali hubs, such as Kampala, where they have received a warmer welcome. This notion emerges from the sense that Eastleigh's development is

INTRODUCTION

displaced. However, I argue that this estate and its economy are very much at home in Kenya, a country which has a long-established and large Somali population and will always offer Somali business networks access to wider markets than those found in Somalia itself. While some still suspect Eastleigh of being somewhere foreign, the estate also has allies in high political places in Kenya, and some powerful people are keen to draw this business hub born of displacement into the mainstream of Kenya's developmental future.

Certainly the many Kenyans—Somali and non-Somali—who rely on the estate and the goods that flow through it for their livelihoods will hope that its vibrant economy stays where it is. Indeed, while the people whose migration and transnational social infrastructure created this global hub are subject to suspicion, the global goods they bring to the estate and to East Africa are embraced much more avidly. More importantly still, the many strong social links between Somalis and wider Kenyan society evident in the mundane activities in the estate, and in the push of many to see beyond stereotypes, show that suspicion between them is hardly the full story, although a tale of separate communities at odds is commonly told.

Somalis in the estate often talk of how trust among themselves underpins the Eastleigh economy and wider Somali business networks, and trust is a key theme explored in this book.[48] But in the many networks within and outside the estate there is much trust evident between Somalis and others in what is actually in various ways a cosmopolitan and open economy. While this is highly susceptible to the changing politics of the region, this wider trust also gives hope that a better relationship is possible between Eastleigh and the Kenya of which it is very much a part.

Researching Eastleigh

The resonance of Eastleigh for key contemporary themes, as well its importance as a source of refuge and livelihood for so many, has attracted many researchers. Indeed, as an accessible centre for urban refugees with such a remarkable economy, Eastleigh has also become a centre of research, one with an identity in policy and academic circles as strong as the likes of Kibera estate on the other side of Nairobi. Thus

17

this book has a wealth of research by others to draw upon, Elizabeth Campbell and Godwin Murunga being particular pioneers. While some research is available from its pre-transformation days,[49] most derives from its more recent past. There are publications from the 1990s that recount the early days of its transformation,[50] but with Eastleigh's exponential growth in the 2000s came a concomitant growth in the number of researchers writing about its current form as well as its historical development. These include, among others, those focused on refugee studies,[51] the history of Nairobi,[52] religious practices in the estate,[53] its economy,[54] and those interested in the social effects of remittances.[55] A number of policy-focused research papers have also been written about the estate.[56] While this research has informed this book strongly, it is rather different in being a historical ethnography focused more precisely on the estate itself and its fascinating past, present and future: Eastleigh is its main character.

I first visited Eastleigh in the late 1990s while conducting research on the trade of the stimulant substance known popularly as *khat* (a substance that features in the present book).[57] Khat is grown in great quantities in Kenya; Eastleigh has long been a prime centre of its trade and consumption, and until recently was a hub for its onward export to Europe. At that time Eastleigh was far from being a no-go area, despite tales of guns being sold there. The guide book I had at the time even recommended it as a place where one could experience a different side of Nairobi. Later editions would excise that section. The influence of Somali trade was already strong then, although the estate's landscape was yet to undergo its most impressive transformation. These initial visits to the estate intrigued me, and over the years it gradually seemed to grow in potential as a subject of research, especially as its ever-booming economy generated yet wilder media speculation as to the source of its success (including allegations of links to piracy by the mid-2000s). An estate with such a strong identity and linked to so many interesting processes of forced migration, diaspora, transnational trade and globalisation had to be worthy of a research project in its own right. I was fortunate to find a home for this project within the Oxford Diasporas Programme of research into the contemporary dynamics of diaspora,[58] and in 2011 began work on the project 'Diaspora, Trade and Trust: Eastleigh, Nairobi's Little Mogadishu', out of which emerges this book.[59]

In a way, this project on Eastleigh was the inverse of my work on khat, which studied the transnational networks of its trade and its links to migration and diaspora through a multi-sited and multi-channelled approach.[60] Eastleigh is a project that also focuses on transnational trade, and migration and diaspora, but through a study of a single site. These two approaches straddle a divide between those who argue that ethnography of the global requires techniques such as multi-sited fieldwork and those who think that more 'traditional' studies of a particular locale can capture the global too. Tsuda, Tapias and Escandell make a good case for the latter, arguing that globalisation can be studied in single sites as it is 'ultimately grounded in and instantiated in territorialized localities as specific transnational processes'.[61] Also, the chapters in the 2012 volume by Mathews et al on 'globalization from below' demonstrate how such processes can be studied both through multi-sited and single-sited studies.[62] Of course, both approaches have their costs and benefits—one sacrificing depth for breadth, the other breadth for depth—but both can offer many insights into contemporary processes of great import, especially when triangulated with other research that can make up some of the deficiencies.

As an anthropologist, my principal research method was ethnographic, and in 2011–12 I spent around eight months in Nairobi, much of the time living in Eastleigh itself. I cannot claim to have lived in hardship, staying mostly in hotels such as the Land Star, Barakat and Grand Royal, key landmarks in the estate. Such hotels are temporary—and sometimes long-term—homes for many Somali diaspora visitors to the estate, and so proved excellent locales for meeting interesting people, including many Somali politicians from Mogadishu and elsewhere in southern Somalia. Staying in such hotels eased concerns over security. My research in Eastleigh began just before the Kenya Defence Force (KDF) launched its invasion of Somalia which has precipitated so much insecurity in Kenya itself, Eastleigh bearing the brunt of much of it. After the invasion, Eastleigh did feel different.

While I have never faced any security problems in the estate—and generally I feel safer there than in downtown Nairobi—fear became heightened post-invasion, not just of grenades and Al-Shabaab, but security service raids too (which had targeted hotels like the Barakat before). While I held a permit for my research, it was easy at that time to feel rather paranoid that my presence would not be appreciated by all, and my Eastleigh friends were always keen to ensure that I reached home before dark, when police swoops were at their height. There was also suspicion of researchers by some residents. My Oxford colleague Jonny Steinberg had visited the estate as part of his research into the life of Asad, a Somali whose epic journey to South Africa he documents.[63] He spent a few days in Eastleigh conducting research alongside a Somali friend of mine. The latter later told me of an acquaintance of his who saw him with Jonny and berated him for helping someone who may very well be 'CIA'. Eastleigh has for decades been a place seen through a security prism, but in the post-9/11 era this has become intensified, especially in the wake of Operation Linda Nchi and the Westgate attack, and this does make researchers people of suspicion. Of course, being people with means and contacts, our stays in the estate are nothing like as difficult as those of refugees, and even Kenyans, can be. The feeling of threat, that was quite overwhelming at times for me, was only a mild taste of the feeling of alienation that can envelop the estate, and is much harder to survive for those with limited means.

However, in general the research went smoothly, allowing me to carry out the standard elements of ethnographic research, participant observation and interviews, as well as a series of surveys. In all this I relied on fellow researchers Hassan Kochore, Hannah Elliott, Emma Lochery and Kimo Quaintance, who all worked on the project at various points. I also relied on well-connected and well-disposed local contacts. Pre-existing links to the Kenyan legal aid charity Kituo cha Sheria (which has an urban refugee programme for a long time based in Eastleigh) were invaluable, especially for gaining access to Oromo informants. I had pre-existing links too to Sky, a school in the estate where I had learnt some Somali in years gone by. This school became a key landmark in my own geography of the estate, a place where refugees and Kenyans interacted in a very welcoming and safe environment. My earlier khat research also provided a wealth of contacts, including Blackie, a Meru man who runs a kiosk in Eastleigh—where I could observe interactions across ethnic lines: it is manned by Meru, yet frequented mainly by Somali.

Another key figure in the research was Kaamil. He works for a cable TV channel offering advertising to the many businesses in the estate, so

Plate 2: The journalist and his contacts

Plate 3: An Eastleighwood concert

has a vast number of contacts, many living in business-card form inside his wallet. Kaamil introduced me to many of his contacts, and was himself a fascinating member of the Eastleigh business world. One person he introduced me to was Burhan Iman and others involved in the Eastleighwood Youth Group, a multifaceted organisation that sets out to provide a social forum for youth and an outlet for its talents. This organisation has subsequently gained media attention for its film- and music-making, and, as a cosmopolitan initiative linked both to refugees in the estate and to the wider Somali diaspora, speaks to a number of themes of the book.

Perhaps most serendipitous was a chance re-encounter with Mohaa, the proprietor of Nasiib Fashions. We first met when he—a Kenyan Somali—worked on the matatus[64] between Isiolo and Meru towns, a route I frequently travelled in the early 2000s. In the intervening years he had moved to Eastleigh in search of—as he likes to put it—'greener pastures', eventually taking over Nasiib Fashions in one of Eastleigh's biggest malls. This shop was truly a haven for me, and I spent many happy days as Mohaa's apprentice, getting to know him and his business, as well as those in neighbouring shops and others in his orbit: these included his business partner Siad, and Siad's cousin Elias, a recent graduate who lives in Eastleigh and who has helped me enormously over the years, especially in introducing me to the Eastleigh Garre, a Somali group of great importance to the estate's economy.

Mohaa was content with me conducting participant observation in Nasiib Fashions, so content that there was some exploitation of his apprentice: 'Neil, you should carry this sack of clothes—remember this is participant observation.' With Mohaa I would also travel to Kampala and Isiolo, following the life of someone surviving and occasionally thriving in the Eastleigh economy. Back in the UK my apprenticeship with Mohaa (someone, by coincidence, nicknamed the 'Masta') would continue too, as with modern forms of communication such as the messenger app WhatsApp we could chat easily across the intervening space. Such technology furthers blurs the boundaries of the anthropological 'field'.[65] As well as Kampala and Isiolo, I also travelled to a number of other towns connected to the Eastleigh economy alongside Hassan Kochore and Elias, including Kisumu, Eldoret and Kakamega. Thus, while single-sited in the main, the project did entail a multi-sited component.

Surveys were conducted to supplement this ethnographic approach. These involved a number of questionnaires that Kaamil and Elias conducted among Eastleigh shopkeepers. Between them they surveyed 129 people in various malls, asking questions focused on various aspects of operating a business in the estate, and the background of the shopkeepers. The survey was very useful for getting a sense of the capital required for establishing a business and the different goods sold, as well as the intermixing of Somalians, Kenyan Somalis, Oromo and others in the shops. Kaamil conducted a further survey of the malls too, obtaining information on forty-two of them and helping clarify those involved in building the malls and the different groupings of people behind them. An Oromo friend, Kemal, conducted a survey of sixty Oromo living in the estate to obtain information on their journeys and experiences there, while two Meru friends—Gitonga and Sofia—surveyed seventy Meru on their migration to and work in the estate. Again, such surveys were extremely useful in generating a broader view of where people came from and what they did in the estate, supplementing and helping calibrate interviews, and providing quantitative data.

The research also involved work in the Kenya National Archives on the history of the estate and Somalis in Nairobi more generally, work which—combined with oral histories from long-term Eastleigh residents—helped to place the contemporary form of Eastleigh and lives led within it into historical context. This context reveals many contrasts, yet also many similarities: Eastleigh is a place transformed, yet in many ways it has always been a place of paradox, one intimately linked to Nairobi and Kenya and suggestive of much of their history; yet also a place apart, viewed as an internal 'other' within the city limits.

Book Outline

The structure of the book is intended to provide a rounded view of Eastleigh, its history and how its economy works. In this way, it resembles somewhat the structure that Mathews uses for his book about Chungking Mansions in Hong Kong, exploring the place, the people who frequent it, the goods that are sold there, the relation of such a transnational and global place to its locality, and imagining the futures of such ambiguous places: one a neighbourhood, the other a building, but both linked into very similar networks and processes.[66]

The first chapter focuses on the historical Eastleigh, highlighting its origins, its history as a place connected yet disconnected from wider Nairobi, and the many waves of migration that have run into and out of it over the years. While strongly identified as an Indian estate in earlier times, this chapter will show how Somalis have lived in the estate before it was even called Eastleigh, forming a population that would help attract more Somali in-migration over the years, including that of refugees in the late 1980s. Chapter 2 focuses on the transformation of the estate into a global hub for commerce and the Somali diaspora, and the transformation of its physical landscape. While deeply formed by Somali displacement and the consequent rise of Somali transnational society and economy, the estate also owes much to its narrower Kenyan and broader global context, as well as to a blueprint of cavernous malls filled with hundreds of small retail shops. This blueprint has spread beyond Eastleigh to other towns in Kenya, and even to southern Africa. Chapter 3 looks at the estate's human infrastructure, introducing its super-diverse 'ethnoscape' of sojourners and long-term residents responsible for and attracted to this transformed landscape.[67] The chapter also considers religious identity, as well as a place-based identity linked to the estate itself.

In chapter 4 we look more closely at economic livelihoods in the estate. There is an 'Eastleigh Dream' of rags to riches that a fortunate few have fulfilled, although most make a more modest living and some barely survive. Mohaa's Nasiib Fashions is a key case study of an Eastleigh business, one that while small in scale offers both a living and a meaningful sense of autonomy, as highlighted by Scott in his cautious praise of the petty bourgeouisie.[68] Values such as autonomy and freedom feature again in chapter 5, which looks at the idealised figure of the Somali businessperson: one who takes risks, can be trusted, and is a good Muslim. Islam is a crucial part of the Eastleigh story, not only socially and culturally, but also economically. Chapter 6 then shifts to a focus on the things that have helped make Eastleigh, suggesting that the volume of goods that arrive in the estate create their own dynamic and momentum that compels their exchange. Exploring the 'social lives' of these commodities that pass through the estate demonstrates how they too are crucial *dramatis personae* in the story of Eastleigh.

Chapter 7 explores in more depth the relationship of Eastleigh to the Kenyan state, putting this into the historical context of the relationship between the state and Kenya's Somali population. It highlights the ambivalence in this relationship, and shows how events such as the Westgate shooting have hardened perceptions of and policy towards the estate and its residents, resulting in the perversities of Operation Usalama Watch. However, there remains optimism for a less fraught future, rendered concrete in the form of the main Eastleigh road—First Avenue—now finally renovated: once symbolic of state neglect, this now might be symbolic of a more constructive state involvement in the estate.

The book concludes by considering further Eastleigh's future, arguing that even if the real Mogadishu continues on its current path to recovery, Nairobi's Little Mogadishu will remain a key hub for Somalis. Despite prophecies of decline, the access this global neighbourhood has to the huge markets of East and Central Africa means that it will continue to attract investment and in-migration from Somalis around the world. The conclusion also returns to the question of the identity of the estate itself as a 'Little Mogadishu', reaffirming the importance of treating place seriously: locality should not be lost sight of in studying the transnational. While formed by the complicated movement of people and things, and through translocal connections to many other places, the particularities of Eastleigh are crucial in this story of urban African transformation.

1

FROM NAIROBI EAST TO LITTLE MOGADISHU

Wood Street was forest then, and you could see monkeys, antelope and lots of birds. Eastleigh was a very good place.

Mzee Gulu, July 2011

Before 1990—as any older resident will tell you—Eastleigh was very different from the trade hub it is today, being principally a lower-middle-class residential zone with a strong history of Asian settlement. Nostalgia abounds for this earlier incarnation, especially among those whose influence has declined in the wake of its Somali-led commercial transformation: the bustle of today is compared with a past of good roads and a peaceful atmosphere where birdsong could be heard. However, this vision of an idyllic older Eastleigh obscures a fraught history bound up with the wider history of Nairobi and its spatial politics of race. In this history, Somalis have played a much longer role than the common emphasis on Eastleigh's Indian past might suggest: indeed, Eastleigh was the Nairobi home of Somalis even before it had been named Eastleigh. This earlier presence is obscured by conceptions of Somalis as foreigners and recent arrivals in Kenya.

As this chapter will show, Somalis have long formed one of the more stable components of the Eastleigh 'ethnoscape'. Indeed, the estate has long been highly diverse, its population formed by complicated patterns of migration linked not just to the collapse of the Somali state in

27

the late 1980s and early 1990s, but also to earlier migrations from the Indian Subcontinent and from Ethiopia, as well as rural–urban migration within Kenya. This book is focused on the commercial transformation of the estate in recent decades, but it is important to remember that it has always been transforming through processes of urbanisation that date back over a century. Understanding how Eastleigh became such a fertile territory for economic transformation requires understanding of the earlier processes that created a diverse district that has long been home to Nairobi's urban Somalis. First, however, we turn to the cosmopolitan young town of Nairobi, and colonial dilemmas over race, dilemmas that would prove highly significant for Eastleigh.

The Segregated Town

In the colonial period, race was used as the most important determinant of one's status and place (literally) in society.[1] (Kefa Otiso, 2005)

Early in the twentieth century the land upon which Eastleigh would be born was simply a boggy plain a few kilometres from the town of Nairobi.[2] Of course, at that time Nairobi itself was a very new urban space, albeit one growing rapidly from its beginnings in 1899 as a campsite that housed workers on the Imperial British East Africa Company's Uganda Railway. So quickly did Nairobi grow that those like the adventurer John Boyes, who had seen the plains from which Nairobi emerged, were shocked: 'What is now known as Nairobi was then practically a swamp, and from the nature of the surrounding country I should never have imagined that it would be chosen as the site for the future capital of British East Africa.'[3] This campsite had grown into a town of 6,000 inhabitants by 1902. By 1907 Nairobi was the official capital of the colony,[4] and by 1908 it 'had cars, trains, banks and clubs, and by World War I commercial European Nairobi had a full range of amenities like electricity, water purification, and permanent stone buildings'.[5] As we will see in regard to Eastleigh, amenities in non-European parts of the young town would take much longer to materialise.

Most of the town was non-European by dint of how cosmopolitan both Nairobi and the railway-building project that created it were. In this regard Nairobi was like other urban centres in East Africa, 'a complex society composed of individuals and groups with varying forms of linkages to and participation in African, European and Indian cultural traditions'.[6] Indeed, along with the railway had come a great mixture of people: Europeans, Indians, Arabs, Swahili and Somali, as well as other Africans from near and far. The Annual Report of Nairobi Township for 1909 lists the population as 14,161, made up of—in the categorisations of the day—799 Europeans, 76 Eurasians, 591 Goanese, 3171 Asiatics, 307 Somalis, 766 'Coast and G.E.A. Natives',[7] 7,232 'Up Country Natives' and 1,219 'Miscellaneous'.[8]

Such diversity was a source of anxiety for the ruling elite, who intended Nairobi to be a segregated town: implicit and explicit forms of segregation were in operation from Nairobi's earliest days, including pass-laws for 'native' Africans, whose presence in the colonial town was begrudged and presumed illegitimate. Nairobi was viewed by white settlers as a town for Europeans, 'even though its African population always outnumbered all others'.[9] Separate residential zones were created in early plans, and given justification by a number of commissions and reports in the early decades, including the Simpson Report of 1913 that recommended segregation to curb plague.[10] Segregation on grounds of hygiene was connected to a 'wider process of normalizing the white image, pathologizing black and setting up black people as a danger to whites'.[11]

Much hygiene-related racial anxiety revolved around the so-called 'Indian Question' of 'whether to allow the expansion of Indian migration and how to shape it should it be permitted'.[12] Despite their great importance for the developing town, the European authorities regarded Asians with ambivalence, and sought to restrict where they could live,[13] especially in the wake of outbreaks of plague in the Indian Bazaar area (now the Moi Avenue/River Road area), the main commercial area of the city. This was blamed squarely on Indians and poor sanitation, and both were seen as a risk to the health of the European population. As Burton notes, the poor conditions of non-European settlements in colonial cities, that often were caused by colonial neglect, led to ill-health and disease, 'thereby fuelling fears of contagion that Europeans in a circular fashion used to legitimate segregation'.[14]

As the above figures suggest, the Nairobi Asian connection was strong from the start, and would only increase in strength as a constant influx of newcomers came to Kenya and Nairobi from the Indian Subcontinent throughout much of the colonial era.[15] While many were of limited means, others were wealthy, playing major roles in commerce in the town, especially in the Bazaar. Ainsworth—the town's first administrator—stated in 1905 that 'fully 80 per cent of the capital and business energy of the country is Indian'.[16] Such wealthy merchants included the likes of Alibhai Jeevanjee—who had recruited many Punjabis to work on the railway, and would become prominent in the future city's politics—and Allidina Visram, an Ismaili from Gujarat. Like other South Asian merchants in East Africa, he became rich through financing caravan traders departing the coast along various routes into the African interior.[17] Not only did he invest in the caravan trade, he also 'established extensive upcountry *duka* (small shops) networks throughout East Africa and invested in real estate, plantations, shipping and ginneries'.[18] Such wealthy figures owned much of the land in the Bazaar, where great profit could be made from subletting plots for accommodation as well as commerce.

Attempts were made to prevent Asians and 'Natives' from living in designated European areas, and 'restrictive covenants were inserted in leases in a number of areas forbidding not merely occupation but ownership'.[19] This segregation would prove extremely difficult to enforce, as would be found in the case of two estates north-east of the town centre that had been imagined as European residential areas of the future: Nairobi East and Egerton, the precursors of Eastleigh.

Speculative Beginnings

These estates emerged out of the rampant land speculation of early Nairobi. To catalyse the town's growth, the authorities offered favourable terms for those willing to buy plots and build. Unfortunately, this attracted people more interested in a quick profit than in construction.[20] Indeed, profits were generous, as the steadily rising population—boosted by the arrival of many European settlers—led to the value of land increasing markedly.[21] In this context, the land that would become Eastleigh was bought by speculators. Contemporary Eastleigh covers over 2,000 acres, including the land that now forms the Eastleigh airbase. Originally the land was divided into two separate estates: 220 acres were demarcated as Egerton Estate, named after the famous family of Maurice Egerton. There are few records in the Kenya National Archives concerning this estate, but it seems it was clearly foreseen as a European neighbourhood, brimming with colonial resonance in its names. As well as the general name of Egerton, planned street names referenced key colonial figures such as John Ainsworth, Nairobi's first administrator.

Neighbouring Egerton to the east, was a much bigger block of 2003 acres that was 'bought freehold in two lots at Rs.1 an acre in 1904 and 1905'[22] by a group consisting of a member of the Municipal Committee, G. P. Stevens, other 'Nairobi residents (H. B. Kendall, A. T. Berry, M. H. Wessells) and other South African speculators'.[23] Then it was designated the 'Nairobi East Township', and the investors formed a development company (known as the Nairobi East Township Company) to control it.[24] Both Egerton and Nairobi East were outside the municipal boundary of early Nairobi, and so were beyond the control of the Nairobi council in these early years.

By 1912, according to Hake,[25] 654 acres of Nairobi East were subdivided for sale into 3,332 plots. Map 4, a reproduction of a 1913 plan of the estate, shows the Nairobi East gridiron system as it was initially conceived.[26]

The layout is very similar to that of contemporary Eastleigh, although much of the land to the east would subsequently be swallowed up by the airbase built in 1940, while First Street to the north would become Juja Road. The plan shows the original demarcation of the land into three parts, Sections I, II and III, with most plots in Section III (1,432), over a thousand in Section II, and around 800 in Section I. Furthermore, the plot numbering of Nairobi East shown on the original of this plan still exists in contemporary Eastleigh. The plan also shows three large areas marked for 'public purposes': the original planners perhaps imagined an estate with adequate recreational land emerging over the years. Over recent years what public land there was has been almost all sold off, and those living in the estate must go further afield to find any greenery.

While initially designated an estate for Europeans—and some plots had been sold on the basis that non-Europeans would not be settled there[27]—there was little European demand for land in Nairobi East, a

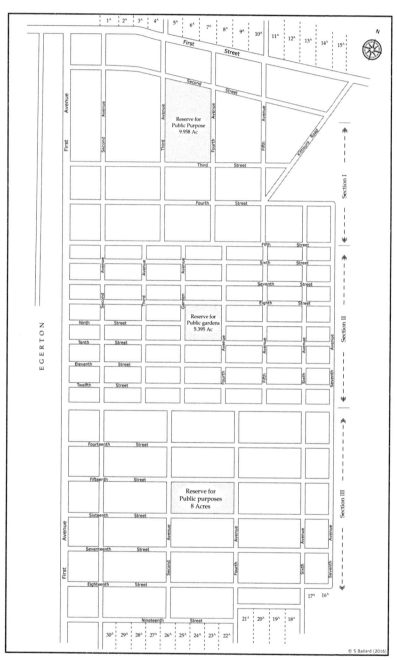

Map 4: Nairobi East plan of 1913

'township' that had no proper road access to Nairobi nor amenities of any sort, and for which the Nairobi Municipality bore no responsibility. The Nairobi East Township Company therefore made the decision to market the estate to Asians instead, advertising Nairobi East Township as an 'Asiatic' estate. Despite the plans to segregate races in Nairobi, Nairobi East was a case in point of how difficult it was to enforce this in practice, especially as the land had been bought with freehold title.[28] Indeed, in a reversal of earlier restrictions, unsold plots in 1913 were advertised as being for 'Asiatics only'.[29] It was at this point that Allidina Visram bought up much of the estate from the company, owning a quarter by April 1913.[30] Three years later he owned 1,078 acres out of the 2,300 acres of what was to become Eastleigh.[31] It clearly represented a good business opportunity, and he reckoned the Asians would not mind residing in that area, despite the distance from town, as long as a tramway was built to connect it to town.[32]

This tramway never materialised, while decent road connections took decades to complete. Essential services and amenities in general were lacking as the Nairobi East Company had done very little to develop the estate, despite having undertaken 'construction of 7 miles of frontage streets and 14 miles of lanes, also drains and water supply "at such time and in such manner as they saw fit"'.[33] The company had wanted guarantees from the administration that no other Indian estate would be established for a period of time, and when no guarantee was forthcoming, they sold off as much of the estate as possible without 'seeing fit' to develop it in a meaningful way.[34]

In this way, their inactivity matched the speculative pattern for much of Nairobi land at the time, as profit came before development, and the government had little power to compel private plot and land owners in townships such as Nairobi East to make them fit for habitation. However, Asians did begin to buy up plots in the estate, setting the scene for its 'Indianisation' over the next half-century as it attracted many different communities with origins in the Subcontinent. But with the death of Visram in 1916 and the final winding up of the Nairobi East Company in 1917, many more plots became available for sale, and it was at this time that the estate began to attract Nairobi's earliest Somali residents.

LITTLE MOGADISHU

The Isaaq Somali

Somalis in early Nairobi were mainly from the Isaaq clan family,[35] one of the five major Somali clan families (Darod, Dir, Rahanweyn, Hawiye and Isaaq), which are divided up further into patrilineal clans and lineages.[36] Somalis were present in the territory that became Kenya long before the country existed, but these particular Somalis had a different geographical origin. They came from the northern Somali regions, the then British Protectorate of Somaliland. Turton describes how the Isaaq came to East Africa as gun-bearers recruited by explorers such as Henry Stanley in the Arabian port of Aden,[37] forming part of an 'auxiliary diaspora', similar to the West Africans (Senegalese and others) who arrived in the Congo Basin alongside the French as 'soldiers, messengers, porters and other labourers' in the late 1800s.[38] They became well thought of and were encouraged to stay. Many became 'clerks and interpreters or joined the King's African Rifles and the East African Constabularies', while the majority became livestock traders.[39] Some worked in the latter capacity for Lord Delamere, one of the most famous British settlers, and this connection is still spoken of by Isaaq in Kenya: one young man in Eastleigh told me with noticeable pride that his 'family came to Kenya with Delamere'. By the time the Isaaq reached Nairobi there were communities in several countries, as many had enlisted in the merchant navy at Aden and subsequently settled in ports the world over, including Cardiff.[40] Indeed, Cardiff still has its population of retired Somali seamen. As well as these far-flung communities, Isaaq also spread throughout East Africa, forming a scattered population whose age-old migration patterns within and beyond Africa challenge conceptions of African transnational mobility as a purely contemporary phenomenon.[41]

In Kenya they settled in various towns, although chiefly in Nairobi, and supplied meat to Nairobi and beyond. Indeed, Somali were key to the livestock trade in early Nairobi, operating a sophisticated barter system between pastoralists such as the Borana and Samburu of northern Kenya, and the Maasai to the south, bringing stock to sell in Nairobi and other urban settlements.[42] The Nairobi District Annual Report of 1912–13 noted how active the Somalis were in this trade, reporting that 'one caravan has just arrived with 3,000 sheep from Samburu, this party is said to have another 3,000 sheep in Kenya ready

34

to come here, and 4,000 in Samburu to go to Jubaland. They have also 800 cattle in Samburu to exchange for more sheep.'[43] They were not just occupied by the livestock trade; some worked in various capacities for the authorities, six forming part of Nairobi's earliest police force.[44]

The Isaaq challenged the racial categories of the colonial authorities, aspiring to be categorised as 'Asiatic' rather than 'native'. They rejected not only the category of 'African'—claiming origins in the Arabian port city of Aden rather than Africa—but also that of 'Somali', as the Somali territory was obviously part of Africa. Their aspiration to be classed as 'non-natives' was seen as credible by some in government, and a Somali Exemption Ordinance of 1919 allowed them that status: indeed, they would pay the same rate of tax as Asians until the 1930s, tax rates being determined by race.[45] This was where the clarity on their status ended: they were considered 'natives under the Native Authority Ordinance but not under its corollary the Native Tribunal Ordinance, while under the Registration of Domestic Servants Ordinance they were considered to be either native or non-native depending on their salary'.[46] The decision in 1936 to classify them as 'native' for taxation purposes (so lowering their tax rate compared with Asians) led to a campaign for them to pay the same rate as Asians again: one of the few campaigns in history to pay more tax.

Not only was pride at stake in this, but they also believed that Asiatic status would confer numerous advantages, including better trading privileges—important for an urbanised people with much interest in commerce.[47] This campaign and its rejection of 'African' and even 'Somali' status is fascinating, especially as it saw the Isaaq attempt to mobilise their diaspora in the UK to help raise support, while appeals to 'home' in the form of Hargeisa were also made: early examples of the 'politics from afar' that diaspora communities engage in. It also spoke to the differences between Somalis, especially between the Isaaq and the pastoralists of northern Kenya, the latter scarcely sharing the same desire to pay more tax. However, this campaign is now elided out of Isaaq narratives of their recent history, due to the politics of Somali identity in contemporary Kenya, Somalis still being the archetypal 'other' for many Kenyans despite their age-old residence in the territory that forms Kenya.[48] A historical campaign that emphasised foreignness is clearly problematic in this context.

Where to Place the Somalis?

By not mapping closely onto colonial racial categories, Somalis disrupted the racial division of space. While the African 'natives' mentioned above in the 1909 Nairobi Annual Report were mainly located on the outskirts of the growing town, the 307 Somalis were living in two villages, one referred to in the 1910 report as the 'Somali Camp' and another as the 'Somali Village'. By the 1912–13 report 279 rupees of hut tax was being paid by Somalis for 93 huts. The location of these villages was to become a contentious issue. They were on the Ngara plains to the north of Nairobi, over the river from the town centre, in an area also populated—then and now—by Indians.[49] Somalis had been given permission by the Nairobi administrator John Ainsworth to occupy vacant land near Ngara Road,[50] but, having no lease or legal rights to the land, they were always in a precarious position, and the authorities had no intention of allowing them to remain there on a more permanent basis.

In 1908 it was proposed that Somalis be given a site in the 'Native Location', precisely where such would-be 'non-natives' would not want to live. This plan stalled, and by 1913 the authorities were once again discussing what to do with the Somalis: now the plan was to establish a new 'temporary location' for them.[51] Such a location was indeed set aside for them 'in order to avoid overcrowding in the previously existing Somali villages and on representations that the number of Somalis in Nairobi was increasing',[52] although few new houses were built on the site.

Pressure for them to move out of Ngara gathered momentum. Being so deeply involved in the livestock trade, Somalis had large numbers of cattle and sheep in the vicinity, leading to fears of smallpox, and the nearby European residents of Parklands demanded that Somalis be removed from an area that had itself been reserved, at least initially, for Europeans.[53] Such pressure led the authorities in 1916 to suggest that Somalis and their stock be moved to Mbagathi, about eight miles southeast of Nairobi. About 126 households were to be accommodated there, and a 'suitable site… was prepared with some care'.[54] However, what was deemed 'suitable' by the authorities was not considered so by the Somalis themselves. They resisted this move, partly because of its distance from town, where many were involved in commerce or employed.[55] Shunning Mbagathi, Somalis instead looked east, and soon had their first foothold in what was to become Eastleigh.

In all this, what the British had not understood clearly was that this Somali population had become distinctly urban, despite their continued involvement in the pastoral economy of the region. Indeed, the Isaaq Somali formed some of the earliest 'townspeople' in colonial Kenya, despite being neglected in the literature on urbanisation in Kenya.[56]

First Footsteps

Almost all the Ngara Somalis took up residence in Nairobi East.[57] With no race restrictions on the purchase of plots, Somalis—some of whom were relatively wealthy from their livestock commerce— could buy plots there. By 1918 an inspection by the Principal Sanitation Officer of 1,000 acres of Nairobi East found there were 3,364 plots, of which approximately 2,500 had been alienated by the following buyers: 'Europeans 86. Eurasians 112. Goans 284. Indians 1839. Somalis 219. Armenians 3'.[58] Few of these plots had actually been built upon, so most were uninhabited. Also, as the freehold titles contained 'no development clauses, or sanitary obligations', there were no roads or drains constructed, while water came from two wells, one of which was dry while 'the other contained a little water much rubbish and dead animals'. Nor were there any police or other forms of formal authority. Not dissimilar to the later 'Little Mogadishu', Nairobi East was in some ways disconnected physically and governmentally from wider Nairobi.

As well as lamenting the great risk stemming from the estate in respect of sanitation, the Sanitation Officer adds a description of the houses found there: 'Many scattered houses of various kinds were seen, some built of stone, and others wattle and daub. Two large groups of buildings inhabited by Somalis and Indians exist; the building line has not been adhered to.' Another description of Somali houses in Nairobi East comes from Isak Dinesen (Karen Blixen) who visited what she termed the 'Somali town' alongside her Isaaq 'servant' Farah Aden. She describes it in a manner typifying early colonial tendencies to essentialise Somalis as a 'nomadic race', despite the urban existence of the Isaaq:[59]

The Somali town lay exposed to all winds and was shadeless and dusty, it must have recalled to the Somali their native deserts. Europeans, who live for a long time, even for several generations, in the same place, cannot reconcile themselves to the complete indifference to the surroundings of their homes, of the nomadic races. The Somali houses were irregularly strewn on the bare ground, and looked as if they had been nailed together with a bushel of four-inch nails, to last for a week. It was a surprising thing, when you entered one of them, to find it inside so neat and fresh, scented with Arab incenses, with fine carpets and hangings, vessels of brass and silver, and swords with ivory hilts and noble blades.

There are still Isaaq in the estate who speak of this early settlement. These include Musa Cige, a man born in the area in 1923. He is the son of an early Isaaq 'settler', and he and his brother (Hassan Cige, who still lives in Eastleigh, running a lodging, Moyale Lodge, on First Avenue) are direct links to these earlier days. Their father was involved in the First World War, later becoming a clerk as well as keeping livestock. Musa remembers the area as being just 'bush', and says that livestock were the major factor in Somalis coming there as their cattle could graze on the land that now forms the Eastleigh airbase during the rains, moving further afield for pasture in the dry seasons.

Such Isaaq families were becoming a fixed part of the urban land-scape in colonial Kenya, but were also part of a wider diaspora, keeping their connections to a 'home' region in Somaliland. For families like that of Hassan and Musa Cige, 'home' was still Hargeisa, where they originated. Their father went back to Hargeisa to find himself a wife, while Musa also was sent to Hargeisa for what he termed *dhaqan celin*, a much-used term today for when a young boy or girl in the diaspora is sent back 'home' to learn their culture and religion.[60] Today many children on *dhaqan celin* are found in Eastleigh, having been sent there by families in Europe or North America. In all this, the transnational lives of these early Eastleigh Isaaq echo down the ages.

Becoming Eastleigh

By official decree in January 1921, Eastleigh became the name of a township that amalgamated Nairobi East and the formerly separate Egerton Estate. This is the solemn notice in the *Kenya Gazette* of 19 January 1921 that proclaimed the formation of Eastleigh Estate:

FROM NAIROBI EAST TO LITTLE MOGADISHU

The East Africa Townships Ordinance, 1903

Proclamation

IN EXERCISE of the powers conferred upon me by the East Africa Townships Ordinance, 1903, I, Edward Northey, Major-General of His Majesty's Forces, Knight Commander of the Most Distinguished Order of Saint Michael and Saint George, Companion of the Most Honourable Order of the Bath, Governor of the Colony of Kenya, hereby proclaim and declare all that area, lately known as Egerton Estate and Nairobi East Township and now known as Egerton, Eastleigh and Eastleigh Extension and more particularly described in the schedule hereto to be a Township for the purposes of the above ordinance and to be named Eastleigh Township.

Nairobi,
The 15th day of January, 1921.
Edward Northey,
Governor.[61]

The name Eastleigh—so redolent of the Home Counties of England—clearly pays homage to the Hampshire town of the same name. This is probably connected to the importance of that town to the growth of the railways in England, and the importance of the railway to the founding of Nairobi. Hake refers to this connection, but does not elaborate on exactly why the name was chosen.[62] A guidebook to East Africa published in 1968 relates that the railway company built houses there in the years between the world wars for its 'expanding Indian and Goanese staff'.[63] Perhaps the company had bought up some land there around 1920, influencing the choice of name, or perhaps the 'East' in Nairobi East Township easily slipped into 'Eastleigh'. Whatever the etymology, by 1921 already 'over 3000 plots' had 'been disposed of mainly to Asiatics and Somalis'.[64] Somalis were thus in Eastleigh even before it was Eastleigh.

Eastleigh Takes Shape

This newly proclaimed township still had few buildings, roads or other amenities. Indeed, the estate was still hardly distinguishable from the plain upon which it sat, and the authorities still had little control over it. However, lengthy regulations covering construction and hygiene were published in 1921 in the *Gazette*, while a 'Superintendent of Conservancy'—Mr. W. W. Ridout, formerly Nairobi Town Engineer and Acting Town Clerk—was appointed with the task of ensuring that these were adhered to, as well as collecting rates.

Despite an increasing population (344 by 1926),[65] progress on the estate's infrastructure was painfully slow. By 1927, despite the colonial government taking over more control of Eastleigh following its purchase in 1925 of many plots sold from the estate of Allidina Visram,[66] matters had not improved, and a group of Indian residents sent a petition to the Acting Governor of Kenya lamenting its state.[67] Indeed, contemporary complaints about lack of investment in infrastructure in the estate are not new. Like other non-European parts of Nairobi, Eastleigh would wait years to see the amenities already in place in some European areas by 1908. Eastleigh residents petitioned the Governor about the poor amenities, also lamenting the lack of water:

> The meagre supply carried by the tanks from rains gets generally exhausted before the rains set in again. ... That the unenviable position of Your Excellency's petitioners will be understood when it is realized that they can wish neither for rains nor for drought! In drought they have to go thirsty, without a wash and greenless gardens: and in rains they have to wade through bogs and marshes for their daily trips to the capital.

The petition further complained of the lack of progress in constructing roads within the estate, as well as the lack of electric lighting. The reply came that money had been allocated for the access road to town, but that matters should wait until a decision had been made on Eastleigh Township by the Feetham Commission, then charged with looking into 'the organization and planning of the municipality' of Nairobi, from which Eastleigh was still separate.[68] This commission subsequently recommended that the original municipal boundary be extended to cover townships such as Eastleigh and Muthaiga, despite resistance from residents of both estates who would now have to pay municipal rates.

The recommendation was followed, and Eastleigh officially became part of Nairobi municipality in 1928, after which amenities were gradually improved, with members of the Legislative Council expressing the desire 'that Eastleigh properties should be developed as rapidly as possible' and promising the early establishment of a water supply and access road.[69] Urgency was felt, as housing for Asians had become very scarce, and Eastleigh was seen as the answer.

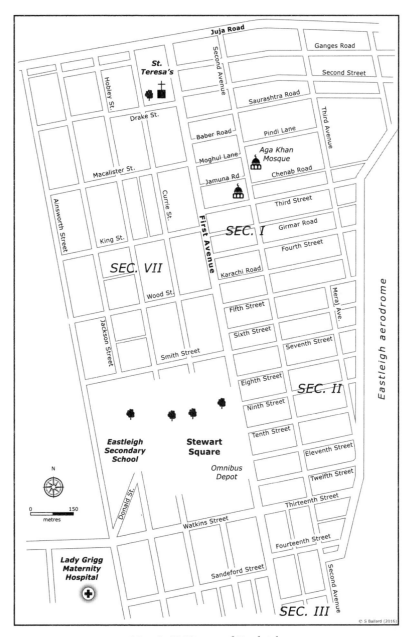

Map 5: 1958 map of Eastleigh

In the next few decades Eastleigh was gradually built upon, although not wholly to the blueprint of the 1913 plans, as revealed by a 1958 map of the estate. This shows its later geography with the estate divided into seven sections rather than the earlier three (compare with the earlier plan of Nairobi East): Section IV was to the south of Section III, Sections V and VI formed the most northerly sections, and Section VII was what used to be Egerton Estate. Map 5 is a reproduction of part of this map with Sections I, II, III and VII marked on. Comparing the map with the plan of 1913, one sees how the 1940 construction of the aerodrome (as a wartime RAF base) had swallowed up much land, leaving only three avenues running north to south, rather than the seven of the 1913 Nairobi East plan.

The airbase eventually became the main airport for Nairobi. This would ensure that the estate's road access to Nairobi was kept in good condition for some time to come, so important did it become to the infrastructure of Nairobi, and Kenya more broadly. Also, in the 1950s the main Kenya bus depot was moved to Eastleigh, leading to the tarmacking of First Avenue (Second Avenue was the main thoroughfare in that era).

Much else on the map speaks of how far it had departed from the earlier blueprint. For example, the map shows how small plots were to become in Section VII, compared with those laid out in the original Egerton Estate shown on the plan from 1916, many having been cut up into plots of an eighth of an acre to maximise the value of the land,[70] while several extra streets had been added to its layout between the numbered streets running east to west. What the map does not show is that many of the plots were still empty, some being used as farmland, as were a number of streets in Section III.[71] That there were empty plots and public land such as Stewart Square by the bus depot suggests a far from crowded estate, very different from today's Eastleigh where even public land has been transferred to private developers.

Identity, Space and Race

In the 1920s Asians attracted to the estate would often move back to town in despair at the lack of amenities,[72] so Somalis formed a relatively large proportion of its population. But while the Somali population grew more gradually, the Asian population grew exponentially; more and more moved into the estate as better amenities began to be supplied.[73] Indeed, the Somali population of Eastleigh was still only in the hundreds—764—by the end of the colonial period, according to the 1962 census.[74] At the same time, the Asian population was in the tens of thousands: 17,811 out of a total population of 29,578.[75] Thus the Asian population soon far surpassed the Somali one, despite the latter's early occupation of the estate, which at this time was in some ways a 'Little India'.

The 1958 map reflects this Asian dominance. While the very British-sounding names of Section VII speak of the earlier European origins of Egerton Estate, Asians had long been the principal plot holders.[76] Meanwhile, the names of the newly added streets to the east of First Avenue demonstrate Asian dominance through their decidedly Indian-sounding names, as the likes of 'Ganges Road' and 'Moghul Lane' make clear. As well as the street names being 'Indian-ised', so was the style of building that came to dominate the estate: the courtyard house, a 'building planned to accommodate a joint family, sometimes also tenants'.[77] This type of building was common in all the Asian-dominated areas of Nairobi, including Ngara, and such a design would dominate Eastleigh until the recent commercial transformation.

'Asian' clearly conflates many different groupings constituted by religion, ethnicity and place of family origin in the Subcontinent. In this regard, Eastleigh has always been the site of much 'super-diversity', (Vertovec's term, popular in analyses of the increasing diversity in the contemporary UK and elsewhere).[78] The term attempts to capture not just ethnic and cultural diversity, but other forms that terms such as 'multicultural' struggle to encompass. Eastleigh and other African urban spaces show that super-diversity is far from restricted either to the West or to the contemporary era. Although Africans and Europeans sometimes conflated Indians as one group,[79] the Asian population of Nairobi was certainly super-diverse, with different populations split along religious, ethnic and social lines. Such diversity was reflected in how Eastleigh's population was spatially distributed. Different populations would, in the main, live separately, although some resident associations united them, and many older children would mix at the Racecourse School (now Eastleigh High School), which was also

Plate 4: Old Indian courtyard buildings among new residential blocks

attended by Somali and other northern Kenyans, including Borana in colonial times. My late Borana friend Abdulkadir Araru—whom I got to know in London—attended this school and vividly remembered a school trip to Government House to see the Queen Mother in 1959 where he and another northern Kenyan friend had to persuade the *askari* (Kiswahili for guard or soldier) that they were indeed allowed to sit with the Asian children—such was still the ambiguous place of Somalis and northern Kenyans in colonial racial categories.

Amongst the Eastleigh Indians were many Goans (1,290 in 1962),[80] and their life in the estate revolved around the Roman Catholic church— St Theresa's, the first building of which was constructed around 1930[81]—in the most northerly section of Eastleigh near to Juja Road. Goan children would usually attend the school at St Theresa's, even those whose parents lived in other parts of Kenya; Mervyn Maciel (a clerk in Marsabit in the 1950s) remembers dropping his children off at St Theresa's before returning back north to his work.[82] Section III, to the south, was 'occupied by the Rajasthani Community. ... This community built the "Ram Mandir" [Temple] in the thirties.'[83] Hindus and Sikhs in general dominated more central sections of Eastleigh, while Asian Muslims were spread throughout, including around the Khoja Mosque in Section I, built in 1958.[84] Economic class would prove another dividing factor, as Section III became seen as the least desirable part of the estate. As Hake describes, 'It was in a cul-de-sac; it was not on the way to anywhere else and nobody visited it without good reason.'[85] Land was cheaper in this part of the estate as a consequence.

As with the Asians, there was much diversity among Somalis. While the Isaaq certainly provided the core Somali population in Eastleigh, a Somali-speaking population in Nairobi proved a resource for other Somalis from north-east Kenya needing a place to stay in the city. In the words of Musa Cige, 'Somalis would come to Somalis' when visiting Nairobi. He remembers a famous Ogadeni visitor from Garissa: Dekow Stanbul—secretary general of the Northern Province People's Progressive Party—who was involved in the so-called Shifta War where Somali secessionists fought a guerrilla campaign against the Kenyan government.[86] Stanbul would come and stay with Cige's family in Eastleigh when visiting Nairobi. Hassan Cige also remembers an earlier movement of Somalians from Barawa (in the south of the former Italian Somaliland territory) coming in the late 1940s with Fiat trucks to instigate trade between Kenya and Somalia.

There was some consistency in the spatial distribution of Somali ethnicity in the estate. Hassan Cige also told me how the Isaaq divided themselves between the different sections by clan. Section I was mainly inhabited by Habr Yunis; Section II by Habr Jalo; and Section III by Habr Awal.[87] He admitted that this was only a rough guide, as although born in Section III, he is Habr Jalo. Another long-time Isaaq resident, Mzee Dekow of Section III, offered the explanation for this spatial separation: that they had fallen out over land for grazing their cattle.[88] Certainly by 1962 Somalis were especially congregated in Section III, where an organisation called the Somali Community Trust had bought up a number of houses. Section III still has some old Isaaq families living there, and is the site for the oldest Somali-built Mosque in the estate, the small Shaafi mosque built by Habr Awal Isaaq in the 1930s on what was then called Banaras Street.

Living among the Asians and Somalis was a population of coastal Arabs and Swahili, another highly fluid ethnic category that fits uneasily into colonial categories. Indeed, coastal Swahili were often keen to emphasise Arab descent in colonial times, to gain 'non-native' privileges in a similar manner to the Isaaq Somali: otherwise Swahili were counted as 'native'.[89] There were even people from as far afield as the Seychelles living there.[90] Of course, there were also many other Africans in the estate, even if 'native' residence there—that is to say, residence of the Africans seen by the British as indigenous to Kenya— was subject to theoretical restrictions. Such restrictions reflected the long-standing anxiety of colonial authorities over the migration of supposedly rural and 'tribal' peoples to urban centres and the potentially dangerous consequences of 'detribalisation'.[91] Apartheid-esque policies were introduced in many colonial cities to counter this, policies the authorities were rarely able to enforce effectively. Certainly in Eastleigh there was much African settlement, perhaps unsurprisingly given its proximity to Pumwani, Nairobi's first 'native' estate.

One of the first to attempt to defy the colonial segregationist policies and purchase a plot in Eastleigh was Harry Thuku, the pioneer of African nationalism in Kenya. In 1932 he wanted to buy a plot in Eastleigh, choosing it as a suitable location under the influence of his wife, a Somali whom he had married in Kismayu—where he had been exiled in the 1920s—and who wanted to be close to other Somalis. The plot in question was in Section III, and became the cause of much debate among the colonial authorities, who were unsure whether he should be allowed to live outside the Kikuyu 'native reserve' in central Kenya. Buying the plot involved a transfer between Thuku and an Indian; this was legally sound as the title was 'free of racial restrictions'.[92] What most worried the authorities was whether a 'native' required exemption to live in any part of Nairobi aside from the 'native location' at Pumwani. Opinion was divided as to whether it was sensible to grant him such an exemption. It later transpired that Thuku wanted the plot for the head office of the Kikuyu Central Association, rather than to reside there himself. The authorities resolved to allow the transfer, happy that they could keep an eye on his association, but advising him of the need for an exemption should he eventually decide to live there.[93]

In these deliberations about Thuku the idea of Eastleigh as a purely Indian, Somali and Arab area was punctured, as it was brought to colonial attention that many 'natives' were also living there.[94] Although the authorities set about removing these supposedly illegal residents, their residence in Eastleigh would only grow stronger. By the 1940s, many Africans had migrated to Eastleigh, and overcrowding was especially severe, 'giving rise to complaints by Indians'.[95] Africans required 'passes from the Municipal African Affairs Officer', but 'large numbers live there, because this officer cannot refuse passes when accommodation is so short. Consequently African labourers have to compete for housing with Indians and prostitutes (these having been given passes to work as "ayahs", but remaining in Eastleigh after they have lost their posts).'[96] African prostitutes were indeed some of the earliest non-Indian or Somali residents of Eastleigh, as White's work on prostitution in colonial Kenya shows.[97] Soon some of these prostitutes were not just residents, but plot owners too: 'Between 1946 and 1948 all the new African landlords in Eastleigh were women, former or still-working prostitutes',[98] and 'by 1948 and 1949 African property ownership in Eastleigh was becoming commonplace'.[99]

Despite the poor nature of the housing available to such residents, colonial Eastleigh was not a cheap place to buy land and to live: indeed, 'rents were constantly forced up and sub-letting increasingly commonplace' through to the 1950s,[100] resonating strongly with contemporary complaints of high rents in the estate. Indeed, land in Eastleigh was more expensive than in European parts of Nairobi, such as Muthaiga, due to the greater demand by non-Europeans. In 1961 the Goan politician Fitz de Souza related in the Legislative Council how an acre in Eastleigh fetched £8,000–10,000, compared with £1,000 for an acre in Muthaiga.[101]

Despite its plots filling up and often cramped buildings, life was less hectic than in contemporary Eastleigh. Mzee Gulu is one of the few Indians who still frequents the estate, owning a restaurant on Third Street. He was born in Eastleigh in 1932, to a father originally from the Punjab—who came to Nairobi with the railway and stayed on to work as a building contractor. It is his quotation that began this chapter, with its evocation of forest and wildlife: a nostalgic image of Eastleigh greatly contrasting with its current incarnation. However, the estate was far from perfect in this era, especially its infrastructure. De Souza, in the same speech to the Legislative Council, remarked how Eastleigh residents had been complaining about the roads for over fifteen years with little progress, although some had been built:

Until a few years ago I know that in the morning at seven or eight o'clock, when the people of Eastleigh went to get to the bus stop to get to work, it was a common sight in the rainy season to see people take off their shoes and their socks and wade across the pools of water which lay outside their houses and walk up to the bus stop and try to put on their shoes to go to work. Such a state of affairs is completely wrong.

De Souza was complaining that despite paying far more in rates than Muthaiga or Parklands (ten times as much, he claimed), Eastleigh residents saw little in return. This again echoes later Eastleigh, where businesspeople and residents have long lamented that despite the estate being a cash cow for the council, the infrastructure was left to decay. While no longer a separate township, colonial Eastleigh was still, in many ways, on the margins.

Post-Independence Eastleigh

Independence brought another phase in the estate's history as many Asians moved not only out of Eastleigh but also out of East Africa. The new era brought them difficult decisions, such as whether to claim local citizenship or make use of the opportunity to obtain a British passport. As the governments of the new nations sought to Africanise their economies, Asians also felt at economic risk, as trading licences became hard to renew and Africans moved into occupations where they had once dominated, including the civil service. Many families would become highly transnational, with some family members remaining in East Africa and taking up Kenyan, Ugandan or Tanzanian citizenship, while others moved abroad and became British, thus taking advantage of opportunities in different countries, just as Somalis do nowadays.[102]

Of those who remained in Kenya, a large proportion moved out of Eastleigh to more upmarket areas, including Parklands. This out-migration affected Section III the most, 'because properties were cheaper to buy, and rents lower, and because the lower-paid Asians were the first to be hit by Africanisation'.[103] Africans from nearby Pumwani and elsewhere moved in, often renting from the departing Asians.[104] As Hake reports, 'By 1970 the area was almost wholly African in character.'[105] Somalis were included in the category of 'African', but they were not alone in buying up plots from Asians, and many Kikuyu moved into Section III. Later, other Eastleigh sections were Africanised, as more people moved in, renting accommodation as well as buying plots from departing Asians. Tiwari describes a 'chain reaction' already operating on the eve of independence, whereby Africans from Pumwani would move into Section III, then into the more high-class sections as they became wealthier, mirroring some Asians who would move from Section III to Sections I and II, before leaving for the likes of Parklands.

Between 1962 and 1969 the population of Eastleigh was swelled by new African arrivals, the main built-up area increasing by around 20,000 people.[106] With the new inhabitants came changes to the spatial use of the buildings, as African residents tended to subdivide houses, even putting up constructions in gardens to house the steady stream of incomers.[107] Little would change architecturally, however, with the courtyard buildings dominating, even as some taller apartment blocks and lodgings began to sprout.

This Africanisation of Eastleigh was also reflected in the new street names, the old Watkins Road becoming General Waruinge Street— named after a Mau Mau general—while the very colonial sounding Ainsworth Road became the very African Muratina Street, *muratina* being the name of a traditional alcoholic beverage. Wood Street became Kipande Athumani Street, named after a well-known Kenyan comedian who used to live in the area.[108] As we will see in the next chapter, Eastleigh's history continues to be inscribed in the names found in the estate, especially the names of the malls that now dominate its landscape.

The general complexion of life appears to have altered little at first, although more shops and lodgings emerged as the estate became seen as a potential commercial centre. Indeed, the city council of this era considered Eastleigh a possible commercial zone that could serve the wider Eastlands areas and reduce pressure on Nairobi's city centre. This was discussed by the council in 1968, at a time when various businesses were moving to Eastleigh from a part of the city centre where a new housing estate was being built.[109] Eastleigh's potential as a commercial centre was discussed again in 1984, while in 1989 a policy plan was submitted recommending that the parts of Sections I, II and VII between Juja Road and what became General Waruingi Road after independence 'be declared the District Centre for Eastlands' and 'accommodate low-level commercial activities that could not find a place at the CBD [Central Business

District]'.[110] Such policy was barely implemented in any meaningful way, but it did mean that the Somali-inspired developments of the 1990s came to an area designated for commerce: in this regard, Eastleigh was already ripe for development.

Many particular post-independence landmarks—as well as the general atmosphere of the estate's earlier incarnation—still live in the memory of former residents. Yusuf Hassan, the current Member of Parliament for Kamukunji (the constituency in which Eastleigh is located), spent time growing up in Eastleigh in the 1970s, and remembers Somali restaurants of the era, including one on Seventh Street run by an Isaaq woman, Mama Fatuma Arr, who now operates a different restaurant in the estate.[111] He also remembers a Mandera café on Sixth Street, as well as several Ethiopian restaurants run by exiles from the 1974 Ethiopian revolution. The Ethiopian-run New Paradiso Hotel on Tenth Street—very much still an Ethiopian-dominated street—had one such restaurant, and even entered the geography of tourism in Nairobi, being recommended for accommodation and food in the early editions of the *Rough Guide to Kenya*.[112] Eastleigh has more recently been banished from such guidebooks.

Paul Goldsmith—a researcher with much experience of the estate—describes the earlier Eastleigh that he remembers:

> Eastleigh [was] a place where Somali transporters parked their double trailers along side streets, coastal Swahili ran lodgings, Gikuyu women sold produce and their men ran bars, and Meru miraa traders hung up their banana leaf flags outside shops. The Kamba sold tires, Ethiopians turned their living rooms into cafes, and the flashes of Luo welders lit up the night.[113]

Mohaa, my guide to much of contemporary Eastleigh, also remembers what it was like before its commercial transformation, as when very young he worked in the transport industry (around 1990) and often visited the estate. He describes the Eastleigh of that era as a *mahali pa starehe* (place of relaxation) where various lodgings—including Garissa Lodge on Jam Street, soon to be the first Eastleigh shopping mall, and then run by a Swahili man—would offer repose. Other places had notoriety as places of prostitution, including a lodging on Fourth Street known as Bahati Lodge. There was a Kamba lodging too—the Mwingi Viewpoint Hotel—which was on Twelfth Street, and another

Kikuyu lodging—Mwaora Boarding and Lodging—on First Avenue, where now one of the biggest shopping malls (Amal Plaza) stands. Eastleigh had also developed some famous bars and discos, including Mateso Bila Chuki,[114] a bar still operating on Second Avenue: this was a central landmark for Eastleigh, attracting revellers from beyond the estate, as did Muungano Point on Third Street, a 'drive-in' bar famous for the residency of the rumba band Simba Wanyika.[115] Both these establishments were also mentioned in guidebooks for tourists.[116]

However, events far away in Mogadishu were soon to precipitate a new era of transformation that would overwhelm this earlier incarnation of the estate.

Becoming Little Mogadishu

Crucial in what would follow, Eastleigh's Somali contingent had remained a constant through all its demographic fluctuations. Many Isaaq would move on to other parts of the city, especially areas such as South C. However, the declining number of Isaaq was augmented in the post-independence period by Somalis of other clan affiliations. A considerable proportion of these were from north-eastern Kenya rather than Somalia. They significantly boosted the population of Eastleigh in the 1980s as drought, insecurity and state policy antagonistic to nomadic lifestyles convinced many in northern Kenya to move away from pastoralism as a livelihood—at least temporarily—and establish businesses in Nairobi and other urban areas.[117] Indeed, for many people Eastleigh is not so much 'Little Mogadishu' as a piece of Garissa or Mandera brought to the city. Other pastoralist residents of northern Kenya—including Borana—also saw Eastleigh as their Nairobi base. Thus, the changing demographics of the estate are not just linked to displacement from Somalia, but also the changing dynamics of pastoralist livelihoods and processes of urbanisation within Kenya.

However, the estate's refugee influx was the key factor in its subsequent transformation. This has a long history, as the estate was hosting refugees from the late 1960s onwards, including those coming from Ethiopia and Eritrea, a number of whom would make money in the lucrative matatu routes—numbers 6 and 9—connecting the estate with the city centre.[118] Somalians have also long been settling in

Eastleigh, though their numbers had been relatively small before the early 1990s and Somalia's full descent into civil war. Some came as refugees from the Ogaden War in 1977,[119] and from Siad Barre's crackdown on groups opposing his rule such as the mainly Majerteen Somali Salvation Democratic Front. The close ties of many Somalis in Kenya with those across the border in Somalia meant that there has always been much intermarriage too, and no doubt many Somali nationals have settled in Kenya (and Eastleigh) as a result of marriage to Kenyan nationals. Forced migration is certainly not the only cause of a Somalian presence in the estate.

With Kenyan Somalis and Somalians both migrating to the estate in the 1980s, Somali identity began to loom large in Sections I and II, and Eastleigh was already known as Nairobi's Somali district. However, it is with the drawn-out collapse of the Somali state in the late 1980s and early 1990s that Eastleigh would see its first major influx of refugees from southern Somalia. In 1991, as Barre fled Mogadishu, a mass displacement occurred as hundreds of thousands of Somalians from the south fled to Ethiopia and Kenya. As opposition groups took control of Mogadishu and much other territory in Somalia, the clan (Marehan) and clan family (Darod) of the exiled president became defined as a 'mortal enemy' of these groups under the lineage-based politics they adopted, a politics termed 'clan cleansing' by Kapteijns.[120] Lindley describes how thousands of Darod—joined by Somalians of other clans too—fled the violence that ensued 'on foot or crammed into vehicles over the border into the NEP [North Eastern Province]; by dhow from Somalia's coastal towns to Mombasa; and by plane to Nairobi'.[121]

After initial attempts to secure the border and prevent incomers, the Moi government allowed 'large numbers of refugees from Somalia to cross the border in 1991 and 1992'.[122] Subsequently, the government received help from the UNHCR in establishing seven camps to house the ever-increasing numbers of refugees (reaching almost 400,000 in 1992, including Ethiopian refugees fleeing the downfall of Mengistu), registering all Somalians reaching the camps as *prima facie* refugees given the impossibility of assessing the claims of each individual.[123]

Refugee life in Kenya is generally seen through the prism of life in refugee camps, especially given the attention to the vast, often insecure camps of Dadaab and Kakuma,[124] where rape and violence have been very real risks.[125] These camps—and their precursors at Liboi near the Somali border and Utange near Mombasa—are the bleak reality for many refugees in Kenya. However, over the years many have migrated to urban areas despite an official policy of encampment, which the Kenyan government has continually tried—or at least threatened—to enforce over the years to keep refugees apart from the indigenous Kenyan population. In this regard, urban refugees are seen by the Kenyan state as people doubly displaced: from their original home country, and from the camps to which refugees are considered to belong. While Kenyan cities are uncertain and risky places to be without legal rights, they at least offer more hope for self-improvement than the camps, themselves uncertain and risky places where protracted dependency can sap morale.[126] The greater opportunities for education, health care and business in urban areas are obviously major draws.[127] Mombasa became home to a number of refugees in these early days, as did Nairobi itself. Some arrived directly on flights from Somalia, and settled there rather than reporting to the camps, especially those who had been urban dwellers in Somalia, and the wealthy[128]—who as in other refugee contexts had the means to leave quickly.[129] Others came from the camps soon thereafter.[130]

Eastleigh, as a home to Somalis who had come in previous decades, was an obvious choice for settlement, offering numerous lodgings for those of means; those without financial capital but with social capital could stay with family members resident in the estate. Such social capital was common for those with cross-border connections between southern Somalia and northern Kenya. This was especially the case for Darod Somalis—especially Ogaden—many of whom have families that span the national divides. Certain Eastleigh lodgings—and certain parts of the estate—would become associated with particular clans too, for example, a Hotel Taleh became a refuge of the Ali Yusuf lineage of the Ogadeni.[131] Not all Somali refugees settled in Eastleigh, however: Goldsmith relates a spatialised settlement pattern in the early 1990s, as wealthy urbanites 'including well-off Hawiye businessmen from Mogadishu or Barre's Marehan kinspeople' moved to higher end estates such as Hurlingham; the less well-off and 'members of the "lower status" groups like the Rahanweyn, ended up in camps like Liboi and Utange'.[132]

In the 1990s—as today—it was very difficult to estimate the number of Somalis in Nairobi as a whole, let alone in Eastleigh. Pérouse de Montclos describes their total number in that era as a mystery, giving a range of 10,000–100,000.[133] Nairobi's Somali population rose in official census figures from 950 (1962); to 6,941 (1979); to 12,988 (1989), most residing in Eastleigh.[134] However, the rise between 1979 and 1999 in Eastleigh's wider population speaks of growth driven by a refugee influx, urban mobility, and rural–urban migration within Kenya: the population rose from 53,562 to 246,420.[135] While only a proportion of this total would be accounted for by Somalis, as other groups were in-migrating too, it is likely that over ten thousand Somali refugees alongside many Kenyan Somalis were living in Eastleigh by the early 1990s.

With this influx, Somali identity had become conspicuous. The language used, the names of restaurants and hotels (including the Hotel Taleh named after a zone of Mogadishu), the greater visibility of Islam, all made Eastleigh seem a very Somali place. Furthermore, Somali food, dress and social habits (including chewing the stimulant substance known as khat) were much more evident too. Even the spelling of its name would be Somali-ised: many Somalis in Kenya and in the wider Somali world write its name not as *Eastleigh* but as *Islii*. Sections I and II in particular were Somali-ised—though not completely, as we will see in chapter 3—and it is this area that would from the 1990s be dubbed by commentators 'Little Mogadishu'.[136]

Perpetual Transformation

While this book takes as its main focus its more recent transformation into a place of hyper-commerce, like many other parts of rapidly expanding Nairobi, Eastleigh had few periods of stasis during the twentieth century. This chapter's survey of the history of the estate shows that while Eastleigh's colonial history of racialised urban policy helped make it a 'Little India', it has long been far more cosmopolitan than this suggests. Hidden by a common narrative of Eastleigh as a formerly Asian estate are the many others who have populated its shifting and super-diverse 'ethnoscape', including Kikuyu and other up-country Kenyans, Swahili, Arabs and even people from the Seychelles. Migratory processes centred on this estate have long had transformative effects, leading to constant demographic and architectural change. However, a Somali thread runs right back to the origins of the estate, showing that their presence is certainly not just a result of displacement from civil war.

In Eastleigh's history we also see a place long soaked in diaspora and lives lived transnationally. Indeed, its connection to far off elsewheres is not a new phenomenon, as its Indian street names of the 1950s make clear. Its very name, Eastleigh, speaks of links to an English homeland far away. Its population—including the Isaaq and its Indians—has also long maintained networks stretching far across the globe. In this regard, Eastleigh's history demonstrates that the hypermobility and transnational connections so evocative of Eastleigh's present incarnation have been a feature of life there right from the start. Sadly, another feature of life in the estate that has echoed through the ages is the decayed infrastructure. This would soon sharply contrast with an urban landscape of malls and multi-storey hotels formed out of the transnational commerce that has become the lifeblood of the estate.

2

URBAN TRANSFORMATION

Look up it's Dubai; look down it's dirt.

Eastleigh resident, October 2011

By the early 1990s the patterns of displacement that resulted from crisis in the Somali regions dramatically increased the Somali presence in Eastleigh, cementing its place as the city's Somali quarter, its Little Mogadishu. These patterns of displacement would soon catalyse economic growth and construction in the estate and provide opportunities to many—Kenyan, Ethiopian and Somali alike. In this way, Eastleigh marks a strong example of what Hammar terms 'displacement economies' whereby out of crisis and destruction can come great creativity and opportunity.[1] That such a strong economy emerged so rapidly in an estate housing refugees has sparked much conjecture of how this was achieved, and a number of sensational explanations—including the piratical—have emerged to account for it.

This chapter adopts a macro perspective upon these developments, interweaving description of the rise of its malls with that of the spread of its networks across the world. In so doing it explores the real factors underpinning its transformation—one that has spilled over from the estate into many other parts of Kenya and beyond. This transformation connects not just to the social and economic impacts of displacement, but also the wider 'low-end' global processes[2] that Somalis have been

57

able to leverage into the landscape of Eastleigh. However, the chapter begins with a look at the shopping mall. Eastleigh's characteristic reinterpretation of this retail model and its use of space are of fundamental importance in understanding what has happened to this part of Nairobi in the last twenty years.

The Malling of Eastleigh

The term 'shopping mall' brings to mind the shopping centres of the USA that became key spaces of consumerist leisure from the 1950s onwards. North America and Europe were well and truly 'malled', as consumer culture came to revolve around these increasingly large establishments, where chain stores compete for custom in an environment that can air condition and security screen out the world beyond. For several decades, as Crawford writes, these structures were an almost foolproof business model in which many were keen to invest.[3] While many have closed in recent years, the mall still remains central to much American social life. Beyond the USA, the model has spread far and wide. Shoppers now throng malls everywhere from Sydney to Dubai to Cairo,[4] spending money or just hanging out in spaces that, while architecturally diverse, generally offer a very similar consumer 'experience'.

Kenya has not been immune to this retail blueprint. The city's wealthy Westlands area has long been home to various malls, beginning with the Asian-owned Sarit Centre, built in 1983. Westlands is also home to the tragic Westgate, perhaps the most high-end of the Nairobi malls when built, and hence an attractive target for the Al-Shabaab militants who stormed it in September 2013. The building of high-end malls appears to have accelerated within the Nairobi metropolitan area (witness the new Thika Road Mall) as well in other towns and cities, and such spaces have been embraced by Kenya's middle classes for shopping and leisure. In Kisumu a newly planned mall has been hailed for the economic growth it will bring through providing business infrastructure.[5] Malls are thus seen not just as spaces of aspirational consumerism, but also triggers for development.

In Eastleigh the term 'mall' currently designates something rather different. Generally, as we will discuss, these are constructions designed to house hundreds of tiny retail shops, selling mostly cheap goods brought from the East by Somali trade networks. Rather than the luxury 'mega-malls' of other parts of Nairobi, these are mostly 'low-end' malls selling the goods of 'low-end' globalisation, although, as we will see, this does not do justice to all the Eastleigh development: more recent constructions are gravitating towards the higher end, including the giant Comesa Mall currently under construction, which resembles the malls of western Nairobi.[6] There is thus some growing convergence between Eastleigh malls and elsewhere. However, the original Eastleigh mall actually began life not as a shopping centre at all, but instead as a lodging called Garissa Lodge. The story of its conversion into a mall is intimately connected with a much older story of cross-border trade whereby cheap, smuggled consumer goods were brought into Kenya over the border from Somalia and Ethiopia, and especially through frontier towns such as Mandera and Isiolo.

Cross-Border Bargains

Such trade has a long history: the Kenya–Somalia border area has always been a hub of trade activity, especially for ivory in pre-colonial times.[7] The colonial border itself, once established, would present many opportunities for those whose social networks straddled it, allowing traders to leverage different economic regimes on either side.[8] Indeed, by the 1980s in the Kenya–Ethiopia–Somalia border area around Mandera, traders were buying textiles and other goods from market towns inside Somalia, such as Bula Hawa and Boru Hache, and carrying them into Kenya, using routes that avoided official check-points, or hiding sacks of contraband behind other goods on trucks to Isiolo (a frontier town between the north and the central highlands). The first edition of the *Rough Guide to Kenya* describes the border area and the trade conducted there in the mid-1980s, with TVs, electronic goods and so forth being sold in Bula Hawa, the 'original duty-free bazaar'. In that town are 'perfumes, cameras, walkmans, TVs, gigantic ghetto blasters, textiles packed in Indonesian canned fruit cartons as well as cut glass, cosmetics from Taiwan and a mass of trinkets and gadgetry'. As the author of the guidebook declared, 'coming across all of this after the wilderness of the desert is simply outrageous'.[9]

Somalis sourced these goods in the Gulf, a region to which they have an age-old connection through earlier patterns of mobility and trade, and through shared religious networks. This connection would grow increasingly strong as many Somalis migrated to work in the Gulf in the 1970s and 1980s,[10] while trading links to Dubai in particular would intensify as that Emirati state became a world hub for trade through its lenient import and export policies and vast range of goods, as well as its transport links.[11] Somalis have long had a presence in the city's Deira District. At the time Barre's regime in Somalia had liberalised trade and reduced import restrictions, encouraging more people to start businesses as the formal economy collapsed.[12] Thus, trade in cheap consumer goods through Somalia increased, while the higher prices they could fetch in pre-liberalised Kenya encouraged their smuggling. Going the other way was often the stimulant drug khat, which had been made illegal in Somalia in 1983, making it a lucrative smuggled commodity. Goods imported through these networks into Kenya were sold by traders who would stay in small hotels in Isiolo and other towns such as Nakuru, Gilgil and Eldoret, where they sold goods from 'under the bed' either to individual customers or established wholesalers.[13]

These earlier networks gradually converged on Eastleigh. While Isiolo and other such towns profited for a time through this trade, none could offer access to as wide a market as Nairobi, and there were people in the 1980s bringing these smuggled goods to the city. One such trader was a Borana from northern Kenya, named Amina, whose husband worked for the Kenyan army. She now lives in Kariobangi, where I interviewed her, and owns a tailoring business in contemporary Eastleigh. After gaining a taste for trade selling khat to soldiers in the Nairobi barracks at Langata in the early 1980s, she moved into the clothes trade. This was facilitated by her husband's transfer to the Kenya air force at Nanyuki, which allowed her to travel on military transport planes to northern towns such as Mandera. There she would cross into Somalia and Ethiopia and buy various sorts of garments and shoes, hiring other women to help her carry them over the border without paying any duty. From Mandera she would catch another lift on the military plane to Nairobi, where she would sell the clothes to women traders in such districts as Ngara, Lungalunga, Industrial Area and Kawangware. She would also sell them in Eastleigh to its increasing number of refugees. Some of these Eastleigh refugees had come with enough assets to survive for a while, but soon turned to trade to make a living.

Garissa Lodge

The earliest to do so stayed at Garissa Lodge, then a two-storey building built by Indians several decades earlier, but owned in the early
1990s by a Swahili man, and a place now synonymous with the
Eastleigh transformation. These Garissa Lodge guests would deck out
their rooms like shops during the day, storing the clothes again at night
under their beds, as had the earlier traders in Isiolo. A number of these
were Reer Hamar (also known as Benadiri), 'people of Mogadishu'
descended from Yemeni Arabs, Indians and other trading populations of
the Indian Ocean: they were an endogamous group, speaking a dialect
of Somali substantially different from the standard.[14] They were known
for their role in business in Mogadishu, and fled early on in the civil
war, bringing with them a keen eye for business and connections to the
Gulf and elsewhere that would soon be mobilised in finding alternative
routes through which to import these goods.[15]

Among the first Reer Hamar to trade in the estate was a woman
known as Mama Fashion, who still operates there. Before the war she
and her late husband had import businesses in both Mogadishu and Dar
es Salaam, selling cosmetics and textiles imported from Dubai. As
Mogadishu became engulfed in conflict in 1990–1 they fled to Nairobi,
seeking shelter in Garissa Lodge. They did not come with much in the
way of capital, and she at first made a living for the family by cooking
and selling samosas to other guests at the hotel and passers-by. However,
her husband—due to his business interests—had a Tanzanian passport.
With this he could travel both to Dar es Salaam and Dubai, and maintain a network that soon allowed them to trade goods brought through
a different route: from Dubai to Dar es Salaam, then over the border
to Nairobi. Like those brought over from Somalia, they could sell these
goods much more cheaply than those sold by the Asian traders of the
city centre who had long dominated clothes retail but had much higher
overheads. With new clothes available cheaply, as well as gold jewellery
from Dubai, word spread among Kenyan traders and shoppers about
the revolutionary Garissa Lodge.

While nominally a lodging, its small bedroom shops gave it the feel
of a bazaar, and bore resemblance to the clothes section of Mogadishu's
Bakaara Market, where there were around 500 clothes stalls by 1990,
a resemblance enhanced by the fact that a number of the Garissa Lodge

traders had been traders at Bakaara.[16] As its fame grew and more rooms and corridors became taken over by trade, it was perhaps only a matter of time before the lodging became converted into a mall, and by 1992 it was renamed as Garissa Lodge Shopping Centre after spilling over into neighbouring buildings.[17] The renovated buildings contained ninety-two shops inside, and a further ninety-two stalls on a wooden structure around the outside of the mall.

An Isaaq woman called Yasmin is credited with this conversion after buying the lodge from its earlier Swahili owner. Now an elderly woman of limited eyesight, she is reckoned by some an unlikely pioneer. However, she clearly had the vision to spot Garissa Lodge's potential as a mall, and her entrepreneurial expertise is evidenced by her wealth and portfolio of investments—not only in Nairobi, but also in Dubai and Hargeisa.

A Successful Model

The speed of the transformation of other plots around Garissa Lodge in the epicentre of Eastleigh's commercial zone—the junction of First Avenue and Kipande Athumani Street—demonstrates how quickly people copied the model, spurred on by the huge demand for retail space that grew as more Somalis—refugees and Kenyan Somalis—saw the business potential. The neighbourhood's second mall opened in 1993 with 185 shops inside and a similar number outside,[18] and was named Dubai Shopping Complex after the Emirati trade hub to which Eastleigh was now connected through people such as Mama Fashion.

The malling of Eastleigh was well under way, a process that gathered pace, especially after 1995 as other buildings were repurposed. By the time of Martin's research in the mid-1990s there were seven main malls and another being built, all within the epicentre of the Eastleigh boom: the junction of First Avenue and Kipande Athumani Street (Wood Street in colonial times, and more widely known within Eastleigh as Jam Street after a famous fast-food restaurant known as Jam Frys). Martin's article contains a map (reproduced in map 6) showing these early malls: they are (with number on the map in brackets) Garissa Lodge (1), Dubai Shopping Complex (2), Al-Maqdis Shopping Complex (3), Tawakal Shopping Centre (4), Towfiq Shopping

Centre (5), Mandera Lodge Shopping Centre (6), Prime Shopping Centre (7) and Bousal Shopping Centre (8).

These malls contained a total of 660 shops and 463 stalls facing the road, according to Martin's figures.[19] The shops at that time were mainly the preserve of Somali refugees, while the stalls were operated by both refugees and also Kenyans, 'attracted by the dynamism of the place'.[20] The whole atmosphere of the malls was informal, especially with the wooden stalls that surrounded them. In fact, the estate was taking on a semi-formal character, as all businesses had to obtain per-

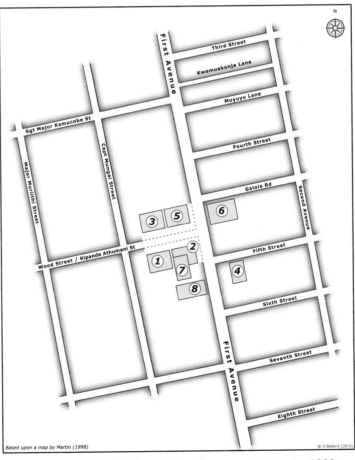

Map 6: Eastleigh in the late 1990s (after a map in Martin, 1998)

mits from the city council, something that local Kenyan Somalis often obtained on behalf of refugees who in reality operated the shops.[21] Thus, while shops were registered formally, many of the people running them did not have the legal right to work in Kenya, and many of the goods sold were smuggled.

However, this initial building boom was not just based on smuggled goods, and networks soon began to circumvent the risky route through Somalia. Facilitating this was a Somali infrastructure of freight and shipping companies, including African Salihiya Cargo, a Kenyan Somali company emerging out of Eastleigh commerce that would help traders there import containers crammed full of goods sourced in the Gulf. Mama Fashion describes how she was an early customer of the company, learning that it could enable clothes to be imported legally yet still cheaply. The Eastleigh economy was also boosted by the opening of Eldoret Airport in 1997, which soon became a hub of air-freight imports for the estate. The low rates charged by African Salihiya—combined with the low overheads of the Eastleigh malls—further consolidated the advantage Eastleigh traders had over Asian traders in the city centre. Demand for the estate's goods grew more intense, prompting more demand for shops, and so encouraging yet more mall development.

The Eastleigh phenomenon was causing consternation in wider Kenyan society as it challenged the old status quo of Kenyan import business. By the early 2000s this consternation was rumoured to be behind a fire that devastated Garissa Lodge in December 2000. Suspicion of sabotage was rife, as a man had been caught two years earlier at night outside the lodge with a jerry-can of petrol, and especially as there was a wider spate of market fires throughout Kenya.[22] While the bales of clothes inside and wooden structures around the building were possibly susceptible to accidental fire, some blamed the fire on arson following a row over a mosque burnt down in another part of Nairobi (South B). However, in the collective memory of the estate, many now suspect that the fire was more likely to have been the work of other business communities—Asians in particular—who were supposedly angry at losing market share to the Garissa Lodge phenomenon. No one was arrested for the fire.

This did not slow down trade in the estate, instead giving the Garissa Lodge owners the chance to build an even bigger money-spinning mall on the plot. Like the proverbial phoenix, New Garissa Lodge emerged from the fire with over 120 shops over three storeys. Traders inside— who had no formal insurance—were able to tap into their networks of cooperation and mutuality to help defray their losses (see chapters 4 and 5). While this redevelopment was prompted by the fire, malls are continually renovated and expanded in Eastleigh, each redevelopment offering the chance to increase income for the owners through obtaining more rent and initial fees to reserve shops (see below on the institution of goodwill). Further building developments would take place from the early 2000s onwards: nineteen of forty-three shopping malls surveyed as part of my project on the estate were built between 2000 and 2006. These were not simple conversions of existing buildings either, but instead most were purpose built as commercial establishments.

There was another boom period post-2006 in the wake of the defeat of the UIC in Mogadishu; it had brought some stability and encouraged diaspora investors to put much money into the city. As Ethiopian forces

Plate 5: Jam Street, as it is colloquially known. Formerly Wood Street in colonial times, the official name is now Kipande Athumani Street (photo credit: Kimo Quaintance)

pushed them out, many Mogadishu businesspeople left for Nairobi and Eastleigh.[23] A wave of Somali businesspeople moved their businesses to Eastleigh, and development once again accelerated: twenty-one malls out of forty-three commercial enterprises surveyed were opened after 2006.

Ever-Expanding Networks

This wave of construction corresponds to the rapid expansion in geographical scope of Somali trade networks. While Dubai remained the principal hub, Somalis were themselves venturing further east and establishing links to India, Thailand and Hong Kong, and, more recently, Turkey. There had been Somali connections with some of these markets even before the collapse of the Somali state in the early 1990s, especially Mumbai and Bangkok,[24] but links to them intensified in the mid-1990s. Hong Kong itself grew in significance as a source of Eastleigh goods around the same time, as Somali presence there increased. Mathews relates how Somali refugees based in Hong Kong have become agents for Nairobi-based Somalis and others.[25] This changing transnational geography of trade is reflected in the changing names of the malls, Dubai Shopping Centre renamed Bangkok, while Al-Maqdis Mall was rebuilt in 2004 as Hong Kong Shopping Mall.

Of course, China itself was to prove the biggest source of Eastleigh goods as economic reform paved the way for it to become the factory of the world. Indeed, 'since the Asian financial crisis of 1997 and China's entry into the WTO [World Trade Organisation] in 2001, China has taken over from other Asian countries as the most important source market in the trade networks supplying African countries, proving much cheaper than its competitors'.[26] Manufacturing exports (in particular clothing, textiles, electronics and plastic goods) have risen exponentially over the last decade,[27] while hubs such as Yiwu and Guangzhou have grown increasingly important for importers from around the world, including from Africa.[28] Indeed, China's growth as a manufacturing hub has been reliant on businesspeople from African countries and elsewhere who live there at least some of the time, acting as middlemen between Chinese factories and markets in the world beyond. In the case of its African traders, they form a key—yet often under-acknowledged—aspect of relations between China and Africa, one that reveals much more agency on the part of Africa than is commonly suggested in one-way portrayals of Chinese migrants coming to Africa. Indeed, as growing research reveals, Africans have transformed parts of Chinese cities through their business and presence, in particular, one district of Guangzhou (a manufacturing city on the Pearl River) called Xiaobeilu has become known by the unfortunate sobriquet of 'Chocolate City', a name suggestive of often tense relations between locals and these many foreign businesspeople.[29]

Somali traders from Kenya, Somaliland, Somalia and elsewhere were soon bypassing Dubai (which is a trans-shipment hub for Chinese commodities) and joining other Africans in places such as Guangzhou, making deals with manufacturers keen to forge connections and sell their goods in bulk. Somalis were helped in all this by the expansion of their transnational infrastructure in the form of companies such as African Salihiya. This company expanded operations to cover these markets, and was soon bringing huge numbers of containers to Eastleigh and a depot in the Industrial Area of Nairobi, not just for Somalis there, but also for the wider Kenyan population. By the time of my research, that company alone was bringing an estimated ten containers to Nairobi daily at peak times (they also have a warehouse in the Industrial Area as well as Eastleigh, located in what used to be the Kenya Bus Service station on General Waruinge Street). The infrastructure also involves Somali brokers in these trade hubs who act as intermediaries between other Somalis and Chinese factories. With improving communication infrastructure too that could connect all these elements—including money remittance companies (*hawala*—see below)—Somalis consolidated their access to these far-away markets.

Despite these expanded networks, the original cross-border trade that fed Eastleigh in its early days remained important for the estate, particularly in the importation of electronic goods.[30] The trade fluctuated, however, hindered by insecurity on both sides of the border. Menkhaus recounts how trade moved from Mandera to El Wak and other border towns at the end of the 1990s while El Wak itself suffered from increased conflict in the mid-2000s.[31] In addition, at various moments the Kenyan state has declared the border closed, though such declarations have been backed with varying degrees of enforcement. The Kenyan town of Garissa—namechecked in the first Eastleigh mall—has also been a crucial node in Somali trade networks linked to Eastleigh, especially those revolving around the livestock trade. It has also grown markedly in the years following state collapse in Somalia.[32] While Eastleigh traders import most clothes and textiles directly from Dubai, Bangkok, Turkey and other such markets through Kenyan ports, other types of goods appear to still enter the estate from Somalia through trans-border networks, many relying on Garissa as a key hub.[33] Thus while networks have been formalised to a large degree with the rise of cargo and clearing companies, smuggling routes are still of some importance for Eastleigh trade.

Networks bringing goods to Eastleigh have thus expanded greatly over the last twenty years; but so have those taking goods out of the estate. As Eastleigh's fame grew, so more traders from beyond Kenya would come seeking goods, and long-term partnerships were developed between Eastleigh wholesalers and those in the likes of Tanzania and Rwanda; trucks are loaded frequently on First Avenue to take goods to these other countries. Matters are complicated, however, as the polarities of these routes can change quickly: as mentioned earlier, Mama Fashion used to import goods to Eastleigh through Dar es Salaam, but goods now more commonly go the other way.

Contemporary Eastleigh

By the time of my research there were over forty substantial shopping malls, as well as countless smaller commercial enterprises. The shopping malls surveyed as part of the research contained over six thousand shops (a tenfold increase since 1998), many around six feet square in area, others double or triple that size. Just how radical an effect the boom construction years of the 2000s had on the landscape of the estate can be illustrated through satellite imagery. Map 7 (based on Google Earth images) shows the main epicentre of Eastleigh (around Kipande Athumani Street) in Section I in 2002, then in 2014 where almost the whole of the block has been filled with purpose-built malls and other new buildings (shaded lighter).

The malls of Eastleigh now stretch way beyond this epicentre, and First Avenue from Thirteenth Street to Fourth Street heaves with them, while others have sprouted on some of the streets that connect First and Second Avenues. Others are now being built in Section III, further

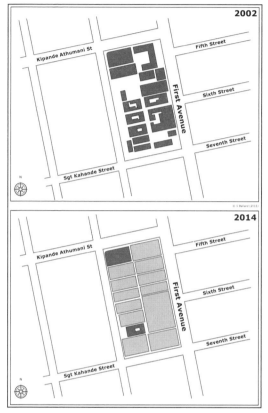

Map 7: Eastleigh's shopping epicentre in 2002 and 2014

south along First Avenue from Thirteenth Street. Map 8 shows the developments along First Avenue that can give some idea of the density of malls, hotels and other structures in the estate.

Some of the more modest earlier malls remain: for example, one of the earliest—Towfiq—remains as it was in its prime location on the corner of First Avenue and Kipande Athumani Street. However, most malls look more modern in design, the Eastleigh mall blueprint becoming grander and more sophisticated over the years. Some of these newer malls are very big indeed, including Sunrise Shopping Mall (renamed recently Mega Shopping). This mall was opened in 2007

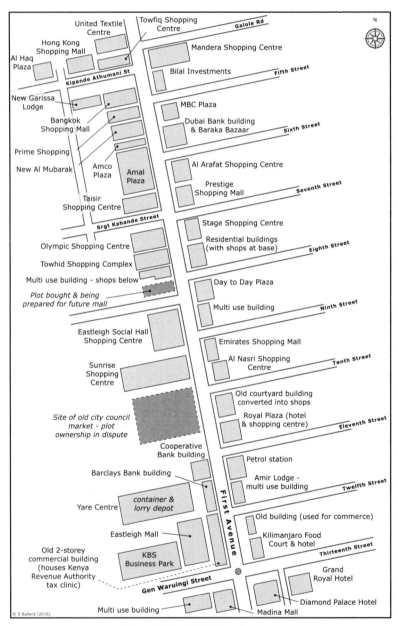

Map 8: Eastleigh First Avenue

Plate 6: Sunrise Shopping Mall

Plate 7: Amal Plaza

(owned by the family of a prominent Kenyan Somali MP from Wajir) and covers a large plot of 0.8 acres. It is filled with 370 small shops, as well as a bank, offices and classrooms.

Amal Plaza—built on three adjacent plots in 2004—is a prime example of this. It is a large mall covering a plot of 0.62 acres, containing over 500 shops, and consisting of three wings and five floors.

Herz describes Amal Plaza, thus, in a chapter on the Eastleigh phenomenon:

> Many of the individual shop units, each around six square metres, are crammed with textiles from floor to ceiling. ... The individual floors are connected by a succession of intersecting double staircases, ramps, bridges, spiral staircases, lifts and arcade-like corridors and galleries. There is a series of air spaces and atriums to channel daylight down through the building to the ground floor. This design creates a complex three-dimensional structure of shopping, access and recreational areas. The building's architecture combines informal and improvised aspects with the formal and conventional. Elements of the standard repertoire of shopping malls such as galleries and atriums are condensed and merged with other spaces and functions such as mosques, ramps or sales areas.[34]

Amal Plaza was long seen as the epitome of Eastleigh sophistication, especially in having lifts, a first for an Eastleigh mall.[35] However, just as with all the earlier malls developed out of older constructions, the same principle underlay its construction: squeeze as many retail units into the building as possible. Malls such as Sunrise and the newly built Eastleigh Social Hall mall are larger in terms of plot acreage (Sunrise covers 0.8 acres), but Amal surpasses them in terms of retail space, filled with shops similar to that of Nasiib Fashions as well as a number of much larger shops at the front of the building. Most shops sell very similar items of clothing, another key difference with high-end malls where shops tend to be more varied in the goods they sell. The clustering of shops selling similar items are more reminiscent of the bazaar as analysed by Geertz,[36] where clustering facilitates search for customers 'in the absence of advertising and posted prices'.[37] Eastleigh shops are lined with all goods on display, blurring distinctions between display and storage space, another factor that saves on the cost of space.

Amal and Sunrise represent the high point of malls designed as warrens of small shops. Nowadays designs are more varied, reflecting what some perceive as a declining market for the classic Eastleigh small retail

Plate 8: Nasiib Fashions

space, and the fact that Eastleigh now attracts large formal businesses, such as banks and supermarkets, able to pay greater sums for an Eastleigh base. In this regard, Eastleigh's architecture is evolving towards higher-end malls and their multi-use retail and leisure space.

Thus, newer malls such as Madina (opened in 2011) house fewer small retail units, but instead have lodgings, clinics and restaurants, as well as mosques—a feature of almost all Eastleigh malls. Madina even has a large Tuskys supermarket (a Kenyan chain) in its basement. The supersized Comesa Mall that is currently under construction on General Waruingi Street will mark a new high point in the shift from low end to high end in the estate, its blueprints suggesting something more akin to the likes of the Westgate. This does not mean the end of the older model, however. The recent opening of the Eastleigh Social

Hall shopping mall (on the site of the old chief's camp and the social hall that gave it its name)—a large mall of three storeys crammed full of shops—suggests that there remains demand for small retail units in prime locations accessible from First Avenue.

Externally, the malls vary greatly. Most are quite functional designs, some inspired by buildings in Dubai and elsewhere. Some, such as the Al-Haqq Plaza and Shariff Building—both near Garissa Lodge on Kipande Athumani Street—have very Arabian-style architectural flourishes, the former possessing small minarets, as seen in plate 9, a photograph of it and the entrance to Hong Kong Shopping Centre.

Eastleigh construction is not just limited to shopping malls, and more and more apartment blocks, lodgings and restaurants have sprouted to service the many thousands of permanent residents and temporary visitors who come to the estate. Indeed, apartment blocks have also been lucrative for real-estate developers, rents and house prices rising greatly in this boom town. Such was the rent rise that many former residents speak of being pushed out of the estate. This is

Plate 9: Al-Haqq Plaza and Hong Kong Shopping Mall (photo credit: Kimo Quaintance)

laden with irony: one of the impacts of displaced people on the estate is to displace other people. Abey interviewed a Kenyan displaced by the Eastleigh transformation, who described how the rise in rents forced her to move to Mathare Valley, while a Somali refugee interviewee of his argued that the rise in rent was due to Kikuyu landlords who 'always like to hike the prices for foreigners'.[38]

As Lindley states: in Eastleigh 'the rent for single rooms after the influx in the early 1990s was five or more times the previous levels, pushing many Kenyan tenants out into other areas of Eastlands, while the refugees often lived in over-crowded conditions, sharing and sub-letting'.[39] Interviewees of mine also referred to this effect, a Luyia man telling me how he had lived in an Indian-owned building in the late 1980s, but was suddenly told to move one day as the building had been sold to Somalis for redevelopment. Some two-bedroomed apartments in the centre of Eastleigh around Garissa Lodge fetch around 60,000 shillings (about $700) monthly, catering mainly for long-term diaspora visitors. Apartments nearer Juja Road as well as in Section III are still much cheaper, however.

An impressive new development is the Grand Royal Hotel, which caters for wealthier Kenyan Somalis and the many diaspora visitors who come to the estate, and is said to be worth 2 billion Kenyan shillings. It is owned by a Kenyan Somali man who had previously built the Barakat Hotel, which used to be seen as the most exclusive hotel, and even hosted meetings of the Transitional Federal Government of Somalia (TFG). The Grand Royal is based on Thirteenth Street near the roundabout junction with General Waruingi Street, where several of the bigger hotels are based. It was opened in 2011 by then Prime Minister Raila Odinga, and its design is typical of the new generation of buildings, being glass-fronted. Indeed, Madina Mall and another new hotel near the roundabout share this same design feature, common too in new buildings around the world. With its uniformed doorman, large conference rooms, gymnasium and other facilities, the Grand Royal very much symbolises the ambition of the estate to develop into a more mainstream destination for visitors to the region, although management admit that Western tourists might be put off by such establishments not serving alcohol.

The very height of the Grand Royal—ten storeys—is also symbolic of the confidence of the estate and its economy. The hotel towers over

Plate 10: Grand Royal Hotel (photo credit: Kimo Quaintance)

Plate 11: First Avenue, 2012

that part of Eastleigh, announcing its presence with its shiny exterior and name in lights up above. However, it is also threatened with demolition: there are by-laws stipulating that with the airbase nearby, Eastleigh buildings within a radius of a kilometre from the runway should not be more than 30 feet high.[40] While planning permission had been obtained from City Hall, it is argued by the government that permission from the Kenya air force should also have been sought. The hotel has been granted a stay of execution through the courts, however, unlike buildings in less prosperous parts of Eastleigh that were torn down on the grounds of being too tall too close to the airbase, suggestive of the power of wealth to insulate itself.

Decaying Infrastructure

While buildings of increasing sophistication—such as the Grand Royal—have been erected in recent years, they have looked out of place in an estate that for years has been blighted by poor infrastructure and municipal services. With little planning oversight the estate quickly outgrew the capacity of its infrastructure: as a densely populated and built estate, the constant arrival of large trucks and containers has long clogged up the roads, causing great congestion, while plot coverage of the malls often exceeds that stipulated by by-laws, further adding to the strain on the environment.[41] Electricity provision is intermittent, and generators often form a loud part of the Eastleigh soundscape, while buildings often rely on water deliveries rather than mains supply. Also, the roundabouts near the Grand Royal have developed into massive rubbish mounds, occasionally picked over by those looking for scrap to recycle. Most symbolic of decay, however, have been the estate's roads, which at times resemble sewage-filled rivers. Until its repair (see chapter 7), crossing the reeking First Avenue after the rains was an unpleasant challenge faced by all in the estate (see plate 11), and queues would form at the safest spots to cross while people awaited their turn, profoundly affecting how people moved around the estate.

Eastleigh's infrastructure is a relic of colonial times that simply has not been able to keep up with the rising population of the estate and all its development and traffic. Of course, as we saw in chapter 1, it was hardly perfect for much of the colonial period either. Asoka, Thuo and

Bunyasi describe the impact of all this growth on Eastleigh's roads, water supply and sewage system.[42] Regarding roads, new construction has often impinged upon road reserve areas, while 'the carriageway is continually being eroded due to construction of embankments from buildings that encroach on the roads, especially on First and Second Avenue. The embankments are constructed in such a manner that they are slanting towards the carriageway, thus, they drain rain and waste water from the buildings to the carriageway which erodes the carriageway.'[43] Regarding water supply, its volume is the same as before the boom years despite such a phenomenal growth in population, while the sewer line was built in 1943 to serve a much smaller population. The result of all this is that Eastleigh can be hazardous for health, especially in regard to waterborne diseases and the risk of flooding and open manholes.

Remedial work had been planned in the 1990s, but constant pleas by residents and politicians went unanswered, and public decay in the face of private development remained the story of the estate. Indeed, rumour has it that the business community in Eastleigh were at one stage so frustrated that they even asked to pay for the infrastructure themselves, only to be rebuffed by the government, perhaps fearful of the state impotence this would have suggested. A key actor in all this is the Eastleigh Business Association, an organisation formed in 2003 to help secure the interests of shopkeepers and others in the estate. They brought a case against the Nairobi City Council in 2010,[44] protesting that much revenue is made by the council from the estate from business permits and rates, yet few results are seen for this money given the state of roads and other infrastructure. They won the case, resulting in a freeze on the payment of council fees until recently.[45] As we will see in chapter 7, major improvements have come to the estate's infrastructure, and renovation work on First and Second Avenues is now complete. However, for much of the last two decades, being a resident in Eastleigh meant inhabiting a very polluted environment with all the attendant risks to health.

The Cost of Transformation

The foregoing suggests the scale of the transformation that swept over Eastleigh's landscape (or at least part of it) in the last twenty years.

Sections I and II in particular are unrecognisable compared to the 1980s. Clearly this transformation involved much capital, although construction methods and materials are not particularly sophisticated. Indeed, the Eastleigh boom came at the time of increasing informalisation of the construction industry in Kenya, where many construction firms 'often have no premises, capital, equipment or permanent workforce. They are mostly ephemeral, comprising a few workers who come together for the duration of a project.'[46] While Eastleigh projects are often large in scale—and generally rely on established Kenyan construction firms and architects—the construction methods rely on the human muscle of casual workforces, and are usually low-tech. For example, plate 12 shows the wooden planks used as supports for the drying concrete of Eastleigh Social Hall. These are typical for the construction industry in Kenya, but contrast with the metal supports that might be used in more expensive projects elsewhere in the city.

However, despite the use of some low-tech construction methods and informal labour in construction, it remains far from cheap to build

Plate 12: Eastleigh Social Hall Mall under construction (photo credit: Kimo Quaintance)

an Eastleigh mall: figures I was given for recent mall developments suggest a range of 100–400 million Kenyan shillings ($1–4 million) for construction costs. Of this, the cost of land is a major factor, one that has intensified over the years as Eastleigh's commercial zone has expanded. Indeed, even small plots in out-of-the-way parts of Eastleigh fetch sums of over 20 million shillings, while bigger plots of around half an acre fetch up to 70 million shillings, according to property websites. Prices rise steeply closer to the epicentre of the Eastleigh boom: a vacant plot near Garissa Lodge of 0.13 acres was on the market for 135 million shillings in 2015.[47] A recent report on land prices in Nairobi suburbs showed Eastleigh to be one of the most expensive at 276 million shillings per acre, only the upmarket estates of Upperhill, Parklands, Westlands and Kilimani fetching more.[48]

In the boom years of the mid-2000s, people spoke of a feverish real-estate market whereby Somali investors would offer plot owners prices way over the odds to secure a quick deal. The manager of one of the malls told me how his company bought their plot in the year 2000. The plot owner would have been content to settle for 35 million Kenyan shillings, but the company paid him 50 million to expedite matters. Many who had bought plots in the pre-transformation period were happy to sell up for such prices, often taking the money to other parts of the country: a man I met whose family originated in western Kenya told me of his father who sold a plot in Eastleigh at the height of the boom. He was expecting to sell for 20 million shillings, but eventually received 30 million. With this money he started a bottling plant in Kisii, his home region; a mall now covers his old plot.

Piratical Capital?

The idea that Somalis could simply conjure up over-the-odds sums in this way has added to a general sense in Kenya and beyond that something extraordinary—and possibly criminal—must be going on in Eastleigh's economy. Indeed, so radically has its landscape transformed that it is understandable that some find it hard to account for this change, especially given its apparent disconnect from Kenya's formal economy and its association with supposedly lowly refugees. It is also understandable how more sensational explanations linking the boom to the growth of Indian Ocean piracy and the laundering of ransoms seemed to fill an explanatory gap. Indeed, pirate money has become a dominant trope in media coverage of Eastleigh, growing in the last decade as Somalis become stereotyped as pirates in global narratives. Hence headlines such as: 'Laundered Somali Pirate Money a Boon for Kenyan Arrr Chitecture',[49] and 'Somali Pirates Take the Money and Run, to Kenya'.[50]

As the most famous example of Somali urban development in Kenya, Eastleigh is under great suspicion for such alleged links. However, most Somalis in the estate will quickly point out a strong piece of contradictory evidence: the boom in Eastleigh started in the early 1990s, well before the rise of Somali piracy in the mid-2000s. This does not quite exonerate the estate in this regard, as it could still be claimed that it is the recent boom in construction there that is linked to piracy. Kimo Quaintance explored the correlation between the rise of piracy and a boom in construction in Eastleigh post-2006.[51] Through historical satellite imagery he counted the new developments in Eastleigh between 2002 and 2011, using images available from those years and from 2004, 2006, 2007 and 2009. He found that in the 2004 there were fifty-five new developments, dipping to fourteen in 2006 and six in 2007, then rising again sharply to thirty-five in 2009 and sixty-five in 2011. The post-2007 rise does show a correlation with increasing incidents of piracy in the Indian Ocean from 2007 to 2010. However, comparing the total value of ransoms in that period suggests that capital raised, while considerable, is dwarfed by other in-flows we will discuss below, such as remittances from the diaspora.[52] While it is quite possible that shady money finds its way to the estate, attracted by the development there rather than causing it, the tendency to link Eastleigh and piracy is certainly based more on stereotypical representations of Somalis than actual evidence.

The real factors underpinning the boom (aside from the hard work, business acumen and innovation of those animating its economy) are much more complex, involving the three dimensions mentioned in the introduction: a Somali transnational dimension; a Kenyan dimension; and a global one. Regarding the latter, the intensification of Eastleigh's links to trade hubs elsewhere is crucial, the proceeds of the trade exponentially sparking reinvestment in the estate: just as a mushroom is the visible fruiting body of hidden networks of mycelium beneath the ground, so the Eastleigh malls are in many ways the fruits of the vast networks of trade that weave through the estate and bring the cheap manufactured goods of the East. That Eastleigh became the focal point of such global networks and the goods they bring is crucial to understanding its transformation (and we will focus on Eastleigh's global goods in chapter 6); however, it is equally crucial to understand how Eastleigh and Kenya more generally offered Somali transnational capital a fertile ground in which to grow, and a means by which relatively small sums could be leveraged into a landscape of malls.

A Very Kenyan Economy

To begin with, Eastleigh has to be understood in relation to the wider Kenyan economy. Indeed, its economy has never merely involved the depositing of people, capital and goods from elsewhere onto the estate, and it is not simply a Somalian refugee economy. There have always been some very wealthy Kenyan Somalis able to finance its growth. Indeed, while Somalian refugees dominate malls as shopkeepers, the more permanent aspects of the boom—the buildings themselves—are often Kenyan Somali owned, including Garissa Lodge, or owned by business groups (often, but not always, linked by lineage) made up of Kenyans and Somalians. Kenyan Somalis with business interests in livestock, transport and petroleum also invest in the estate. The presence of Kenyan Somalis in Eastleigh has also been significant in providing a co-ethnic buffer between Somalians and the Kenyan state, especially in dealing with its bureaucracy. They thus form a key store of cultural and social capital upon which Somalians have drawn.

Furthermore, a great deal of money supporting construction in Eastleigh comes from non-Somali sources. For example, one mall was built by Kenyan Indians before being sold to a Kikuyu firm. Also, many of the apartment-block developments that have emerged to cater for the rising population were built by Kikuyu developers. And while it is the international goods from the East that really sparked the transformation, some initial capital for malls—including Garissa Lodge—came from the trade of that very Kenyan product, khat, from the Meru district in central Kenya (see chapter 6), for which Eastleigh became a hub.

However, Eastleigh's growth also depended to a large extent on wider transformations of Kenya's economy and society in the early 1990s. Crucially, Kenya was adopting liberalisation policies almost simultaneously with the disintegration of Somalia and the growth of the Somali diaspora. Kenya had signed up to structural adjustment in the 1980s to secure a World Bank loan, but the switch from import-substitution policies to the reduction of trade tariffs, import controls and restrictions on foreign exchange was only implemented in practice from the mid-1980s, most policies coming into effect in the early 1990s, at the same time as the Eastleigh boom was beginning.[53] The loosening of foreign currency exchange was a key factor paving the way for the Eastleigh transnational economy and money-remittance infrastructure, one based around the US dollar.

Thus, while cross-border trade networks that brought goods to Eastleigh in its earlier days relied on Somalia's 'economy without state',[54] with liberalisation there was a retreat of the Kenyan state from the regulation of formal imports and foreign exchange, a retreat that Somalis—Somalian and Kenyan—with their connections to Dubai and expanding transnational networks, were exceptionally well placed to exploit.[55] They could afford to import goods in large volumes adopting a 'pile it high, sell it cheap' model of retail, providing competition for the more expensive Asian shops of the city centre. Meanwhile, structural adjustment as enacted in Kenya and elsewhere led to spiralling rates of formal unemployment and rural poverty, thus multiplying those seeking work in the urban informal sector:[56] the economy of Eastleigh thus had access to an ever-expanding pool of labour, as well as the informalised construction industry mentioned above. Eastleigh's transformation also resembles in many ways that of the wider Kenyan informal economy of clothes traders, and the conversion of buildings in city-centre Nairobi into 'exhibition stalls', small, Eastleigh-like retail units, that Kenyan women dominate, as Kinyanjui discusses.[57]

A much-lamented facet of Kenya's social fabric is also relevant: its corruption, also something that increased in significance in the early 1990s (although Kenya was far from corruption free previously, perceived levels of corruption spiked with the coming of multi-party democracy).[58] While Somali life in Eastleigh often involves paying bribes to police and other officials to avoid arbitrary arrest and harassment, in other ways the corruptibility of Kenyan officialdom can be beneficial, allowing those with means to circumvent legal hurdles: corruption as 'facilitation'. As Daniel Smith recounts for Nigeria, while most people lament corruption as a bane for society, it can offer opportunities for them too, hence its intractability.[59]

In an economy as big as Eastleigh's within a country as corrupt as Kenya, it would be naïve to imagine that corruption is absent from Eastleigh's economy. For example, the allocation of land has apparently been subject to corrupt practices in some instances, especially with regard to obtaining planning permission and purchasing public land. There is scarcely any public land now in Eastleigh, and such is the suspicion over the sale of the former City Council market (next door to Sunrise Mall) that there are two ongoing court cases attempting to unpack what happened. The land was sold by the City Council in 2008 to some Somali businesspeople on a public–private arrangement, but they fell out over what to do with the land, so sued each other. Meanwhile, the former market traders were suing the council for their ejection from the site. This site is now being developed, although former market traders have appealed to Evans Kidero—Governor of Nairobi County—and Mike Sonko—Senator of Nairobi—and the case continues.[60] This is only one recent example of the land-grabbing rife in the wider Nairobi economy.[61]

Corruption said to occur at Kenya's ports—both at Mombasa and at Eldoret airport for goods reaching Eastleigh—is also reckoned a factor in the Eastleigh economy. Corrupt practices at ports include the mislabelling of goods to lower import tariffs (a practice, it must be emphasised, not limited to Somalis, but widespread, and even practised by large companies in the formal sector), and such practices may well play some role in the sale of consumer goods at cheap prices in Eastleigh. How big a role is impossible to say, and evidence is obviously difficult to obtain. However, a freight company based in Eastleigh was investigated by reporters from the KTN channel in 2009 on irregularities in import-duty payment, irregularities the company denies.[62] Ironically, this investigation appears to have boosted business significantly for the company in question, advertising to Kenyans the cheap rates it charged.[63] Such mislabelling and port corruption is a global phenomenon, however, as Mathews et al. make clear in relation to the smuggling of goods out of Asia. Such tax evasion is very hard to curb, too, as only a tiny proportion of containers are ever checked at ports around the world.[64]

Clearly in an economic environment such as Kenya's, corruption is something that all have to navigate to some degree, coping with its demands, and exploiting the advantages it can offer. In many ways the legal vulnerabilities of refugees and the difficulties in navigating Kenyan officialdom for even those Somalis with Kenyan citizenship make Somalis especially prone to the corrosive impact of corruption. However, Somalis may well have a comparative advantage in one respect. Corruption has produced an environment in Kenya where trust in others, and society in general, is in short supply. As Burbidge describes it, it is a society where there are 'widespread expectations of widespread corruption'.[65] In this context, the strong social bonds and networks maintained by Somalis, and their great emphasis on the need for trust in business (see chapter 5), help generate mutual security in an environment where suspicion often prevails. This also offers Somalis advantages in other environments seen as risky by others, for example in the spaza shop (a small retail outlet) economy of South African townships, where Somalis are dominant despite the xenophobia and related violence that they have faced.[66]

A City Built on Goodwill

However, there is another Kenyan institution far more central to the growth of Eastleigh: goodwill. This term is used in business accounting the world over to refer to the intangible assets of a going concern (the customer base, reputation etc. that add value above material assets and liabilities). In Kenya's formal economy the term is used in this way, but it has also evolved a more particular usage, referring to payments made by would-be shop owners to reserve the right to rent a shop for a certain time period. The institution of goodwill has a long history in Kenya, and there was concern post-independence that Africans could not afford to establish businesses in the Nairobi city centre as Asian landlords were asking for large goodwill payments.[67] While that debate was highly racialised, nowadays such payments are charged by landlords of all ethnicities where demand for shops is strong, and ironically goodwill is a source of much ill-will for those who raise enough capital for stock, rent and deposit, but then have to raise more for goodwill.[68] Payments in central Nairobi can be millions of Kenyan shillings for small premises, while even a tiny kiosk might fetch 300,000 shillings (about $3,500) for a five-year period, following which more goodwill is paid. As we will see in chapter 5, these payments are considered by some in Eastleigh as immoral and un-Islamic as they open the way for profit gouging. There has been a move away from them in some recent developments.

In Eastleigh usage of the term 'goodwill' is not uniform, and is sometimes conflated with 'buying the key', also used for a payment made to reserve a shop. Mohaa considers the terms distinct, and the example of his shop, Nasiib Fashions, might help clarify usage. Mohaa and his then business partner Siad took over Nasiib Fashions in 2008 when the shop became vacant. They did not buy it outright, but came to an arrangement with a Somali (originally from Ethiopia, but now a US citizen) who had bought the 'key' to the shop for $5,000 (US dollars are normally used in buying the key) when the mall was being built a decade ago. For his $5,000 the landlord obtained the rights to the shop for ten years, after which a new arrangement would be negotiated. Instead of running the shop himself, he bought the key so he could sublet it and be paid goodwill each year. When Mohaa and Siad took it over, they agreed to pay goodwill of 10,000 Kenyan shillings a month for this shop, paid in a lump sum of 120,000 shillings (around $1,000) each year. They were also paying the shopping mall 9,400 Kenyan shillings in monthly maintenance fees and rent, meaning they effectively paid 19,400 Kenyan shillings per month for the shop. Now the arrangement has changed following the expiry of the ten-year arrangement, and as a result of negotiations between the same shop owner and the mall management, Mohaa (now working on his own) pays an extra 6,000 shillings to the management, on top of the rent and goodwill, meaning he now pays 25,400 shillings per month. As the owner bought the key for $5,000 initially, we can see that he has doubled his money over the ten-year period without having to busy himself with trade.

However, there is little consistency in such arrangements or in usage of terms such as 'goodwill' and 'buying the key'. Matters are complicated by the numerous different types of arrangements and fees those who own the rights to shops and their tenants negotiate. Shops in

Eastleigh often have intricate layers of ownership and rights and, while initial payments for the rights to shops might be standardised, as individual shops are sold on or sub-let over the years consistency tends to be lost. Shops also fetch different rates of goodwill depending on where they are located and their size.[69] In the survey of shopkeepers undertaken for this research, the highest reported sum was $80,000 goodwill for a five-year right to a large shop. The current going rate for the key to a shop at the front of Amal is said to be $45,000. In the survey most shopkeepers report paying 300,000–600,000 shillings yearly, usually to those who bought the key to the shops, rather than to the mall owners. These shopkeepers also have to pay rent to the malls, like Mohaa, and the fees range from 10,000 to 120,000 shillings depending on the size.

These initial payments to reserve shops have been crucial to the Eastleigh transformation, providing funds for the construction or refurbishment of most of the malls. Early malls such as Bousal were redeveloped from older buildings through these payments. Martin relates how in the mid-1990s, 210,000 Kenyan shillings (then around $3,500) were required to reserve a shop at Bousal even before it was finished.[70] Indeed, many were financed as follows: a business group—often connected by family or lineage—invests in land in Eastleigh, then erects a sign saying that a mall will be 'coming soon', urging prospective shop owners to reserve their shops. To do so requires paying goodwill or buying the key. As we have seen for Nasiib Fashions, a shop within Amal Plaza, the owner of the key paid $5,000 to reserve it, though bigger shops facing the street fetched double or even triple that when it was being built. As that shopping mall has hundreds of shops, up-front payments of goodwill raised significant funds that could be used in construction.

A manager of another mall on First Avenue told me how it was capitalised. It was first opened as a mall in 2000 by an Isaaq-owned cargo company that had emerged out of the early boom years. They bought an old building from its Kikuyu owner and converted it into a mall. Then in 2009 they decided to redevelop the mall, constructing a much bigger building in the process. Shops at that time were very much in demand, and so 120 prospective shops were soon snapped up by people willing to buy the key, paying $25,000 each for the privilege. Thus, the company received 120 payments of $25,000, giving them $3 million with which to build the mall, and enough for a considerable profit too. This system can also be used to renovate and expand malls. It is quite common to see malls where the lower floors are occupied by retail and wholesale businesses, while above them new floors are being built, paid for by yet more goodwill payments. The mall in question was further developed in this way, as extra storeys were gradually added: now it is one of the tallest malls in Eastleigh, with seven storeys.

Goodwill is not just paid when a building is initially constructed; if malls are taken over, new owners aim to profit from charges too. In such instances there can be disputes if tenants face new demands for large payments, having already paid the previous management. This happened in the case of Al-Haqq Plaza, and the tenants took the new owners to court over demands for goodwill payments of between $20,000 and $140,000.[71] Here we see a more predatory face of business in Eastleigh and Nairobi more widely, where existing tenants are vulnerable to attempts by new owners to gouge out profit through demands for goodwill.

Given that there are more than forty malls today, with thousands of shops, billions of shillings have changed hands over the years as goodwill. Also, as Asian property owners found in the Indian Bazaar of colonial Kenya, the ability to subdivide retail space into ever smaller stalls can increase profitability greatly. The size of shops such as Nasiib Fashions offer opportunities to the likes of Mohaa, but they also multiply the takings for the property developers. Paying thousands of dollars to reserve a shop may seem exorbitant, but such was the demand and the profit to be made that many would—and still will—pay. Indeed, it should be remembered that such payments in Eastleigh are much lower than those required to secure shops in the city centre.

The scale of these sums also helps explain how Somalis have been able to pay what to some seem like exorbitant amounts to buy up land in the estate. Some malls have been built as partnerships with current plot owners. For example, mall developers might make a deal with the plot owner to construct the building and profit from it for a number of years, before turning ownership over to the plot owner. However, those who pay outright are so keen to expedite matters that rather than haggle they would agree to pay inflated sums so as to start the construction process sooner and rake in goodwill. Furthermore, an increasing formalisation of Eastleigh business (see below) has increased possible pre-construction windfalls. Nowadays Eastleigh malls—including the under-construction Comesa—are not just built with the typical small shops of Garissa Lodge, but incorporate banks, restaurants and supermarkets. These companies pay hefty sums—often also in advance of construction—constituting a substantial proportion of the construction costs and profits for developers.

The Diaspora Connection

The institutions of goodwill and buying the key are thus channels for much capital in the estate, often providing more than enough to cover initial construction costs and give profit to developers even before shopkeepers have sold a single item or paid any rent. But how can Eastleigh shopkeepers afford to pay all these sums, especially as many are refugees? Even the smallest sums charged, such as the $5,000 paid by the owner of Nasiib Fashions, might be seen as beyond the reach of most in Eastleigh. Indeed, stereotypes of refugees bring to mind people of few means facing shortages of all sorts of resources, from money to food to shelter to security.

While many refugees do often face extreme duress through scarcity of resources, their economic capacity can easily be underestimated and discounted.[72] Indeed, not all refugees lack means, especially those able to flee directly to or settle in an urban environment such as Eastleigh. Some came to Eastleigh with cash or (in the case of women) gold brought over when escaping Somalia in the initial throes of the civil war, and more recently in 2006, when many businesspeople fled the insecurity created in the overthrow of the Union of Islamic Courts (UIC). Somalian businesspeople with ongoing concerns in Somalia itself have also invested in Eastleigh.[73] Such people can afford to invest in Eastleigh shops.

As the survey undertaken for this research suggests, those of fewer means—refugees and Kenyans—raise capital in other ways.[74] Some pool resources in joint ventures: 10 out of 129 respondents in the shopkeeper survey responded that they obtained capital through being part of a 'business group'. Others rely on money-go-round schemes known as *ayuuto* or *hagbad* by Somalis,[75] or through petty trade: indeed, savings and previous business were given as the source of capital for twenty-nine out of those surveyed; some in this category proudly insisted that no one helped them but 'Allah'. There are traders who operate wholesale outlets capitalised by their previous business selling smuggled clothes in Isiolo back before the rise of Eastleigh. Another source of income reported was the selling of livestock. Though only two shopkeepers in the survey reported this method—both from Somalia—it is probably more common, especially among Kenyan Somalis who have moved from north-eastern Kenya to Nairobi. Another 'asset' sold by one survey participant to raise capital was a car.

Tellingly, only one shopkeeper surveyed reported getting start-up capital from a bank loan: he was one of the few non-Somalis surveyed, a young Kikuyu man selling shoes. Of course, as Muslims, interest-accruing loans are *haram* for Somalis (though see below on the growth of Islamic banking in Eastleigh), while for the many in Eastleigh with insecure legal status, dealing with banks is difficult. In this respect they contrast with some informal traders in other parts of Nairobi, including the women studied by Kinyanjui who were able to obtain bank loans to capitalise their small shops in the city centre in the 2000s, at a boom time for Kenya's banking industry.[76] Rather than bank loans, the predominant response in the survey (76 out of 129, or 58.9 per cent) to the question of the origins of their capital was: 'family'. Indeed, Eastleigh relies on networks of kin and friendship-generated solidarity to source capital.[77] Whether Kenyan Somali or Somalian, there is a strong ethos of mutual support reflected in this that we will return to in chapter 5. Out of these seventy-six, forty-four specifically mentioned that they secured help from family abroad, that is to say, the diaspora.

As discussed in the introduction, increasing focus has recently been placed on remittances from diasporans overseas and their role in aid and development: the enormous scale of remittances are a key reason for so much current interest in diaspora and development.[78] Somalia itself has received much business start-up capital from the diaspora: estimates suggest that 80 per cent of start-up capital for small and medium-sized enterprises in Mogadishu was sent from the diaspora in the West.[79] Eastleigh too is a major recipient of diaspora remittances. Much money is sent through hawala—money remittance—companies such as Dahaabshiil:[80] these form a crucial part of the Somali diasporic infrastructure. Indeed, by allowing deposits of money in one location to be picked up in many other locations around the world, they constitute an infrastructure more suited to transnational populations than nation-state-grounded banks, though they have long been suspected in our securitised era of facilitating terrorist finance.[81] International anti-money-laundering regulations have recently forced many banks to close accounts of hawala companies, leading to a vigorous campaign among the Somali diaspora to save them and their valued services, so critical are they to Somali diaspora society. In Eastleigh the scale of transactions is certainly very large, although accurate figures are unavailable for the in-flow of remittances. Dahabshiil estimates that it alone remits $200 million to the wider East Africa region each year, much of which would go to Kenya and Eastleigh, and this is just one of several companies operating there.[82] Such remittances bring much foreign exchange to Kenya.

Horst has described how refugees living in Dadaab often survive through remittances sent from family members overseas or in Nairobi, and the same is true of Eastleigh.[83] Many people there rely on remittances from relatives in such countries as the UK and the USA for subsistence, and thousands of such small sums play a significant role in boosting the Eastleigh economy through their circulation. However, some remit funds for goodwill and initial stock to help the receiver start a business and become more self-sufficient.[84] Thus, while war and conflict have had a devastating effect on the social fabric of Somali society, the consequent creation of a vast diaspora capable of leveraging resources in countries that vary greatly in terms of wealth means that Somalis often obtain financial help from relatives far away.

Those surveyed mentioned the location of family members supporting them, mostly Western countries including Norway, the USA, the UK, New Zealand and Denmark. However, there was also help coming to these Eastleigh traders from Somalia and Puntland in a few cases, while one respondent reported obtaining help from family in Yemen. Such remittances are not one-way traffic. A number of Eastleigh traders reported sending money to help family in Somalia; the successful also send money from Eastleigh to the West, reversing the standard notion of remittance flows, including an Eastleigh wholesaler I met who ran three shops in the estate and uses profits to help family in North America. While the Eastleigh boom is thus fertilised with much money from the West, some in turn goes in the opposite direction.

Most remittances sent in this way seed small-scale businesses; however, larger projects—including real estate—are also funded through diaspora investment.[85] This has become a theme in recent years as Eastleigh business became more attractive as a boom area for diaspora investment, and business opportunities are promoted by global media in the form of cable and satellite TV channels, and websites. Such ventures seek shareholders to invest for mutual profit in the long term and resemble standard global business practices. A good example from the wider Somali business world is Pontus Marine, a fishing company aiming to exploit the seas off the coast of Somaliland, which seeks investment through very professional advertising.[86]

Some of the newer Eastleigh malls have sought investment in the wider Somali world, especially those connected with a company called Al-Bushra, now developing property not just in Eastleigh—where they are behind Madina Mall and others—but in other parts of Kenya, for example, Mombasa and Kajiado. Such malls are not typical of the Eastleigh transformation, not being based on goodwill, but do demonstrate the significance of shareholder-style investment opportunities to the estate's economy. It is not just malls that are built this way: a Somali friend now living in Bolton in the UK told me in 2011 of a Canadian Somali company funding an apartment block in Eastleigh by offering shares at $10,000, guaranteeing investors a 100 per cent return on this investment. In this way, Eastleigh can be seen as a major site of foreign investment, as wealthy Somalis—as well as those of more humble means—throughout the world take up its investment opportunities. Some invest not just their capital, but also their time and energy, coming to the estate in person to start up businesses or join already-established ones. We will meet some of these diasporans who live and work in the estate in the next chapter.

Eastleigh and the Official Economy

The earliest origins of all this economic activity certainly lie in informality and contraband, but this scarcely captures the current nature of the Eastleigh economy. As the literature on informality highlights, there is rarely a straightforward binary between the formal and the informal, the two intertwining and interacting, often being dependent upon each other in complicated assemblages.[87] Even in terms of legality, the two are often blurred: as Bop states for Senegal, 'illegal practices are also performed in the formal sector, while so called informal economic networks operate with well-established hierarchies and are fully integrated into social life'.[88] Some point out how the state itself is often informalised, as, for example, when state officials routinely ignore laws regarding immigration when in their interests: for example, in China the 'illegal' presence and business of some of its migrant traders is often ignored, as such traders are crucial to China's export success.[89] Furthermore, for Hart, who first coined the concept, the informal economy 'seems to have taken over the world, while cloaking itself in the rhetoric of free markets': no longer is it merely a term useful for understanding those marginalised by the world economy—as corporations, banks and others ignore global attempts to regulate their activities, the informal economy has become the world economy.[90]

Eastleigh has long bridged formality and informality. Defining aspects of the informal economy—lack of regulation, few contracts and a reliance on personalised business relationships (see chapter 5)—still dominate. Yet the estate has been increasingly formalised over the years.[91] For example, once its shopping-mall blueprint was established, its economy became more formalised as business permits and so forth were required. However, a significant part of a trend to formalisation in Eastleigh's economy is the growth of banking in the estate. While goodwill and diaspora remittances continue to provide much capital, formal banking institutions have strategically moved into the estate.

Islam is a factor here. The religion runs deep in Eastleigh—perhaps even more deeply in recent years, a subject covered in chapter 5—and the question of interest (*riba*) and its morality in the view of Islam has made most Somalis steer clear of banks. However, First Community Bank, Gulf Bank, Barclays and others all offer Sharia-compliant loans, and now have a strong presence. While Islamic financial products are considered dubious by some who view their differences from mainstream financial products as merely semantic, these products have the backing of influential Islamic scholars in the estate, and are increasingly popular.

Many people still prefer to use hawala for savings (especially those refugees without the alien card required to access banking), but these companies too are increasingly formal and mainstream, having adapted to stringent new financial rules against money-laundering since 9/11 and accusations that they helped fund terrorism. Hawala in Eastleigh are all formally registered companies, paying tax to the government.

Connections to banks have also played a direct role in funding Eastleigh construction. This is especially so in the cases of Sunrise Mall and the Grand Royal Hotel. While the former was partly funded through goodwill payments, a bank loan was taken out by its Kenyan Somali owners to fund its development, and recently the mall was auctioned after the owners failed to keep up with repayments of a loan of 220 million shillings.[92] Developments such as the Grand Royal also involved bank financing. Thus, Eastleigh is not disconnected from the formal Kenyan economy and its institutions—on the contrary, it has become deeply entwined with them: indeed, such has been the scale of Eastleigh's growth that the formal economy could scarcely avoid it.

Beyond Eastleigh

There is a danger in all the above of giving the impression that Eastleigh is more exceptional than it actually is. In fact, many of the processes that helped form it have transformed other places in Kenya and beyond. Mathews' 'low-end globalisation', and the 'low-end malling' of urban areas, are occurring throughout the world, as is the high-end malling analysed by the likes of Crawford.[93] Indeed, the period since the 1990s, when many countries have embraced trade liberalisation, and cheap products from the East have also become more globally accessible, means that other parts of the world have seen similar transformations.

Furthermore, as Mathews emphasises, one can speak of low-end globalisation of such goods and their often informal trade as a key feature of contemporary life for millions in India, Africa and elsewhere.[94] Markets in Lagos, Kampala and elsewhere—even in the Western world—resemble Eastleigh in products sold, in the timescale of their growth and in the nodes to which they are connected. Indeed, post-liberalisation brought many Asian companies to Nairobi in the 1990s to promote goods at 'exhibition shows'. From the 'exhibition show' evolved the 'exhibition stall' in Nairobi's central business district (CBD), small shops that resemble the likes of Nasiib Fashions, offering opportunities to small-scale businesspeople (women, as Kinyanjui describes,[95] being some of the key agents in this retail development) to establish business in an area with valuable real estate. Older buildings that once housed large Asian shops have been subdivided, turning them into Eastleigh-style shopping malls,[96] where traders in the informal economy could find retail space free from city council harassment. Some of these traders have done very well, many travelling the world in search of the in-demand goods found in Istanbul, Dubai, Hong Kong and elsewhere.[97]

However, Somali networks have made Eastleigh a hub for much of this trade, while diaspora remittances helped supercharge its transformation. It has also provided a trade model replicated throughout Nairobi, Kenya and beyond. In parts of central Nairobi, Somali traders linked to Eastleigh supply chains have become dominant: for example, in Luthuli Avenue Somali-operated mobile-phone shops have taken over much of the street from previously Asian-owned electronics stores. There are also Somali-owned malls in the city centre modelled on those of Eastleigh. Jamia Mall—next door to the large Jamia Mosque—is the most impressive of these, offering an Eastleigh-like experience and Eastleigh goods (though sold at higher prices) for those unwilling to make the two-kilometre journey into Eastleigh itself. A more direct link to the estate is 'Garissa 2', a mall in the River Road area built by a Somali Garre man influenced by the original Garissa Lodge. This is not in a prime retail area, however, so is unable to attract goodwill in the way that Eastleigh malls—and Jamia Mall—do. Beyond Nairobi, mini-Eastleighs are also found. There are Somali-run malls in Nakuru, another key town for Somali trade, while a part of Eldoret is nicknamed 'Eastleigh', and Kisumu has its own 'Garissa Lodge', an old residential building that like the original Garissa Lodge had been converted into a warren of small shops, selling goods brought from Eastleigh by bus and sold mainly by Kisumu's population of Kenyan Somalis and Somali refugees.

The Eastleigh model has travelled much further still, however. Eastleigh is home to many Ethiopian Oromo, as we will see in the next chapter, some of whom move on to South Africa. Tanya Zack, an urban planner, has studied the transformation of part of Johannesburg into a 'Little Addis', where hundreds of Eastleigh-like shops have filled older, underused buildings.[98] Similar goods are sold, and similar systems— including that of goodwill, and the Eastleigh mix of semi-formal trade—are found there too. While Eastleigh is not necessarily a blueprint for this urban commercial transformation, the similarities and the pathway that many Oromo take to South Africa through Eastleigh, suggest it has been something of an inspiration. Meanwhile, Somalis in the USA have started similar malls in such places as Minneapolis, where there is the famous Karmel Mall, which started in the late 1990s, and where mainly women have established themselves in small businesses. Somalis have thus taken their version of the mall back to the original home of malls.[99] In a further demonstration of the global interconnections so important for Eastleigh and the wider Somali diaspora, one of its restaurants is named 'Karmel'.

Eastleigh has also served as a stepping-stone for Somali diaspora investment into the wider Kenyan economy. A number of its real-estate

Plate 13: New Garissa Complex, Kisumu

companies encourage investment in properties elsewhere in Nairobi, and Somali presence is felt in such attractive districts as Hurlingham, South C and Kileleshwa. Somali investment has also intensified in the East African transport sector: Somalis have long been involved in this, but the growth in import–export activities around Eastleigh has spurred further expansion. Some elite Eastleigh businesspeople also have interests in the fuel sector. Somali involvement in the latter has grown quickly over the last decade, from four petrol stations in Kenya in 2002 to fifty-six in 2009.[100] Hass Petroleum in particular has grown in strength, with operations throughout East and Central Africa. Thus, while it is principally a centre for trade in cheap clothes and electronics, Eastleigh has helped those most successful in its economy to diversify into yet more lucrative sectors within the wider East African economy.

In short, from humble, highly informal beginnings inside the rooms of an old lodging, Eastleigh's early refugee economy led rapidly to the malling of the estate, and to the creation of a hub for vast transnational and diasporic networks: Eastleigh became a global Somali hub built on global goods, goodwill and diaspora investment. Its shopping-mall economy itself became a model for mini-Eastleighs in other parts of Kenya and beyond. But all this private enterprise has left the estate's public infrastructure behind, making it a place of decayed streets as well as mushrooming malls. We will return to this stark contrast in chapter 7. For now we focus more closely on the people who animate this vibrant and cosmopolitan estate.

3

MORE THAN LITTLE MOGADISHU

'Kenya has 42 tribes; but Eastleigh has 48!'
Mzee Roba, October 2011

Somali identity is very much to the fore in Eastleigh, especially in Sections I and II. Somali language is heard on every street corner, Muslim dress is much in evidence, hotel and restaurant names often allude to the Horn of Africa, and food served in the estate often has a distinctly Somali flavour. But Eastleigh is far more diverse than the name Little Mogadishu suggests. As long-term resident Mzee Roba suggests above, Eastleigh's diversity goes well beyond the Kenyan norm: indeed, Eastleigh is 'super-diverse', with intricacies of identity revolving not just around ethnicity, but clan, nationality, religion and place of origin. It is a place where Somali unity is often emphasised, yet where clan distinctions are still salient; it is a place where national identities go beyond Kenya and Somalia, incorporating also Ethiopia, Djibouti, the UK, the USA and Norway, among others; furthermore, despite all this mobility and flux, there are traces of an identity in being someone 'from Eastleigh'.

This chapter focuses on those who live and work in an estate marked by movement: where migrants from within Kenya and beyond constantly arrive, and from which others constantly depart. Of course, Eastleigh is well known as a key node within Somali networks, and the

Somali-ness of the estate is regularly reproduced by new incomers from northern Kenya, Somalia and the diaspora. However, contemporary Eastleigh is also a hub for others, most notably Oromo, who form a large population within the estate, and Meru of central Kenya, for whom Eastleigh has become a migration destination thanks to demand for khat, the stimulant substance grown in their home region. Thus, Eastleigh is a highly complex social field where, in the words of Baumann in his study of the multicultural London suburb of Southall, there are 'communities within communities as well as cultures across communities'.[1] Much might therefore be lost by focusing solely on one ethnicity or nationality. However, the chapter begins with a look at the broad identity of those Somalis whose presence underlies its nickname of Little Mogadishu.

Being Somali in Eastleigh

A vision of Somali society as constituted by people of one religion, one culture, one language, one livelihood and one ethnicity is still widely cited,[2] and one shared by those Kenyans for whom all Somalis are Warya, a term derived from the Somali word for 'hi' that has become a generic—and sometimes pejorative—ethnonym. Such an homogenous vision of Somali society—and the concomitant idea of Somalis as a 'nation' separated by arbitrary territorial boundaries—belies the many intricacies within that society, intricacies formed by cleavages of various forms, including national origin, class, gender relations, sedentary versus nomadic livelihoods, religious differences, linguistic differences and so forth. Of course, clan is the most commonly cited—and most controversial—source of division in Somali society, and is much focused upon in studies. The classic work of those such as Lewis have made clan and patrilineal descent and the 'segmentary lineage' principle central to much analysis of Somali society, suggesting that allegiances at various levels (family, sub-clan, clan and the six clan families of Darod, Dir, Isaaq, Hawiye, Digil and Rahanweyn) connected through patrilineal descent served to govern traditional pastoral Somali society, and even to explain many of the contemporary dynamics and politics of Somali society. This focus is criticised for obscuring salient markers of difference such as class, race, gender and religion,[3] as well as the colonial and post-colonial context in which clan emerged as the master-concept, being reified in the process, especially during the civil war of the 1980s.[4]

In Eastleigh, while there are evident divisions between Somalis that sometimes become socially significant, as we shall see, there is in general a broad and strong self-identity as Somali, and many forces join Somalis into some degree of *midnimo* (Somali for unity). Unifying forces include shared social activities, attending prayers and, of course, business. Another is a strong discourse against 'tribalism' and 'clannism' amongst Kenyan Somalis and Somalians alike. The former are sensitive to ethnicised politics, especially in the wake of the 2008 post-election violence in Kenya, while the latter often cite clannism as the cause of their country's conflict. In the diaspora too 'tribalism' is blamed for, in the words of a Somali informant of Bjork, 'unprogress'.[5] Much unity discourse centres on the 'one ethnicity, one language, one religion' pan-Somali ideal of *Soomalinimo* as a counter to tribalism and 'the culture of violence and anarchy that pervaded the homeland in the aftermath of the civil war'.[6]

More negative forces unifying Somalis include the insecurities and challenges of life in a city where Somali identity is treated as suspect (see chapter 7), though these can also act to highlight divisions too.[7] 'Them' and 'us' boundary making in Eastleigh thus often becomes a matter of Somali versus non-Somali, creating the 'bounded solidarity' reckoned by Portes and Zhou as characteristic of foreign minority populations.[8] Relatedly, conflicts between clans and sub-clans in Somalia or other parts of Kenya do not necessarily translate into conflict in Eastleigh, recent clashes between Somali groups such as the Garre and Degodia in northern Kenya being a prime example.[9] Despite heavy fighting and competition in the town of Mandera, Garre and Degodia interact with little difficulty in Eastleigh, even doing business together.

Thus, in Eastleigh the wider category of 'Somali' has much purchase in its cosmopolitan space. Yet this unity is occasionally rather brittle. Despite the above example of the Garre and Degodia, tension between clans can flare up in Eastleigh based on events elsewhere, just as Horst describes them doing so in Dadaab,[10] while political debate in Eastleigh can bring clan discourse to the surface. This was so in the victory of current MP Yusuf Hassan over Johnny Ibrahim in the Kamukunji by-election of 2011,[11] where much campaigning took place in Eastleigh. While the election was peaceful, some Isaaq claimed that the result was due to clan politics, and in particular the strength of the Darod in Eastleigh (Yusuf Hassan is a Darod and Johnny Ibrahim an Isaaq). Politics in Somalia itself can produce contestation along clan lines in Eastleigh too: at the time of the 2004 election where Abdullahi Yusuf was elected interim president of Somalia, there were demonstrations from opposing groups of Hawiye and Darod which became fraught and led to some outbreaks of violence.[12]

While most Somalis in Eastleigh would see talk of clan as something to avoid, it often bubbles up to the surface, especially in the stereotypes of particular clans that are sometimes the source of banter. Such banter risks causing offence even when meant as light-hearted. For example, an Ogaden friend of mine joked to a Garre man that he must be a 'bad man' because of his clan affiliation. This was not met with the smile he anticipated, but instead with a flash of anger as the Garre man responded by questioning the Ogaden contribution to Kenya: 'What have the Ogaden ever done for Kenya? We Garre were at Lancaster House!', referring to the Lancaster House conferences of the early 1960s where the terms for Kenya's independence were debated.

Clan and lineage are also reproduced in more positive ways, as such connections can offer protection and support to those finding their way in the estate, or seeking investment in business. We shall explore their role in underpinning networks of solidarity in chapter 5, but for now it is worth highlighting that lineage and clan connections are socially reproduced because they are socially useful, not because they represent some primordial instinct among Somalis.

Being a Muslim

Being a Somali in Eastleigh also entails being a Muslim. Indeed, Islam is hugely influential spiritually, and in wider social life and business (see chapter 5). There are several major mosques frequented by Somalis, some dating back before the commercial transformation, others more recent. Also, most Somali-owned malls have prayer rooms, Islam being built into the concrete fabric of Eastleigh commerce.

Islam structures life in the estate in many ways. Temporally, it punctuates every day with prayer, while the congregational prayer on Friday closes business in the malls from 11 a.m. until 1.30 p.m. The malls close their doors between these times while the main mosques fill. Some get so busy that if you do not arrive early you cannot get a place inside, especially at the popular Sixth Street Mosque. Islam also structures space in the estate. While some parts of Eastleigh—especially Tenth Street, where there are bars, khat kiosks and a casino—are distinctly un-Islamic, some streets are very much the opposite, Sixth Street in particular. One of the main Eastleigh mosques is there, surrounded by Islamic bookshops, while khat kiosks are conspicuous by their absence. Some newer malls bear Islamic names, including Madina and Mecca. Furthermore, space has also been increasingly gendered in the estate under Islamic influence, as most Somali restaurants have separate areas for men and women.

Although Islam is a unifying factor for many in Eastleigh, both Somalis and non-Somalis (see below on the Oromo), and one perceived as transcending clan divisions,[13] it can be a source of difference too. Jacobsen explores religious distinctions that are salient despite all Somalis being Sunni Muslims. There are the Salafi (often referred to as Wahhabi), who 'self-consciously aligned themselves with more global, conservative paths of Islam that rejected the moral and religious pollution identified in Western countries and in impure practices undertaken by other Muslims'.[14] A Kenyan Somali who grew up in the estate in the 1960s and 1970s described how in those days Salafi preachers were rare. One of the first was a relative of his who had studied in Saudi Arabia. This relative even preached against mourning at funerals on the grounds that it is un-Islamic. The Salafi contrast with the Sufi, 'those men and women who, while they also engage in activities associated more generally with Sunni Islam, also practice devotional activities … and the veneration of the Saints usually associated with the mystical tradition of Islam called *tasawwuf*'.[15] The Sahaba Mosque on Twelfth Street caters for Sufi worshippers.

Islam among Somalis has generally been moderate, a 'veil lightly worn', as Menkhaus expressed it.[16] However, increasing Salafi influence is rendered visible in various ways, and is an important aspect of social change that has intensified with Eastleigh's increasing trade links to the Gulf regions (see chapter 5). Salafi imams are highly influential, and many seek to heed their words regarding correct behaviour. This was brought home to me when a friend in one of the malls rushed up to me the day after I'd taken a picture of him with a digital camera, asking me to delete the picture. He had heard the imam at the mosque preach that photography was immoral as it tried to imitate God's creation. He also tore down a picture of himself that had graced his shop's signboard. In this era of widespread ICT technology, advice on proper moral behaviour is not just sought at the mosque but also through online Islamic advice forums, and popular Islamic scholars on YouTube, such as Zakir Naik from India.

Religious difference is also marked by dress. Most Somali men wear tunics for Friday prayers but Western clothes most other days. However, Salafi men wear tunics as well as prominent beards. For women, *abaya*s (long, often black, robes) or heavier *jilbaab*s and *burqa*s are commonly worn, and there is much social pressure to dress modestly, essential for Salafi women. Many women in Eastleigh also wear the *niqaab*—the face veil. Some see such dress as un-Somali, however, and as an imposition of the Salafi.[17] Abdi analyses this adoption of conservative dress among Somali women as one of several 'invented traditions' of the civil war that 'consolidate patriarchy and exacerbate women's social subordination'.[18] Indeed, there is some nostalgia for the Eastleigh of the 1970s, when Somali women dressed in multi-coloured fabrics, and wore their hair uncovered. A Somali woman who left Eastleigh for the UK in the late 1970s before returning recently conveyed the more liberal atmosphere of that era through changing hairstyles: back then she had an Afro; now her hair must remain covered.

The politics of Islam in Eastleigh link to those of Somalia itself. There was support in Eastleigh for the UIC movement that had gained much control of Somalia by the mid-2000s, bringing an uneasy peace to the city and encouraging businesspeople from the diaspora to return and invest there. By the end of 2006, however, combined Ethiopian and Somali government forces had ejected the UIC from power, the consequent instability forcing many businesspeople to leave, some coming to Eastleigh.[19] As groups such as Al-Shabaab have become ever more militant in Somalia, and within Kenya and Eastleigh itself, religious figures in Eastleigh have moved away from giving them support (see chapter 7). However, there remains an undercurrent of threat felt strongly by some in the estate, especially those involved in music and the arts.

Members of the band Waayaha Cusub who once lived in Eastleigh were very open in criticising the likes of Al-Shabaab in its music, and one of them was attacked, forcing them to move to the other side of Nairobi. More recently, those involved in Eastleighwood, the youth group whose film and music activities are seen as immoral by some of the more hard-line in the estate, have also felt threatened, one member moving out of Eastleigh on grounds of security.

Being Kenyan Somali

Somali identity in Eastleigh, and Kenya more generally, is also complicated by national citizenship. While the Little Mogadishu tag suggests that most Somalis there come from Somalia, there are thousands of Kenyans of Somali ethnicity in Eastleigh originating from all over the country, but especially such counties as Garissa, Mandera, Wajir and Marsabit.[20] Some were born in Eastleigh itself, while most have moved to the city in search of what Mohaa terms 'greener pastures', whether lured by the opportunities of the Eastleigh economy and the educational opportunities Nairobi more broadly, or pushed by fluctuations in the pastoral economy of the north.

For most, Eastleigh is a hectic place of work rather than of permanent settlement. While some settle themselves and their families in the estate, many—including Mohaa—keep strong ties to their home areas. In his case, his family remain in Isiolo, an important town north of Mount Kenya, where he hopes to build a future in the concrete form of a family home, as well as a future business. Isiolo itself is a place of much future hope for Kenya, being the planned site of a 'resort city' and infrastructure development connected to the Lamu Port and Lamu– Southern Sudan–Ethiopia Transport corridor project (LAPSSET).[21] Anticipations of development there and in other parts of northern Kenya mean that the likes of Mohaa ensure that they keep stakes in that region. In this regard, most Eastleigh Kenyan Somalis do not vote in Nairobi, but return to their 'homes' at election times—these are some of the only times when Eastleigh feels deserted.

One aspect of being a Kenyan Somali is that Somalians are often dismissive of their knowledge of Somali *dhaqan* (culture), and this is reflected in the term that Somalians give to their Kenyan fellows:

Sijuis. 'Sijui' is Kiswahili for 'I don't know', and was supposedly the frustrated response of Kenyan Somalis when pressed by Somalians to recite their genealogy beyond the few generations back that they could remember.[22] Not all Kenyan Somalis are quite so unaware of their genealogies, however, and those from areas bordering Somalia tend to be more attuned to such matters.

Language is key in how Kenyan Somalis and Somalians can be distinguished. Kenyan Somalis like Mohaa (who grew up in Nakuru and Isiolo) are often teased by Somalians for their *garamgaram* pronunciation, garamgaram being an onomatopoeic term for the sound of somebody speaking Somali badly. A shopkeeper on the same landing as Nasiib Fashions with whom Mohaa shares much banter was incredulous when I told her he was helping me learn Somali: how could Kenyan Somalis teach me when they do not even know how to distinguish 'she' and 'he' in the language? It would be far better to learn from a Somalian like her. Mohaa and other Kenyan Somalis—especially those who grew up in towns such as Isiolo, Nairobi and Nakuru—readily admit their lack of fluency in the language, accustomed as they are to speaking Kiswahili.

For Mohaa this is far from a source of shame, and he self-identifies strongly as being Kenyan: when asked if he would like to visit Somalia, he told me that there is no reason why he would ever venture there, a place that means little to him, having never experienced it. He also takes pride in his Kiswahili, and in speaking some other Kenyan languages. Indeed, Mohaa might accede to the recent Kiswahili catchphrase used by the Kenyan government to encourage unity: *najivunia kuwa Mkenya* ('I am proud of being Kenyan'). However, the history of marginality in Kenya's north-eastern region where most Kenyan Somalis reside—as well as a history of state-perpetrated atrocities—means that many others feel themselves treated as second-class citizens, and embrace the slogan 'not yet Kenyan' used to highlight this treatment. This history will be covered in more depth in chapter 7.

Perhaps the classic Sijui are urban Kenyan Somalis such as the Isaaq, who were such a large presence in early Eastleigh. Isaaq are still important players in the estate's economy, with investments in a number of malls, restaurants and other businesses. However, in terms of population they now form a small proportion of Eastleigh Somalis. Some still live there, including Hassan Cige, the owner of Moyale Lodge, who featured in chapter 1. He told me how many Isaaq moved out in the early 1990s after becoming a minority, some moving to Europe, others to Tanzania. Many, however, still live in Nairobi. These include his brother and sister-in-law who now live in the middle-class suburb of South C. Like Eastleigh's Asians before them, therefore, some Isaaq have moved to more salubrious suburbs. Many do see themselves as distinctly 'Kenyan', having played such a long role in its history. They prefer speaking Kiswahili to Somali, and have links to elite Kenyan politics. There are traces of ambivalence to Kenya, some lamenting that it can feel hostile, especially with much recent anti-Somali and anti-Muslim sentiment, while they maintain some allegiance to their ancestral homeland in what is now the independent state of Somaliland. Yet they do not entirely feel at home in the latter either, leaving them somewhat 'betwixt and between': a well-connected Isaaq woman of South C expressed this to me explicitly when she said, 'We feel at home neither in Kenya, nor in Somaliland as there too we are outsiders.' However, events celebrating Somaliland's independence draw large crowds of Kenyan Isaaq.

While Isaaq residents are now few in Eastleigh, Darod, Hawiye and Garre from north-eastern and northern Kenya are plentiful. People from these groups had been in Eastleigh prior to the transformation, but as Eastleigh boomed many more arrived. For Darod in particular, their influx had a great symbiosis with the arrival of Ogadenis (a Darod clan) from southern Somalia,[23] and their networks are deeply interconnected. Kenyan Ogaden are politically and economically influential in Kenya, having produced such powerful politicians as Yusuf Haji, the former Minister of Defence, and Major-General Mahmoud Mohamed, who famously helped save the Moi regime at the time of the 1982 coup. They are powerful in Eastleigh too: many businesses there are Ogaden owned, including the Nomad Palace Hotel, an upmarket hotel that serves a wide business and tourist clientele.

The Garre are another group also present in Eastleigh in large numbers. Their home region straddles the Kenya–Somalia border at Mandera and the Kenya–Ethiopia border at Moyale,[24] and, while an influential group in Eastleigh, their identity as Somalis is not necessarily assured in the eyes of others. This has much to do with the fact that amongst themselves they commonly speak Oromo or the Somali dialect of Af-Maay Maay,[25] rather than standard Somali. Garre identity is as complex as their history of alliances with groups in their home region on the borders with Somalia and Ethiopia, and their knowledge of Oromo allowed some strong alliances to develop with Oromo-speaking peoples.[26] Some designate the Garre as an Oromo group, others as Somali, and yet others as an entirely separate group. A website called The Garri Nation[27] ran a poll asking what 'ethnicity' should the Garre be categorised within: Oromo; Somali; neither; or other (40 per cent said Somali, 37 per cent Oromo, 19 per cent other).[28] In Nairobi, while Garre I knew always emphasised their Somaliness, they also took great pride in their Garre identity, and saw themselves as the epitome of Eastleigh success: some of the big new developments are Garre-owned, including the Grand Royal Hotel. Garre pride in the latter is expressed by nicknaming it the 'Garre Royal'.

Eastleigh's booming economy is clearly the key draw attracting such northern Kenyans to the estate, especially those with relatives who can help them settle. This ramifies further connections between Eastleigh and towns such as Garissa, Mandera, Moyale and Wajir. A relative in Eastleigh can be a great resource, as my friend Elias found when his young brother arrived unannounced from Moyale on his doorstep one evening, expecting accommodation. He had finished school but had few opportunities for work in Moyale, so came to the estate, where he soon found work tending the shop of a cousin. Elias described how he was given no warning of the arrival of his brother, as he could have refused had he been told in advance. Better for the young man simply to arrive as a fait accompli and for familial duty to take over. Elias and his brother ended up sharing a tiny Eastleigh flat for the next few months.

Being a Somali 'Refugee'

Interwoven with Kenyan Somalis are the thousands of Somalians resident in Eastleigh. These, of course, include those who would be officially—and sometimes unofficially—designated as 'refugees', although this is a label that many Somalians shun, especially those more successful in the Eastleigh economy. In the camps too, 'refugee' has been seen as pejorative,[29] and, in general, many are uneasy with the notions of dependency and victimhood that the term often conveys. As Bakewell emphasises, it is important not to use policy categories uncritically at the expense of other sociological categories that may be more salient depending on the person and the circumstances.[30] In a complicated place such as Eastleigh this is especially true as Somalian networks blur into Kenyan Somali ones, giving people different kinds of support and opportunity beyond those they can access as a bona fide refugee. While I use the category 'refugee' for convenience, this complexity should be borne in mind.

Population levels of Somali refugees have fluctuated over the years, depending on conditions within Somalia itself. As Betts argues, the 'predominant drivers of displacement have shifted over time and across regions of Somalia'.[31] While conflict and persecution dominated causality for much of the last two decades, the devastating famine of 2011 was a critical factor in the more recent peak in Somali refugee numbers. Although most refugees live in Dadaab and Kakuma camps, many live in Nairobi, principally in Eastleigh. UNHCR statistics suggested that by the end of 2011 there were 520,000 Somali refugees and asylum seekers in Kenya, of whom 30,790 were registered in Nairobi.[32] Clearly there are likely to be many more living in Nairobi, but unregistered. New arrivals in Eastleigh are predominantly those with lineage connections to Kenyan Somalis from Garissa and other Somali-dominated Kenyan counties. Certainly most Somalians in the survey of Eastleigh businesses conducted for the project who gave their clan-family affiliation were either Hawiye or Darod, the majority being Ogaden from Mogadishu or Kismayu. However, there is a significant presence of Somalis from smaller clans in Eastleigh including the Reer Hamar mentioned in the last chapter. Also, I met a number of Dabare in Eastleigh, a branch of the Rahanweyn from around Dinsoor in southern Somalia, who congregated in an apartment block near the Grand Royal, while there are also some 'Somali Bantu'[33] residents.

Connections between Eastleigh and those in the camps are socially and economically important. Families are often split between the two, Eastleigh and the camps forming a translocal social field. Indeed, despite the increased cost of living in Eastleigh, people are continually attracted to the greater opportunities the estate offers for livelihoods, education, healthcare and so forth, while a family member in Eastleigh can make a great difference to the income of households in the camps.[34]

Many refugees come individually before encouraging other family members to join them.[35] Those who move to Eastleigh generally keep options open, however, often returning for the periodical headcounts in the camps to maintain registration (important for the right to rations). Buses from Eastleigh to the camps are often full around the time of headcounts. Thus camps are resources, and offer both greater opportunities for resettlement in the West than Eastleigh and a place to return to if life in Eastleigh becomes too hard.

Indeed, Eastleigh is not an easy place for urban refugees, both in terms of security and the risk of harassment by the authorities, given the difficulties in accessing legal documentation to remain in the city (see below and chapter 7). Poorer refugees find themselves sharing cramped accommodation, while even the wealthier in the many fine apartment blocks have to face the often sewage- and garbage-filled streets. Eastleigh can also be tough as so many refugees there are physically separated from loved ones, including spouses and children in the camps, but also further away in the diaspora. Many live transnational family lives: even newlyweds often spend much time apart, while maternity is something many women negotiate alone in Eastleigh while their husbands are far away.[36] For my friend Kaamil, this was a very difficult aspect of his life—his wife and son were resettled in the USA without him several years ago. While divorced now from his wife, the many photographs of his son growing up in Minneapolis stored on his phone remain testament to a sense of loss and longing. Women have faced particular difficulties in the city, some reporting more gender-based violence in Eastleigh than in the camps.[37]

While some refugees thrive in Eastleigh (see chapter 4), others struggle. Many refugee households eke out only a meagre living despite the promise of the malls, workers earning only 200–400 Kenyan shillings a day ($3–5).[38] A 2012 report suggests that over half of refugee households in Eastleigh can be categorised as either 'poor' or 'very poor'.[39] The poorest often sleep in cramped rooms crammed full of mattresses without beds, as do many Kenyans staying in an estate where good accommodation has become more expensive. There is a significant proportion of refugees who do better in the Eastleigh economy, however. Newcomers need to learn rapidly how to navigate both the social networks and the muddy streets of Eastleigh, where threats from police and security services, as well as from thieves and other criminals, are constant concerns.[40] It is here that clan and lineage can be vital, and many come to Eastleigh in the knowledge that there are people there who will feel obliged to help them settle. Steinberg describes his research subject Asad's arrival in Eastleigh as a young boy in the 1990s and how soon he was brought to a hotel owned by members of his lineage.[41] Even more evocatively, Steinberg recounts how upon reaching Johannesburg many years later, Asad was taken to a man who had notebooks full of names of Ogadeni living in South Africa: this man through his mapping of the Ogadeni was able to direct Asad to his uncle, who instantly agreed to look after his 'son'.[42]

Family and lineage connections to the diaspora are also hugely important for Somalis, modern ICT technology, mobile phones and social media ensuring that lack of physical presence does not mean that bonds of care diminish through distance. Perhaps even more than commerce, remittances that both derive from these transnational bonds and help reinforce them support the lives of thousands of Somalis in Eastleigh.[43] Lineage and kin connections are thus crucial, both in helping refugee newcomers adjust to the estate and in ensuring their survival. However, new arrivals have to deal with others beyond their lineage and even their ethnicity, and in this regard learning to speak Kiswahili and securing identity documents of various kinds can be key to survival, and even to moving on, an aim of many Somali refugees in Eastleigh.

Kiswahili, Documentation and Citizenship

Learning at least some Kiswahili helps to navigate everyday life in Nairobi, and is important for those working in retail shops and dealing with Kenyan customers. Eastleigh is well provisioned with several community-based colleges which teach the language. One such establishment is Sky, a small courtyard compound with a number of rather worn classrooms located on Second Avenue. Sky offers classes in computing, mathematics, English and Kiswahili among other subjects, and was established to cater for refugees both in Eastleigh and in the camps. For 1,000 Kenyan shillings a month (around $8), students can study a variety of courses; while waiting for other options to materialise, some refugees turn to education and obtaining certificates to help negotiate an unknown future. At Sky the Kiswahili taught is tailored to Eastleigh-specific encounters: rather than learning how to order coffee, the text-book used features a practice dialogue of a policeman demanding a Somali's *kitambulisho* (ID card).

However, not every Somali refugee wants or needs to learn Kiswahili. Given the protracted nature of refugee settlement in Kenya, many have spent most of their lives there, and some were born in the country: for many, speaking Kiswahili comes naturally. A number also speak Sheng, a language associated with urban youth that combines Kiswahili, English and other languages,[44] just like their Kenyan peers. However, some older Somalis have an intense dislike of Kiswahili and refuse to learn it. An old man I met in a restaurant was very happy to hear me learning Somali, but when I asked if he spoke Kiswahili he made an aggressive spitting gesture suggestive of the disdain he feels for a language associated with the Kenyan police. For some, learning Kiswahili also implies protracted displacement within Kenya and a reduced chance of returning 'home' or being resettled in the West: many in Eastleigh are 'sojourners' little concerned with—and some-times resistant to—integration with wider Kenyan society.

However, even for those who wish to integrate in Nairobi and Kenya more broadly, there are great difficulties, as the legal status of urban refugees is so uncertain, and rendered more so recently by security fears (see chapter 7).[45] Being registered with UNHCR and Kenya's Department for Refugee Affairs conveys some—precari-ous—rights that can make a difference in surviving Nairobi.[46] These rights include greater access to help from the UNHCR and other organisations in Nairobi. With the Kenyan government's encamp-ment policy, urban refugees in the 1990s and the early 2000s had little legal protection from harassment, although the UNHCR launched a Nairobi Initiative in 2005 that led to some positive devel-opments, including promotion of refugee rights, as well as some health-care provision.[47] Urban refugees can also obtain help from Kenyan NGOs offering pro bono legal assistance such as the Refugee Consortium of Kenya and Kituo cha Sheria's urban refugee pro-gramme. However, the aftermath of Operation Usalama Watch and the stated intention of the Kenyan government to enforce encamp-ment has made the lives of refugees in Eastleigh yet more precarious, undoing much of the work of the UNHCR and civil society organisations to uphold the rights of urban refugees.

Before Operation Usalama Watch, refugees registered with UNHCR were—in theory at least—able to live in Nairobi legally if they held documentation of their status.[48] As Campbell states, 'documentation is the foundation of protection for refugees residing in Nairobi',[49] providing some defence against detention and extortion by the Kenyan police. Without documentation, Somali refugees can feel confined to Eastleigh, where at least they can blend in more easily than other parts of the city. Documentation can thus expand their horizons, although the rights these documents bring seem ever more tenuous.

Crucial forms of documentation include the UNHCR Mandate Refugee Certificate (MRC) and the Refugee Identification Pass, issued by the Department of Refugee Affairs until 2013, when their distribution was suspended in the wake of security fears. Many Eastleigh refugees have these documents, or carry an 'appointment letter' that confers temporary protection while waiting for the MRC.[50] Older forms of the MRC attested that the holder was a refugee, but stated that they should report to Kakuma or Dadaab camps within a certain number of days, thus limiting their rights to remain in the city. Now the MRC does not link refugees to a particular place, reading: 'X is a recognised refugee in Kenya under the 1951 Refugee Convention and the 1969 OAU Convention'. Many refugees keep the originals of these documents safely at home, carrying a miniaturised and laminated version with them. As harassment from security officers in the estate is a very real threat, Somalis—even Kenyan Somalis, who often have trouble accessing identity cards in northern Kenya (see chapter 7)—are aware of how essential keeping identification on their person can be.[51] Those without documents face greater difficulties making a living, as the right to work and obtain business permits is dependent on possessing them,[52] although it is relatively easy to find work—albeit often menial and insecure—in Eastleigh's informal economy without them.

There has long been a trade in identity documents, including ration cards in the camps, and Kenyan identity documents that allow greater mobility.[53] Indeed, the marketing of identity is an important business both in Nairobi and in the camps.[54] It is not uncommon in Eastleigh to meet Somalis who claim to be Kenyan nationals from towns such as

Garissa and Isiolo, but whose knowledge of these towns is minimal. I met some who obtained Kenyan identification documents through the help of fellow clanspeople in Kenyan towns. Here, the illegibility of Somali identity for the Kenyan state[55] can work to Somali advantage, especially for those who can afford to pay for the privilege of becoming 'Kenyan'. However, the Kenyan state has been complicit in this allocation of citizenship, using it as a political tool to gain support during elections. As Campbell describes for the late 1990s: 'An increasingly powerful group economically, the Moi government sought Somali electoral support during the tense multi-party elections of 1997. In exchange, thousands of Somali nationals were granted blanket citizenship.'[56]

More expensive than ID cards are Kenyan passports, which can be bought in Eastleigh for around $2,000. A Kenyan passport has some power in the world—certainly more than a Somali one—according to a ranking of relative passport power, and offers better prospects for mobility for the many who wish to leave Eastleigh for other migrant destinations.[57] Often these are obtained from *mukhalis* (brokers) as part of arrangements for onward migration to South Africa and elsewhere,[58] including European countries through Sudan and Libya. Obtaining a passport, and paying fees for smugglers and trafficking brokers, requires much money, sometimes sourced from relatives in the diaspora,[59] or from selling jewellery, livestock or resources still held in Somalia.[60]

These Kenyan identity documents become a burden once in Europe or North America, however, as Kenya is seen as a stable country and so asylum is likely to be refused to someone holding Kenyan citizenship. Thus documents that perhaps cost thousands of dollars in Eastleigh become a liability and are disposed of en route:[61] Kenyan identity is sometimes disposable. While it offers increased mobility in some respects, it can hinder obtaining the more desired citizenship of countries such as the UK and USA.[62] Conversely, Kenyan Somalis sometimes adopt the identity of Somalians. Kenyan Somalis have been able to obtain refugee resettlement abroad, and it is no secret that a small proportion of Somalis now resident abroad are actually Kenyans who were able to persuade immigration officers in the West that they originate from war-torn Somalia. Indeed, there has been a thriving business in the sale of resettlement slots, though new biometric screening processes apparently make this harder.[63]

Dreams of Elsewhere

This willingness to pay a high price for resettlement slots and illicit transport to other countries should be put into the context of the desire for onward migration more broadly,[64] a phenomenon known to Somalis as *buufis*: a longing to escape to elsewhere that is seen as something of a mental illness.[65] The term is also used in a broader sense for symptoms of depression.[66] Horst in her study of Dadaab has analysed the concept within a wider Somali culture of mobility, as well as within Somali awareness of the greater security and economic opportunities abroad,[67] though of course the idea that to progress in life means to move to a 'first-class' place such as Europe is common throughout the Global South, as Ferguson and others have emphasised.[68]

Jacobsen focuses on its use in Eastleigh. One of her informants there stated that 'the person who has buufis is someone who is crazy; his mind is not settled. He is here, but his mind is elsewhere'.[69] Eastleigh is seen by many as a stepping-stone to elsewhere: it is not just a hub for the goods of its commerce, but also for the movement of people. Indeed, such is its association with opportunities for onward travel that some venture there for that specific purpose rather than for straightforward refuge. This was the case for Hawa, a young Hawiye woman I met, who lived in Mogadishu until 2009 when her parents sent her to Nairobi in anticipation of resettlement in Norway with an uncle. This fell through, however, and now she is left to survive in Eastleigh. A friend of hers—also a Hawiye originally from Mogadishu—left Somalia for Dubai in 2005. She remained there for two years, but in her own words left 'because of buufis', coming to Kenya to seek resettlement to Europe. However, her plans have yet to materialise despite having relatives abroad in Europe and North America, and she has already spent a number of years in Eastleigh. Lindley recounts a similar case concerning her informant Fadumo. She came to Eastleigh in the hope of resettlement with her aunt's family in the USA but was rejected in the screening process and 'left high and dry in Eastleigh with her small daughter, with no resources and few contacts'.[70] Instead of moving to the USA she remained in the estate, establishing herself in the clothes business to make ends meet.

Not every Somali in Eastleigh is fixated on resettlement in the West. Many regard it as a place to wait until Mogadishu or elsewhere in

Somalia becomes safe and they can go home. This was the case with Mohamed, a refugee who moved from the camps to Eastleigh in the early days of its transformation. He was the principal of a technical institute in Mogadishu who fled to Kenya at the start of the war, first staying in Utange camp near Mombasa, one of the original camps set up for Somali refugees. When that camp closed he was moved to Kakuma. There his educational background helped him get a job as a translator with the US embassy and the Joint Voluntary Agency. He was soon posted to Nairobi, moving to Eastleigh despite not knowing anyone there. Over the years he established a business importing second-hand pieces of medical equipment for clinics in Eastleigh, sourcing them from contacts in Europe.

Despite this business, he described Eastleigh as just a 'transit' zone. Indeed, his accommodation has a very transient feel: a lodging in Eastleigh, his accumulation of belongings in his room the only sign that this is actually his long-term residence. In this respect he is not alone as many get by in Eastleigh living out of such lodgings. Mohamed stated that he avoids putting down too many roots in Kenya so as to be ready to go home to Mogadishu; but, sadly, Eastleigh has developed into a place of protracted displacement for him. Mohamed's desire to return home was shared by many with nostalgia for an idealised Mogadishu where there was peace, a good climate and beautiful beaches (contrasting the city's charms to the dirt, cold and squalor of Eastleigh). Indeed, a longing for 'home' over the border and a pride in the Somali nation despite its travails remain strong among many refugees. Throughout Eastleigh there are signs of Somali national identity: Somali football strips and flags are sold throughout the malls, and decorate many offices and shops. When I first met the Eastleighwood team, their members were keen to pose in front of the Somali flag.

Dreams of elsewhere can become oppressive when life in Eastleigh becomes protracted. Indeed, there are many who lament their immobility. However, there are others for whom remaining in Eastleigh can be a boon, especially those with business interests and enough resources to obtain work permits or Kenyan identity documents. Economic security and a more secure status can mean that Eastleigh's trials and tribulations—especially those related to police harassment—are more easily navigated.

Plate 14: A member of Eastleighwood, in front of the Somali flag

Furthermore, an anti-buufis sentiment is quite common, especially amongst those making a decent living from the Eastleigh boom. This connects with the ease of communication with those in the West through social media. Some told me how relatives and friends abroad lamented lives led in cold northern climes, especially in countries suffering economic decline. People are also aware of how educated refugees in the West might end up doing menial work or suffer racial abuse.[71] This was the lament of Mohamed, the trader in medical equipment introduced above, who knows of a Somali doctor who moved to the USA, where he works as a night watchman. Such sentiments are less surprising in a vibrant economy full of livelihood opportunities such as Eastleigh than they would be in the harsher environment of Dadaab where Horst found so much buufis.

117

Diasporas

Mohamed also described how Somalis in the West often suffer buufis, developing a differently focused longing for elsewhere, one that urges them to return to Africa. This is especially so, in his view, for Somalis in Europe, who he said often idle time away on welfare. He related how many Somalis he meets in Eastleigh tell him they are on 'holiday' from Europe or North America, seeking the many things—tangible and intangible—the West cannot provide. I too met many Somalis in Eastleigh who were settled in the West but had come to the estate for a 'holiday'. These visitors give Eastleigh a very cosmopolitan soundscape, as their Western accents can often be made out. While Eastleigh may not seem an idyllic location for a holiday, it offers much for a Somali visitor, especially those with family in Kenya or in Somalia. Its new plush hotels such as the Grand Royal and Nomad Palace provide decent accommodation for those coming to visit relatives in Nairobi, or hoping to travel on to Somalia itself (Nairobi's international airport now has many flights to Mogadishu and elsewhere in Somalia). Such hotels are also the base for numerous Somali NGO workers on their way into Somalia. So common are such visitors from the West that they are referred to by other Eastleigh residents as *diaspora* (or *dayuusboro* in the Somali spelling given by Hammond in the case of Somaliland).[72]

That 'diaspora' has become a common noun in Eastleigh shows how widespread a term once restricted in general usage to the Jewish Diaspora has now become. Its semantic restriction in Eastleigh to Somalis resettled in the West is interesting too, even though technically its Somalian population could be referred to as a diaspora, especially as many maintain strong links to their 'homeland'.[73] Furthermore, in usage in Eastleigh, exactly whose diaspora the 'diasporas' constitute is not necessarily clear. While many who come to the estate from the West were born in Somalia itself, others grew up in Kenya while waiting for resettlement, or are actually part of the Kenyan diaspora; many Kenyan Somalis have also settled in the West over the years, often merging socially and economically with the wider Somali diaspora. Of course, the awkwardness of the colonial border between Kenya and Somalia means that many families straddle the border, further complicating the question 'whose diaspora?'.

'Diasporas' are a varied category, including those coming to find spouses: Eastleigh is an important hub for marriage arrangements and ceremonies, and there are many awaiting the chance to join spouses in the USA, UK and elsewhere. Some ceremonies even involve substitute brides or grooms where someone in the West has not yet secured the required documents to safely travel. The wedding goes ahead anyway, sealing their bond transnationally. There is a website (www.guurso.com (*guurso* is Somali for 'marriage') to help single Somalis throughout the diaspora find partners. Diaspora financial power and the attractions of life in the West means that some in East Africa see those seeking spouses in places such as Eastleigh and the camps as unfair competition.

Many diasporas are young boys and girls sent to Eastleigh from the USA, UK and elsewhere to spend time with relatives as part of what is known as *dhaqan celin* (cultural rehabilitation).[74] This usually consists of spending months at a *madrassa* learning to be better Muslims, as some of the children are regarded as having gone astray in their life in the West. Such children are sent to Eastleigh rather than Somalia itself as it is safer, yet 'home-like' enough, so that they might escape Westernisation for a while, while still living in a place dominated by Muslims.[75]

During fieldwork I encountered Adan, a twelve-year-old boy with a Somali mother and Tigray father, who had come to Eastleigh from Arizona. We first met as I was on my way with some friends to a restaurant. It was a Thursday, a day on which he would often hang out with retailers he had got to know on First Avenue. Most other days he attended a school where he was the only 'diaspora' in his class. He regaled us with stories, and took great delight in recounting his mischief at school back in Arizona, which is what had prompted his mother to send him to stay with an uncle in Eastleigh. Like most sent for *dhaqan celin*, *dhaqan* seemed less the point of the trip than *diin* (religion), although Adan was using his time to learn better Somali, a language which he can understand but speaks with some difficulty.

Life in Eastleigh appeared both exciting and daunting for Adan. He had friends in the estate, but felt cut off from his friends in the USA, though he remained connected to them through Facebook. He emphasised the difficulty of life for a diaspora in Eastleigh, telling us that he was 'tricked' into coming by his mother, who had told him that life in Eastleigh was 'just like the USA'. Some of the difficulties he found were at school: he claimed that he was teased for being different (his American pronunciation being a particular target), and that the teachers caned him, something American teachers would not dare do. Life was not all bad, however, and Adan had the freedom of the estate with friends on most corners.

Young women and girls sent from the West to places such as Eastleigh for *dhaqan celin* can find life there restrictive, especially in how they dress. There is pressure in the West too for Somali women to dress 'modestly',[76] and those who wear their hair uncovered, for example, can face abuse. However, not wearing modest Islamic dress in Eastleigh is almost unthinkable nowadays for Somali women. I met Mariam, a young woman in her late teens who had grown up in Minneapolis, and more recently Milwaukee, where she lived a very Western life. Her mother was quite liberal regarding religion, having left Somalia for the USA in the 1980s at a time when Somalia itself was more secular under Siad Barre. Mariam was learning Arabic at a college in Pangani while staying with relatives. In the end she stayed about a year in Eastleigh. She was very American in many respects, from her accent, to fondness for American food, a taste satisfied in Eastleigh by restaurants such as Kilimanjaro Food Court that cater for diasporas. While dressing conservatively in Eastleigh, on trips out of the estate she would make the most of the freedom to wear Western clothes, slipping her abaya back on before heading home.

Diasporas in Eastleigh also include investors in its economy.[77] Such investors tend to be from south–central Somalia, as people from those regions often have family and clan connections with Kenya and Eastleigh. They have not necessarily lived in Kenya before, although having family or clan connections is usually seen as important in navigating Nairobi. Some who grew up in the refugee camps or Eastleigh before resettlement in the West often are more familiar with Kenya than Somalia, and hence see it as a more natural place to invest. An Eastleigh friend, now living in Bolton in the UK, grew up in Dadaab and spent much time in Eastleigh. He told me that if he was in a position to invest back in Africa, he would more naturally consider Kenya as it is so much more familiar a country for him than Somalia. However, some would rather invest in Mogadishu, but find Eastleigh the 'next best thing' given the insecurity in the former.

It is easy to find people who had lived for a long time in London and elsewhere, and have come to Eastleigh for investment opportunities. Most diaspora investors I met were men, perhaps reflecting similar dynamics to that seen by Hansen in Somaliland, where more men than women return. Hansen links this to ideas of men as emasculated in the West seeing return to Somaliland as a way of regaining masculinity in the homeland.[78] While I would hesitate to make such an argument for investment in Eastleigh, men do seem to outnumber women as investors.

Diaspora investors are motivated by a number of factors: some by the desire to invest in a boom before it ends, others to invest somewhere considered more profitable than the West, yet with a business-friendly economy. One diaspora investor, with a strong London accent, told me that I should forget about the UK and set up business in Kenya, saying, 'Listen mate, England is finished.' This links to a common sentiment that the West is already developed, so more opportunities lie in Africa, a feeling common too in Hargeisa.[79] Establishing business in Kenya is regarded as easier and cheaper than in the West too, with fewer overheads, cheaper labour costs, and the ability to speed up bureaucracy. Indeed, one supermarket owner, who also ran a business in the UK, told me that those from the UK appreciate the familiarity of Kenya's bureaucracy, but also how a payment here and there can facilitate matters. In Hargeisa, diaspora investors find a similar ease in opening businesses in an environment with few regulations and restrictions.[80]

Some previously worked in the West in what they perceive as lowly occupations for which they are overqualified, so the desire for more 'respectable' work is also a factor. Sheikh Shakul—the managing director of a major real-estate developer based in the estate, and himself a diaspora who spent much of the last twenty years managing grocery stores in the USA—told a reporter how his business involved helping those who had saved hard in the diaspora in humble jobs to find investment opportunities.[81] Furthermore, as Hansen suggests for Somaliland investors, another drive is to invest where you are known and your achievements appreciated.[82] To become 'someone' entails building up conspicuous success in a Somali place—and Eastleigh is such a place in the geography of the Somali diaspora. Experiences of racism and living in non-Muslim countries are also motivations for some, as Abdi relates in her account of life for Somalis in the USA.[83]

Also, as the cost of living is less than the West, good lifestyles can be had, especially for the successful who have built up considerable savings. Such investors may have businesses in Eastleigh, but often live in more prosperous residential estates such as South C. However, some prefer living in the estate itself, especially as Nairobi's notorious traffic can make reaching it so arduous, and as Eastleigh now offers a number of comfortable apartment blocks aimed at the diaspora market, as well as many opportunities to socialise with fellow Somalis. Eastleigh may seem a place dedicated to business, but for those with resources, life there can be pleasant. Another recent investor saved money while working as a limousine driver in Arizona, doing arduous shifts; now he has built a restaurant and hotel in Eastleigh and lives, as he told me, a far more relaxed lifestyle.

In the words of one diaspora investor—a woman who had spent many years in the UK—diaspora Somalis enjoy an 'Out of Africa' lifestyle in Kenya, many living in comfortable parts of Nairobi where they have maids and drivers. The dream of a romantic life in Africa is thus influencing a new generation of settlers to move to Kenya from the West. Many make sacrifices, however, especially with regard to family. A number of diaspora men I met preferred their families to remain in the West, often not wishing to disrupt their children's education. Some support their families in the West through money raised in Eastleigh, a clear disruption of standard notions of remittances travelling from the Global North to the Global South.

Visiting places where they stay and socialise, such as the Grand Royal, is a very cosmopolitan experience, so many nationalities are represented. While Somali identity is emphasised in Eastleigh, these other nationalities are extremely salient, to the point that one diaspora speculated that in the future clan identity will cease to make sense, as Canadian Somali, British Somali and other such diaspora-level identities take over. Another said how home-town loyalty was evident, as diasporas were always pleased to meet another from Manchester, Milwaukee, and a huge range of other towns and cities.

These diasporas form some of the Eastleigh elite, and their secure citizenship of a Western country allows them an escape route, should things go wrong.[84] However, while diasporas often come to Eastleigh with both financial and social capital, there is another category of

Somalis from the West seen as almost their opposite: 'deportees'. There are many in the estate—Somalian and Kenyan Somali—who have had asylum claims rejected in the West and so have returned to Kenya. Being recognised as a deportee can mean being considered a failure in the common dream to attain social improvement through international mobility, and there is much fear of this social category characterised by lost hope. This is epitomised by the fear shown towards the Super-powers, a gang that has terrorised Eastleigh in recent years, and is thought to consist, in part, of deportees. To return to Eastleigh from the West is not always to return in triumph.

The Eastleigh Oromo

The foregoing might reinforce the impression of Eastleigh as a Somali space. However, there are groups with many other identities in the estate, including among its refugee population. Indeed, submerged somewhat under Somali identity are many refugees from Ethiopia, whose story of life in the estate is also worth recounting.[85] According to the UNHCR's statistical summary, there were 35,185 Ethiopian refugees in Kenya in 2012, of whom 10,796 were resident in Nairobi.[86] Most of these are Oromo, and most live in Eastleigh, especially in the most northerly part of Section I where there is an Oromo mosque.[87]

Oromo form the largest ethnic group in Ethiopia, although it is composed of several smaller groups, including the 'Raya, Wollo, Karaiyu, Kotu, Leka, Mecha, Tulama, Guji, Arssi and Boran', among others.[88] They also have a fraught history of relations with the Ethiopian state.[89] Despite their size, they have found themselves marginalised under successive regimes,[90] most recently by the Ethiopian People's Revolutionary Democratic Front (EPRDF), which came to power fol-lowing the 1991 revolution, which brought down the authoritarian Derg regime of Mengistu. There has been much political and economic oppression in their province—known as Oromia—following the with-drawal of the Oromo Liberation Front (OLF) from the Transitional Government of Ethiopia in 1992, and its subsequent designation as a terrorist organisation. This oppression has forced unknown numbers to leave the country, which means that many Oromo now live abroad, some as far afield as USA and Australia following refugee resettlement.[91] However, for many, heading south to Kenya is an important first step on their migratory journey.

While Somali refugees in Eastleigh report leaving their homes for a variety of interrelated reasons, for Oromo the reason given for leaving is almost always state persecution. Indeed, meeting Oromo in Eastleigh and hearing narratives of detention, persecution and flight is a moving experience. Most interviewees—men and women—described being imprisoned following accusations of association with the OLF. In fact, in mapping out other places that connect to Eastleigh, Ethiopian detention centres loom large in importance, especially notorious ones like Mekalawi. Oromo also complain of a lack of education opportunities for them in Ethiopia, which they see as an attempt by the authorities to keep them marginalised and submissive. The story of Gennemmi is emblematic:

> This man was detained in Dire Dawa in the late 1990s after leading a student protest against conscription for military service in the Ethiopian–Eritrean war. As a member of the student council, he called a meeting to object to the conscription of students as it would disrupt their education. The meeting was broken up by the military, and many students ran away. He was accused of sending them off to fight for the OLF, and was abducted during a night raid before being detained and tortured in a military camp for eighteen months. After failing to get evidence against him the authorities released him, but with harsh conditions restricting his movements. He was told to return to his studies, where he was even expected to inform on Oromo teachers. He gained sufficient qualifications to enter university, but was refused permission to leave Dire Dawa to attend, and he was subsequently arrested and detained once more after protesting. Released soon after—again with the precondition not to leave Dire Dawa—Gennemmi defied the restrictions, and registered at a university near Harar. He was subsequently tracked by the authorities, and it was then that he decided to leave for Kenya, helped by his aunt who gave him money for the journey.

All Oromo interviewed had similar accounts of the factors behind their decisions to leave, which reflected not just their actual shared experiences of oppression in Ethiopia, but also the need to have a consistent narrative of 'trauma' to give UNHCR and officials from countries of resettlement.[92] Most also gave very similar accounts of their journeys to Kenya and Eastleigh. This is because while they come from many different parts of Ethiopia, most of their journeys south funnel them through the town of Moyale that straddles the Ethiopia–Kenya border, and most trucks that connect Moyale to Nairobi end their journeys in the heart of Eastleigh at the junction of Second Avenue and Tenth Street, an area known as 'Moyale Airport'.

So common is the journey made by Oromo refugees that an industry has developed in Moyale to facilitate the border crossing and onward travel to Nairobi. These brokers charge 400–2,000 Ethiopian birr (around $18–92) for their services, though other reports give figures as high as $700.[93] One man interviewed pretended to be a porter to cross the border, then paid a Burji broker 2,000 Ethiopian birr for the journey to Nairobi on a cattle truck. Some secure free passage by travelling on trucks carrying livestock and tending to animals that fall over on the journey. One interviewee described how he barely slept for three days on the journey from Moyale to Nairobi as he tended goats.

Oromo arriving at 'Moyale Airport' in Eastleigh find themselves in a place full of familiar tastes, sights and sounds. There are Eritrean- and Ethiopian-owned restaurants that do a brisk trade in *injera* and spicy stews, while smaller shacks run mainly by Oromo sell Ethiopian commodities such as *teff*, *shiro* and *berbery*. Oromo women sell bundles of khat from tables outside. The Ethiopian feel of this area is bolstered further by the profusion of Amharic and Oromo names daubed on several businesses, often in Amharic script. The area is suffused too with distinctly Oromo music, while the majority of voices there speak Oromo. It is here that the newcomers find support. Some have contacts they can trace, such as Demeni, a young woman resident in the estate, who found a friend from her home region living at Tenth Street, who helped her to navigate the bureaucracy of the UNHCR in the quest for a mandate certificate. For those without contacts, help can be found through a strong sense of Oromo 'moral community'.

Moral Community

While regional and other differences in identity among Oromo might be salient in Ethiopia, in Eastleigh there seems to be a real sense of moral community amongst Oromo, supported by shared narratives created in exile, similar to those described by Malkki for Burundi in Tanzania.[94] A moral community was reflected in the most common response to the survey question asking if the respondent had relatives in Eastleigh when they arrived: 'Oromo are my family.'

As with Somalis, solidarity is important in the face of a potentially hostile environment, and this is bolstered in the case of Oromo by a strong political consciousness. Oromo in Eastleigh are deeply aware of the wider context of persecution and of the global dimensions of the Oromo cause, and this acts as a unifying factor.[95] All know of Trevor Truman, the British campaigner for Oromo rights and chair of the Oromia Support Group, and there is much communication through Facebook between Oromo around the world. However, most Oromo interviewed stated that they did not maintain communication with family in Ethiopia. This was explained as a necessity, as there is a fear that by getting in touch they might be putting families at risk should the authorities find that they have been communicating with an exiled 'subversive'. There is much fear too in Eastleigh that Ethiopian and Kenyan authorities work together to repatriate Oromo—talk of Ethiopian 'agents' is common, and there are numerous reports of abductions and disappearances, including recently of an Oromo scholar and leader who had been living in Kenya for many years—Dabasa Guyo.[96] Another real fear is insecurity in general, and a number of interviewees reported being attacked by thieves in Eastleigh and on nearby Juja Road.

Furthermore, Oromo have two major disadvantages compared to Somali refugees. Firstly, they do not get prima facie refugee status in Kenya, but instead have to be processed to get their MRC, which can take months or even years. Some live in Eastleigh without MRCs, having been rejected by UNHCR. Secondly, while Somalians have always been able to rely on the substantial population of Kenyan Somalis to help them embed in the Eastleigh economy and in Nairobi and Kenya beyond, Oromo have no such co-ethnics with Kenyan citizenship to help them. There are Kenyan Borana in the estate who speak Oromo and are considered part of the wider Oromo people, but they do not have the great presence and power of the Somali in Eastleigh.

Thus solidarity is a necessity, and is certainly much in evidence. Those who arrive alone at Tenth Street can expect to be taken in by other

Oromo, the latter perhaps reciprocating for good deeds done to them. Sometimes refugees find not just fictive kin within a wider 'Oromo family', but also actual kin. One young man came as a refugee and unexpectedly found his father, who had lived there for well over a decade, having fled following detention in Mekalawi. His son had been told to forget about his father as he was 'probably dead', having been out of contact since 1993 when he was detained. Eventually, however, he himself was targeted by the authorities and decided to flee to Kenya. He found himself in Eastleigh, and was amazed to be reunited with his father.

Another form of solidarity and moral community transcends being Oromo: being Muslim. Indeed, what is known as *Islantiti* ('Muslimness') by Oromo is a significant factor in how they survive and tap into Somali business networks.[97] Just as for Somalis, being a good Muslim means being seen as trustworthy, and hence gaining greater access to Eastleigh's economy (see chapter 5). A number of Oromo related how Somali families looked after them or gave them work as 'fellow Muslims'. This reflects a wider shared identity with Somalis, especially for those Oromo from the Harar region, many of whom interacted much with Somalis and even spoke some Somali in Ethiopia. While Christian Oromo might find Eastleigh not an especially welcoming place, for Muslim and 'Somali-ised' Oromo it offers many opportunities for livelihoods.

Transience and 'Stuckness'

In a survey conducted among the Oromo for this research, there was a high proportion of relative newcomers. This fits an impression that most do not stay for too many years in Eastleigh before moving on, whether through the legal channel of resettlement abroad, or through illegal channels to places such as South Africa. An estimated 17,000– 20,000 people from East Africa and the Horn are smuggled to the latter destination each year.[98] These smuggling routes pose a great many dangers, tragically illustrated by the deaths of forty-three Ethiopians and Somalis in a container in Tanzania in 2012.[99]

Certainly, like those Somalis with buufis, most Eastleigh Oromo hope that the estate does not become a permanent home. Even those with shops apparently feel little attachment to the estate, leaving businesses to others once the opportunity to move comes along. Unlike Somalis—for some of whom the estate can be a land of opportunity and one where becoming 'Kenyan' can be an attractive option—for the Oromo it is almost wholly a transit zone, and desperation can ensue if stays are protracted, which is often the case as resettlement can be denied, especially for those with political pasts. As Elliott recounts, the increased securitisation since the Patriot Act of the Bush administration means that anyone associated with supposedly 'terrorist' groups like the OLF will not be granted resettlement there.[100] The story of Aseffa, an Oromo in his fifties, illustrates this.

Aseffa spends his days at an Ethiopian restaurant in Eastleigh watching the world go by. A member of a banned Muslim organisation, he fled Ethiopia and arrived in Eastleigh in 1993. Initially optimistic that he would be resettled, constant setbacks began to sap his confidence. In the late 1990s he attributed the reluctance of the UNHCR to process his resettlement claim to the immense corruption of the era, but now he also thinks that he has been labelled a terrorist, and this has held back his claim. Disappointment at his plight has descended into paranoia. An eloquent man with good English, his talk of helicopters searching for him in Eastleigh is alarming. His claims that everyone— from the UNHCR to evangelical Christians and the general Eastleigh population—is out to sabotage his life make sense, given his experiences of such a precarious existence within an estate where much credence is given to conspiracy theories.

While Aseffa constitutes an extreme example, narratives of victimhood and conspiracy are common among Oromo in Eastleigh, and further reinforce the sense of Oromo moral community that helps them survive in an estate to which they have only tenuous feelings of attachment. Some are supported by money sent from family in the West, but few Oromo in the wider diaspora would consider returning to Eastleigh to invest. In this they differ markedly from Somalis, whose attachment to the estate—although soaked with ambivalence—is much stronger.

A Sub-National Diaspora

It is not just Kenyan Somalis who keep the Kenyan flag flying in the estate. The Kenyan Asian and Kikuyu dominance of earlier Eastleigh has faded, yet neither is a spent force. While many sold up to Somalis, capitalising on the rise of real-estate value in the Eastleigh boom, some remain, as do some earlier landmarks. The latter include bars such as Disney on Fourth Street and the famous Mateso Bila Chuki, a bar and disco on Second Avenue. Kikuyu still own most residential buildings in the estate, leading a prominent Somali businessman to reflect that in some ways Eastleigh is more 'Little Kiembu' than 'Little Mogadishu'. Also, Kenyan Asian businesses in Section I remain, although owners now live in Pangani, Parklands and elsewhere. Given Eastleigh's links to northern Kenya, it is unsurprising that the estate is home to Borana and other non-Somali people of the north too, who, as Cushitic pastoralist groups, often have cultural and religious affinity with Somali and Oromo.

Furthermore, different sections of Eastleigh have different population ratios. Thus, Sections I and II are dominated by Somalis and Oromo, but Section III has a much more mixed population, with many Kenyans of various ethnicities resident in a lower-middle-class area offering access both to Eastleigh and the city centre.[101] Eastleigh stretches beyond these sections too. The boom has attracted an increasing influx of Kenyans into the likes of Kiambiu, a slum part of Eastleigh to the south-east of the airbase, Zawadi Village, bordering Section III to the south, and Kinyago-Kanuku, between Eastleigh and Shauri Moyo to the south-west of the estate. These house many Kikuyu, Kamba and others, some of whom form a labour pool for Eastleigh. Historical satellite images available on Google Earth show the homes in Kiambiu and Kinyago-Kanuku expanding between 2002 and 2014 to fill all available land. The Eastleigh transformation is thus not limited to the commercial zones of Sections I and II.

However, within Sections I and II, something of a third 'diaspora' exists, constituted by another group whose roots in the estate were laid before the commercial transformation: the Meru (principally the Tigania and Igembe sub-groups from the Nyambene Hills district north-east of Mount Kenya)[102] whose cash crop *miraa* (khat) is hugely in demand in the estate, both for consumption there and for onward export to Somalia, Europe and elsewhere (see chapter 6). Khat has been consumed there since at least the 1930s, and Meru themselves have come to the estate for decades to establish khat kiosks. In more recent times many young Meru men found work in Eastleigh packaging khat for Somali exporters sending it to Europe, work which has diminished in the wake of a UK ban on the substance in 2014 (see chapter 6). Most such young men have returned to Meru, life being too expensive in Nairobi without work. However, there are still many Meru in Eastleigh, and there is scarcely a street in the estate without at least one Meru-run khat kiosk.

A questionnaire survey conducted by two Meru friends evokes the lives of some sixty-nine Meru residents. The majority of these come from Muthara, a Nyambene town populated by Tigania, and many of the men (twenty-four) were khat traders, while a smaller number sell *mokhokha*, a cheaper khat from Embu County. The original khat connection has encouraged other Meru to move to Eastleigh and establish different types of enterprise. Many Meru women are now resident too, and they tend not to sell khat. Instead, they have established hair salons, greengrocers and M-Pesa (mobile-phone-based money-transfer) businesses or *hoteli* (small cafés selling central Kenyan specialities). Not all men sold khat either; and some had established themselves as milk traders or butchers. However, the Meru presence in Eastleigh was initially at least a commodity-led migration, which, when established, attracted other Meru in turn. Indeed, whether selling khat or involved in another trade, all except three of the Meru surveyed had family or friends in the estate before they came. With this population, Eastleigh has thus become a key node in Meru networks, one consolidated by its similar status for Somalis and Oromos, ethnicities known for their consumption of khat.

The literature on Kenyan khat[103] suggests that there is a standard pattern of migration for young Meru men from the Nyambenes, whereby they apprentice themselves to Meru khat traders in towns around Kenya, eventually establishing kiosks of their own before retiring back to the Nyambenes and using savings to buy bars and hotels, or investing in livestock. While the presence of families in the estate shows that Eastleigh is a home of sorts for Meru, this idealised career trajectory still appeals to Eastleigh Meru, and most still regard the Nyambenes as home. The survey showed that only eight Meru envisaged staying permanently in Eastleigh; the rest expressing a desire to return to Meru. This is backed up by the age-range of those

Plate 15: Meru in Eastleigh

surveyed, with the oldest being in their forties, and most being in their twenties.

Meru seem very much at ease in Eastleigh these days, many living around Fourth Street in particular, and most make a decent living thanks to the presence of keen chewers with money to spend. There has been tension between Somalis and Meru over the international khat trade, especially in the late 1990s, with Meru accusing Somali export-ers of exploiting them.[104] However, this has subsided over the years, the interdependence of the two sides requiring good relations. Most Meru are Christians, and so do not share a religion with Somalis (though some Meru have converted to Islam), but in Eastleigh, daily life requires Meru–Somali interaction, and much socialising occurs between them. Some Meru even speak a little Somali, while there are Somali who know a little Kimeru in return. Thus, while trade in khat initially linked the two ethnicities, wider social interaction in Eastleigh has forged yet stronger connections.

Reer Islii

Eastleigh thus draws its population from within Kenya, the refugee camps, Ethiopia, Somalia and the wider Somali diaspora. Rather than being a site of uniform Somali ethnicity, it is also an important place in the global geography of Oromo, while remaining very Kenyan through its population of Kenyan Somalis, Meru and others. Indeed, while Eastleigh's cosmopolitanism in its pre-transformation era is obscured by its depiction as an Asian estate, so its current portrayal as a Somali estate similarly obscures a yet more 'super-diverse' population. While outsiders often see in the estate a mono-ethnic 'Little Mogadishu', many non-Somali networks thread through Eastleigh, drawing people from different parts of Kenya and East Africa to seek opportunities there.

Eastleigh's cosmopolitanism does not mean that all its residents and workers interact smoothly, however. Many—often for reasons of language as much as the desire to exclude or fear of the other—are only integrated within a narrow part of Eastleigh's social field, and interact seldom with those from other parts beyond business. Even within Eastleigh's Somali contingent, people sometimes limit interactions to those of the same lineage: there remains some spatial separation of clans, as in colonial times when different Isaaq clans settled in different parts of the estate. This lack of integration relates sometimes to suspicion, often of a racist or xenophobic nature. The xenophobia and even fear some Kenyans of other ethnicities display towards Somalis and 'Cushites' is well documented, as is the disdain some Somalis have for 'Bantu' Africans, with words such as *adoon* ('slave' in Somali) known to be used in Somalia to describe the Gosha and other Bantu groups,[105] and sometimes heard in Eastleigh to describe Kikuyu, Meru and others.

Intermarriage between different groups sometimes occurs—usually involving a Muslim convert marrying a Somali woman—but is rare, and casual inter-ethnic flings can be frowned upon. A Somali friend told me how he once dated a Kikuyu woman, but got peculiar looks from other Somalis when he took her to a café in Eastleigh. Such prejudice and social pressures can lead to exclusion. Furthermore, with such mobility and so much effort to leave by many living there, it is difficult to see how a wider feeling of *communitas* related to being someone from Eastleigh—a *Reer Islii*, as Somalis sometimes put it—might emerge. Indeed, there are laments that the great amount of litter strewn in the estate results not only from poor council services, but also from an inadequate sense of ownership of the estate and its public space: some are so fixated on elsewheres that they care little for Eastleigh itself.

Despite all this, however, some do develop a strong feeling of attachment to Eastleigh, and there is a sense of a place-based identity revolving around it. As such a powerfully evocative place with links throughout Kenya, East Africa and the world, and as one of the most identifiable Nairobi estates, there is a certain cachet in being from Eastleigh. Shared business interests, schooling and socialising patterns do generate a feeling of *communitas*, while multi-ethnic organisations such as the Eastleigh Business Association and the Eastleigh Residents Association—an organisation headed by Mzee Roba, the Borana long-time resident who made the remark that opened this chapter—further encourage this. Eastleighwood is a case in point once more, having broadened its membership to incorporate non-Somali artists, technicians and actors, building up a youth culture that crosses communities, to refer back to Baumann's quotation at the start of this chapter. There is also much work done by organisations such as the Centre for Christian–Muslim Relations in Eastleigh to bridge religious divides through various initiatives, including the joint mapping of Eastleigh and its landmarks by Eastleigh residents recounted in a 2013 publication.[106] While there certainly are elements of national, religious, ethnic and clan chauvinism in the estate that can lead to exclusivity, the work of Eastleighwood and others encourages a more inclusive outlook suited to somewhere that is far more cosmopolitan than the name 'Little Mogadishu' might suggest.

4

LIVING THE EASTLEIGH DREAM

In business there is yaum asal and there is yaum basal.

Mohaa, 2011

The Eastleigh story is one of mobility in the sense of migration and dreams of migration; but it is also one of social mobility and dreams of social mobility. Indeed, there is an 'Eastleigh Dream' whereby small-scale retail enterprises can be transformed into business empires. For Somalis, Eastleigh has numerous role models of rapid economic advancement. Yasmin, the Isaaq woman who took over Garissa Lodge and expanded it, is a classic example. Of course, for most the Eastleigh Dream remains just a dream: generally business is on a far more modest scale that that of Yasmin, and many eke out a living in service jobs rather than thriving as shop owners. However, so much capital flows around the estate that it appears a land of opportunity, tempting many to in-migrate from other areas of Kenya as well as from the refugee camps. As we have seen, Somalis in the diaspora also come seeking opportunities in Eastleigh, while many come to the estate hoping to go in the other direction and join the diaspora: social mobility appears intricately connected with physical mobility.

This chapter examines the Eastleigh economy and these opportunities. In particular, it looks closely at commerce inside the malls, people's varied pathways to becoming shopkeepers, and the social world within them that undergirds its success. We get a micro-level look at the trade in the malls through Mohaa and his shop, Nasiib Fashions, and consider the fulfilment a small shop in Eastleigh can offer its 'petty bourgeoisie'. The chapter ends by considering the fluctuations in the Eastleigh economy, encapsulated by Mohaa's fondness for the Arabic phrase *yaum asal, yaum basal*, which demands a fatalistic embrace of both days that bring you honey (*yaum asal*) and those that bring you onions, and hence tears (*yaum basal*).

Equal Opportunities?

The early days of under-the-bed trade in Garissa Lodge scarcely hinted at the scale of the economy that would emerge within Eastleigh. What began as an economy of smuggled goods that helped refugees sustain themselves in the wake of displacement grew exponentially into a source of employment—and wealth, in some cases—for a far wider demographic. In this regard it is important to remember that Eastleigh is located in the centre of Eastlands, the poorer side of the city, surrounded by Mathare Valley to the north and Pumwani to the west, both districts with large populations without formal wages and in need of work; the wider Eastleigh district also contains slum settlements such as Kiambiu. Indeed, Eastleigh has two key labour pools tapped by investors in the estate: poor Kenyans in Nairobi and beyond, and poor refugees.[1] For investors, this proletariat class underpins the opportunities the estate offers by providing a cheap source of labour.

Although accessing the Eastleigh economy might be relatively easy at the bottom rungs, becoming an Eastleigh shopkeeper is more difficult (as we soon discuss), while gaining the transnational networks necessary to become a major importer or large-scale wholesaler is harder still. There is differential access to these networks, even for Somalis: for example, a Somali Bantu spokesperson from Eastleigh, at a conference on the estate in Nairobi, lamented at how they were excluded from Somali business networks and hence Eastleigh business. Also, some Kenyan Somalis I met complained that they are disadvantaged compared to Somalians in having fewer transnational networks to leverage. The inclusivity or otherwise of the Eastleigh economy works on several levels: its need for labour provides informal work opportunities to Somalis and non-Somalis alike; its retail shops mainly offer opportunities for Somalis (and, to a lesser extent, Oromo) capable of earning the trust of others in its economy; the elite level of wholesale and import trade usually requires significant financial and social capital. Indeed, Eastleigh opportunities are far from equal despite numerous rags-to-riches tales.

The situation appears to be closer to equality in terms of gender. Indeed, it is striking how many key figures in the story of the Eastleigh commercial revolution are women, from Kenyans bringing clothes to Eastleigh from the borderlands region to Yasmin of Garissa Lodge fame. Many of the pioneers who first travelled to Dubai to bring goods to Eastleigh, like Mama Fashion, are known also as Mama Dubais for their transnational trade. Women are highly visible as shopkeepers in the malls, forming, if not the majority, then at least almost half, and their business activities earn much praise, as well as economic freedom. Studies of the transnational lives of Somalis have highlighted how gender relations have been transformed in the last two decades as women have often become heads of households in the diaspora or in refugee settlements:[2] this is certainly the case in Eastleigh.[3] In Somalia itself, many households have become reliant on a female breadwinner, with so many men killed in the conflict. In these situations women's role in economic enterprises has expanded greatly,[4] although examples such as Mama Fashion and her pre-war business in Mogadishu show that Somali women engaging in business is hardly new.

However, Eastleigh businesswomen are less vocal in the media, and form only a small proportion of the management of the influential Eastleigh Business Association. A (male) friend organised a focus group in Eastleigh of a number of businesspeople operating there. The only woman invited lamented how it was rather typical that 'men were doing all the talking'. Nonetheless, while an increasing Salafi influence in business (see chapter 5) may marginalise them from some business networks,[5] women remain key to the Eastleigh economy, and the Eastleigh malls provide a relatively safe urban environment for their businesses.[6]

Eastleigh Industries

Eastleigh opportunities do not just revolve around the core Eastleigh business of trade in imported goods: its boom has created a number of satellite industries, and there are several sectors in its economy. Key areas include construction and real estate, which have transformed the Eastleigh landscape in the way discussed in chapter 2. Also crucial are those relating to the transnational movement of people, goods and capital, attesting to the notion that 'the most successful migrant businesses arise in the very interstices created by transnationalism; for example in shipping and cargo companies, import and export firms, labour contractors and money transfer houses'.[7] In Eastleigh, with goods and people pouring into and out of the estate from near and far, transport in general is one business emergent from these interstices. Somali-owned travel agents are numerous in the estate, often specialising in flights to Somalia and locations important in the Somali business world: Dubai, Bangkok, Hong Kong etc. Such agencies are a key part of the transnational infrastructure that runs through the estate, as are freight companies such as Africa Salihiya, introduced in chapter 2. It was one of the first of a number of freight companies to operate in Eastleigh, although its headquarters are in Dubai. The company formed in 1993, right at the start of the Eastleigh boom, and now has offices throughout Kenya—in important towns such as Mombasa, Nakuru, Eldoret (whose airport is used for much importation from Dubai, and mainly deals with Somali-operated imports), Garissa, Mandera and Wajir—and throughout the world in China, Thailand, India, the UK, USA as well as Dubai.

Industries revolving around the mobility of people are also strong in Eastleigh. Locally and nationally, transport is also an important Eastleigh sector, and always has been, given that the main Kenya Bus Service depot used to be in Eastleigh. Eastleigh acts as a node for transport to the Somali regions of Kenya: Kakuma and Dadaab camps as well as Garissa and Mandera are well connected to Eastleigh, while Isiolo is served by a number of Kenyan Somali and Boran companies. Such bus services bring not just passengers, but also many Eastleigh goods destined for sale in northern Kenya.

The area around Tenth Street—'Moyale Airport'—sees many trucks leaving for the north of Kenya, generally laden with goods and people. The bad roads of the north have traditionally made trucks the main form of transport, and Eastleigh has long been their Nairobi hub. Meanwhile, local transport is provided by the famous numbers 6 and 9

Plate 16: Bus services to northern Kenya, Thirteenth Street, Eastleigh (photo credit: Kimo Quaintance)

Plate 17: A number 9 route matatu cruises through a muddy First Avenue

matatus that run in a loop between Eastleigh and the city centre.[8] Number 9 matatus are on the quickest and most lucrative route, charging passengers 40 shillings to come anti-clockwise from the town centre, along Racecourse Road and General Wairungi Street then into Eastleigh as far as Garissa Lodge. There is a long economic history to these matatu routes, which were once run mainly by Eritreans and Ethiopians. Eritreans have mostly left the industry, and both Kikuyu and Somali own a number of the vehicles on these routes.[9]

Taxi drivers can do good business in the estate too, ferrying Somali international guests between the airport and Eastleigh hotels. Some diaspora Somalis fear matatus, and so use taxis to visit the city centre. Many taxi drivers in Eastleigh are Kamba, Meru and Kikuyu, but there are Oromo, Kenyan Somalis—and some Somalians—who also drive customers around the city. Taxis are also seen as good investments, providing opportunities for kin and friends of owners to work for them as drivers. This was the case with Ahmed, an Oromo taxi driver whose friend—also Oromo—had a number of businesses in the estate, and who had bought a second-hand Toyota which Ahmed could drive. Ahmed claimed he was choosy with his clientele, often refusing business from non-Cushitic customers (i.e. non-Oromo and non-Somali) as he has been carjacked in previous years by those he termed 'Bantu' (referring to the likes of the Kikuyu); a job such as this that takes you out of the confines of Eastleigh is seen as dangerous by many, demonstrating a palpable distrust of wider Nairobi and Kenyan society.

Within Eastleigh, much of the economy flows through *mkokoteni* operators—the cart pullers who are often seen navigating the flooded streets of Eastleigh with heavy loads of goods.[10] In Eastleigh there will always be luggage in need of transportation from point A to point B: mkokoteni drivers are the professionals who do much of this transportation. The men—*hamali* (porters in Kiswahili)—who pull these carts mostly come from estates such as Mathare, although some live in Eastleigh while others come from Huruma, a few kilometres further away. My friend Elias interviewed some of these drivers, all of whom came to the business through lack of work, and some of whom walk several kilometres each day even before they begin work. Drivers do not own the carts they pull, but hire them from others, in some cases former drivers who have saved enough money to invest in their own carts. Drivers hire the carts for around 50 to 100 shillings per day depending on their age, and charge customers per distance and the type of goods carried, charging more for fragile loads such as television sets than for basic sacks of clothes. They reckoned they generally made 500–600 shillings ($7–8) per day. The recent parlous condition of First Avenue itself provided opportunities for enterprising hamali: they earned money by ferrying people across First Avenue when its river of sewage was in full spate.

The Eastleigh economy also has a strong service industry, as supermarkets—Somali-owned and Kenyan chains such as Tuskys—hotels and restaurants are all found in plenty. The recent arrival of a Tuskys branch in Madina Mall is itself a sign of how Eastleigh is interconnected with the wider Kenyan economy. Restaurants come in a variety of forms and scales, and are often staffed by members of the same ethnicity or nationality, though this is not always the case: bigger restaurants such as Kilimanjaro Food Court on Thirteenth Street have a broad mixture of Somalis and non-Somalis working there. Some refugees working in restaurants are recompensed with accommodation and food, rather than money. Bigger shopping malls often have restaurants inside, but also are populated by itinerant hawkers selling fruit, tea, coffee, ice cream and other refreshments.

With so much money flowing through the estate, financial services have also boomed. While some years ago there was only one bank, now there are many, almost all of which offer Islamic banking services. The scale of investment of the formal banking sector in Eastleigh is itself testament to its radical commercial transformation. However, many there remain more likely to use hawala.[11] The current largest company in this sector—Dahaabshiil—has a branch in Eastleigh, but other companies operate too, forming the main financial infrastructure for the Eastleigh economy. There are also business opportunities in money exchange in Eastleigh, and one building in particular near Garissa Lodge houses many young men with dollars, euros and other currencies to exchange informally, while there are more formal forex bureaux too.

Being at the centre of so many global networks, Eastleigh requires good communication infrastructures and cybercafés have long been plentiful. With mobile technology more accessible, and with mobile coverage extended to the refugee camps in 2004,[12] there is now little

need for the *taar*, the radio communication system developed by
Somalis to connect relatives and friends in Somalia, in Eastleigh and in
the refugee camps.[13] Global media also throws up its own opportunities. Eastleigh is home to a number of cable TV channels, including
HornCable, that span the Somali globe with branches in Somalia,
Somaliland, the USA and the UK. Studios in Eastleigh broadcast news
reports from Nairobi, many focusing on business and politics in the
estate. These channels are also a major medium for business advertising, a significant source of their revenue: the likes of my friend Kaamil
spend time scouting out new businesses to offer them advertising.

As some refugee and diaspora residents only leave the estate when
strictly necessary, fearing both crime elsewhere in the city and the
authorities, the estate has developed much educational, religious and
medical infrastructure to support the needs of an Eastleigh-bound life.
In the last chapter we visited Sky, one of the many educational institutions in the estate. Its many mosques also provide opportunities for
employment. For example, at the Grand Royal I met the imam of the
hotel's mosque, a young Garre from Mandera. He had practised as an
imam in Mandera, and applied for the post in Nairobi after seeing an
advertisement for it in his home town. Medical, as well as spiritual, aid
is available too. Pharmacies and medical clinics have proliferated, as
many residents have little trust in state-run hospitals.[14] These include a
clinic at Madina Mall where facilities are impressive and some clinicians
are from the diaspora, including an ophthalmologist who had worked
in the British National Health Service for years before getting the
opportunity to work in Nairobi. He told me how Eastleigh medical
services are not just for Eastleigh residents, but that some come from
Somalia to the estate's clinics when they need medical treatment, again
demonstrating how important a hub Eastleigh is for the Somali world.
He himself had treated a Somali dignitary who had come to Eastleigh
to treat an eye condition: he discovered the man had also spent time in
the diaspora in Canada, and that his spectacles had been prescribed in
Toronto. For such elite Somalis, the world is a small one.

With all this business comes a niche for those able to offer business
advice. Burhan—pioneer of the youth group Eastleighwood—began
his entrepreneurial life in Eastleigh with a venture called Iman e-Business. This offered online advertising and also business consultancy

services. He had previously owned a shop in Jamia Mall in central Nairobi, and so was experienced with business regulations. As part of his later business in Eastleigh he had an office in Garissa Lodge, where he advised on procedures for registering enterprises with relevant authorities, as well as on issues such as paying tax and obtaining an account with the Kenya Revenue Authority. He had contacts at Sheria House, where companies are registered in central Nairobi, and acted as middleman between the state and Eastleigh businesspeople. Being savvy in terms of branding, he also advised clients on designing logos and registering names for their enterprises: this idea came to him when a Somali trader wanted a business card printed, but had no logo and the rather uninspiring name of 'Miss Koll' (a pun on 'missed call').

As in the rest of Nairobi, not all sectors of the Eastleigh economy are legal. A key industry linked closely to Eastleigh's transnational connections is the trade in identity documents and the brokerage of people smuggling, as well as the sale of resettlement slots discussed in chapter 3. There are other illegal trades too. As White suggests,[15] sex work has long been an Eastleigh industry, and newspaper reports suggest that it remains so.[16] The estate has also long had a reputation for illegal drugs. An investigative TV report showed a building on Twelfth Street being used for the sale of valium, rohypnol and other such pharmaceuticals.[17] Cannabis from Ethiopia is sold in some parts of the estate. Eastleigh (Sections I and II at least) is reckoned relatively crime free compared with some other parts of the city (though crime statistics are hard to find), but there are still many incidents of theft and fraud, as Mohaa has found to his cost: he lost 70,000 shillings in a recent venture as an agent for M-Pesa (Kenya's famous mobile money business), as a group of conmen tricked him into releasing cash. There have also been incidents of theft through a Trojan Horse-type technique whereby a trader is asked to look after a large box of goods overnight, inside which is a man who then steals the goods in the shop and breaks out. Mohaa told me of one Somali woman in Eastleigh who was the victim of an online scam, sending someone she met on Facebook money for importation fees for goods he claimed he would send so they could start a business. She sent the money, but the goods never arrived.

Another form of livelihood in the estate is the extortion practised by gangs such as the now infamous Superpowers. This gang is constituted in part by deportees from the diaspora, and began as a vigilante group supported by Eastleigh business people fearful of crime, but it morphed into something more sinister and violent.[18] Of course, those charged by the state with curbing crime—the police—are notorious in Eastleigh for targeting Somalis for extortion. Such is their reputation that rumours abound of police seeking postings to Eastleigh where money can be made from Somali refugees seen as walking ATMs. Indeed, a large economy of corruption is sustained in the estate, feeding off the wider economy's success, but also the access Somalis often have to money from the diaspora. Such insecurity—and the state's inability to curb it (see chapter 7)—has made the security industry in Eastleigh another burgeoning sector, an influential member of the Eastleigh Business Association running a business there supplying guards and CCTV equipment.

This survey of Eastleigh opportunities is scarcely comprehensive, but serves to show how the original Garissa Lodge economy has evolved into something far larger and more diverse. However, these other economic sectors were built on the back of the estate's primary economic activity: the wholesale and retail of imported goods sold within thousands of shops within numerous malls.

The Eastleigh Petite Bourgeoisie

Not all trade of imported goods takes place within these malls. Indeed, much trade activity is often outdoors, and Eastleigh teems with hawkers—often selling the same goods as sold in the malls—as well as traders with outside stalls. Alfresco trade can be profitable, with lower overheads than traders in the malls and more passing trade, and First Avenue often clogs up with it, to the disgust of some businesspeople who accuse hawkers of disrupting the flow of customers to the malls. However, hawking outside is risky for those without correct permits (who are often harried by *kanjos*, a slang word for Nairobi County Government workers), and often disrupted by the elements. Thus, despite these outside opportunities, the thousands of small shops within the malls remain immensely popular. For shoppers the malls are a more pleasant place to browse and try on clothes, cocooned from the hectic streets; for traders malls not only provide a secure business base free from harassment from the kanjos, but also access to the social networks of support within them, and, importantly, a sense of autonomy and ownership.

As discussed in chapter 2, the design of the malls with their small shops—usually around six square metres or so—has been replicated around Kenya in an attempt to meet the demand for accessible retail space, and Kinyanjui argues that the Eastleigh mall is a potential blueprint for improving conditions of informal traders in general.[19] These malls reduce the barriers to becoming a member of the shopkeeper class—the petite bourgeoisie—where owning a business is a source not just of livelihood but also of meaning. As Scott suggests in his guarded praise for the oft-denigrated petty bourgeoisie, the 'desire for autonomy, for control over the working day and the sense of freedom and self-respect such control provides, is a vastly underestimated social aspiration for much of the world's population'.[20] Having rights to a shop in Eastleigh and a small business has much meaning for the likes of Mohaa, who can creatively make the space of the shop their own.

Plate 18: Eastleigh market stalls on First Avenue (Photo credit: Kimo Quaintance)

The Eastleigh blueprint has given thousands this opportunity for self-employment; in contrast, the large chains that fill higher-end malls in Nairobi might provide much employment, but only give a select few the chance for this sort of autonomy. The next section looks in detail at how one establishes oneself among the Eastleigh petite bourgeoisie.

Paths to a Shop

Despite being more accessible than similar retail space elsewhere in the city, becoming an Eastleigh shopkeeper is not easy, as the capital required to buy the key, or to pay goodwill and rent, restricts access. We sketched out some ways people capitalise Eastleigh businesses in chapter 2. In this section we flesh this out with some case studies of Eastleigh entrepreneurs.

While bank loans are used in the financing of bigger businesses in Eastleigh and real estate, few smaller-scale traders seem to seek them. Many, like Mohaa, do not trust bank loans even though Eastleigh now offers Sharia-compliant loans (see chapter 5), and many others would not be eligible. Some refugees come to the estate with means, perhaps money they were able to bring with them or have sent from Somalia after selling up businesses and property. These include Fatuma, who fled from Mogadishu in 2007, selling up her stock and property (she had traded in Bakaara Market). She used her pre-existing contacts in the Gulf and Asia to start importing textiles and carpets to Eastleigh, initially from one shop, but expanding to three in recent years. However, for those of less means a strong Somali ethic of mutual help means that many gain access to the economy through contributions from family, especially those in the diaspora, as discussed in chapter 2. For example, Hadija—a retailer of men's clothes in Amal Plaza—is married to a man living in the USA. They met in Nairobi, where he lived as a refugee before being resettled. She also came to Kenya as a refugee—her family is originally from Puntland—and hopes that he can eventually sponsor her to come to the USA too. In the meantime, he gave her $3,000 to pay the goodwill on her shop, allowing her to establish herself in business.

For others, securing an Eastleigh shop is a long process, relying on perseverance and hard work, as well as mutual support. There are many narratives of a trajectory of petty trade leading to an Eastleigh shop, including the following:

Abdi Warsame is a refugee from Mogadishu whose path to relative prosperity began on a small scale in the pioneering days of the Eastleigh transformation. He reached Eastleigh in 1991 with almost nothing to his name, relying on remittances from relatives living in the USA for his survival. From these he saved up $200, which he used to capitalise a small business selling watches on the Eastleigh streets. Beyond subsistence, he made enough from this trade over a few years to save up some money: $2,000. Once he reached that figure, he asked friends in Eastleigh to give him another $2,000 on credit, and then, in 1997, he started a shop in Kisumu, where he saw there was an opportunity to trade clothes in a less competitive environment than Eastleigh. He was one of the founding traders at Kisumu's very own Garissa Lodge.[21] His entrepreneurial character led him to expand beyond clothes, selling also fish and fuel in Western Kenya, then returning to Eastleigh 'when his pocket was full' and he could compete with other traders there. Now he has a shop in a mall selling textiles imported from China where he has numerous contacts, a herbal medicine clinic on Jam Street, and is also involved in the leather trade in northern Kenya.

A similar story is told by Hassan, an Oromo refugee:

Hassan came as a refugee to Eastleigh in 2005, arriving alone with few belongings. His first employment was at a Somali restaurant where he worked as a cleaner. He was paid poorly, but was given a place to stay and food. Next he moved to an Ethiopian restaurant on Fourth Street where he felt more at home as he could understand the language, and earned 3,000 shillings per month as a cook and given accommodation. He worked at Fourth Street for just over a year, before getting a job in a Somali shop in Garissa Lodge. By then he understood Somali and Kiswahili fairly well, at least knowing the words for clothes, and secured work through an Oromo contact who was asked if he knew another potential worker and recommended Hassan. Having worked there for a year and a half and saved much of his salary, his next enterprise was to make juice, which gave him his nickname Mr Juice. He bought a blender and sold juice to shoppers and traders at Amal. This enterprise became profitable, eventually allowing him to secure a shop in the mall where he sells men's clothes with an Oromo partner. This shop is in a lower-demand section of Amal where shops are just rented from the mall management. They took it over from another Oromo who moved to the USA. He and his partner had $1,000 capital between them, but only needed a fraction of this for the rent and deposit. They had to buy their initial stock outright, but soon built up a name for themselves among wholesalers, allowing them to obtain credit.

Mama Fashion—the Reer Hamar woman introduced in chapter 2— also exemplifies this trajectory, and is a classic example of a refugee living the 'Eastleigh Dream':

> In fleeing Mogadishu in 1992 (on a UN aircraft bound for Nairobi) she and her husband lost much of their capital, and her cosmetics business in Mogadishu was pillaged by militia. She emphasises her humble beginnings in Eastleigh by recounting how she survived at first by selling home-cooked samosas to other guests in Garissa Lodge. However, she and her husband had a highly valuable resource: transnational connections to Dubai and Tanzania, and the travel documents that allowed them to begin importing clothes to sell from her Garissa Lodge room. From these beginnings she was able to make sufficient money to obtain retail and wholesale shops in prime Eastleigh locations, buying the keys to these premises: the retail shop alone required 4.5 million shillings in goodwill for a ten-year period, as well as rent of 14,000 shillings per month. Her business success has also taken her and her family far from Eastleigh, travelling as far as Dubai, India and China to source goods for her shops. Indeed, she is well travelled in China, having visited Shanghai, Hong Kong and Guangzhou, where she knows a number of agents and dealers able to help her get what she needs; she brings back a quarter to a half container of clothes from such trips.

Many shopkeepers in Eastleigh begin by seeking employment as shop assistants. Kinship and ethnicity can play a role here, as employees working in the shops are often either related by family or lineage to the shopkeeper, although friendship can also lead to opportunities. Indeed, many shops are family businesses. Goldsmith describes a trip to an Eastleigh shop and the nature of its family organisation:

> I go looking for textiles from the revived looms of Barawa,[22] and find two-piece sets of these original kikoi wraps in a stall in the Amco shopping complex. It is a typical family enterprise—the husband, a former high court judge in Somalia, mans the stall; his wife is the main buyer; their son does the accounts and deals with licences and bills, and the daughters spend shifts relieving the father.[23]

For Mohaa, his first opportunity came from an Ogadeni relative from Habasweyn who had a shop in Amal:

> After earlier attempts at making a living in Nairobi had met with little success, this relative helped him settle in Eastleigh, providing him with

accommodation and 100 shillings each day. Mohaa describes how he impressed the relative once when he was left in charge of the shop. In his absence, Mohaa's sales charisma led to many sales, and he was given 300 shillings, and, more importantly, a job in the shop in 2006. He worked there until 2008 when his relative moved to Norway after marrying a woman from Kakuma with resettlement rights. In showing that *anaanimika* ('he can be trusted') both to be honest and effective in sales, he could build up networks capable of advancing him goods on credit, essential when an opportunity came for him and Siad—whom he had befriended as they worked in neighbouring shops in Amal—to obtain their own shop in the mall when its previous occupier moved to South Africa in 2008.

They still needed to raise the capital to pay initial goodwill for the shop, however, and had to find 100,000 shillings each. Here their experience of working in the malls no doubt loosened the purse strings of their relatives who could see they would work hard in the business. They both were loaned the money by family, Mohaa by his father (a man of some means and influence in Isiolo), Siad by a brother, allowing them to start Nasiib Fashions, so beginning a partnership that at one stage included a second shop on the same landing. This partnership lasted until Siad became disillusioned with life in Eastleigh, returning to Moyale to start a shop there in early 2014. Mohaa was then able to attract a 'sleeping partner' to the business: a friend of his brother in Mombasa invested in the shop, allowing Mohaa to buy out Siad's share of the business. For his investment this partner will receive a share of Mohaa's profits (35 per cent), as well as the money back in full. [24]

Bigger businesses—such as wholesale shops, which generally are larger and require far more rent and goodwill—are often begun by business groups, very often related by lineage. These can be quite large, allowing the pooling of resources from a number of people able to raise capital from savings or loans from relatives. For those without help in the diaspora, pooling resources in this way is critical, as it was for a group from Mandera—mainly brothers from one particular Hawiye sub-clan—who had bought the key to a shop on First Avenue for $10,000. There they sell rice, powdered milk and other foodstuffs, sourced from both Kenya and Pakistan. They had no relatives they could call upon in the diaspora, but still managed to raise that sum between them through other enterprises and family contributions. They regarded the Eastleigh shop as a great investment, reckoning they could sell on the 'key' to the shop now for ten times the amount they had paid, so good is its location.

Another way to raise money is through saving groups, the classic money-go-rounds that are known as ayuuto and hagbad by Somali. Many smaller-scale shopkeepers raise money through these means, some using ayuuto savings to pay off wholesalers on a regular basis for stock obtained on credit. Oromo and other non-Somali Kenyans in the estate also have their groups, some of which are multi-ethnic. Ayuuto are common in the diaspora too, one Somali woman living in London telling me how she puts £1,000 each month into an ayuuto alongside twenty others. She works at a ticket office on the London Underground, and so this amount of money is considerable given her likely wages: however, she does not pay it alone, and told me that her husband contributes half the money, though secretly. Women in her ayuuto do not trust men with the money, she told me, so have banned them from taking part. However, ayuuto savings both in the diaspora and within Kenya are invested in Eastleigh shops.

Of course, having the capital to start a shop is only the first step in being a successful Eastleigh shopkeeper, and the next section looks at how individual skill and experience, alongside the ability to access credit and social networks in the estate and beyond, are key ingredients in operating an Eastleigh shop, in particular focusing on Mohaa and Nasiib Fashions.

The Eastleigh Shop

Mohaa came to Eastleigh with transferrable skills from his time working in the matatu industry, experience that had sharpened his ability to handle money and deal with customers. This was enhanced while he was apprentice to his relative in the men's clothing trade. While a good salesman like him could sell anything, he is now well versed in clothes, being able to gauge a man's suit size just by looking, and has learnt to keep himself up to date on the latest Kenyan fashion trends. He has also learnt the value of eye-catching displays that pull in shoppers and make Nasiib Fashions stand out from the many competitors selling similar stock. Many times when I visited, Mohaa would be in the process of rearranging his shop, meticulously searching for the just-right way to display his shoes, shirts and suits. As well as such experience and care, the social capital that comes in being embedded within Eastleigh networks is also a key ingredient of success. For Mohaa, being an apprentice in the Eastleigh economy allowed him to enter the dense nexus of wholesalers and retailers that runs through the estate and its malls, cemented by a complicated web of credit and debt.

Indeed, while some goods are paid for upfront, the Eastleigh economy relies on goods being advanced to trading partners on credit, and not just in Eastleigh: wholesalers visiting China in search of stock related how some Chinese trading partners would advance even container-size loads of goods to cement relationships. Debt links many in webs of dependency in the Eastleigh economy, as it does in economies throughout history.[25] Power is ambiguous in such relationships as this dependency is mutual: wholesalers rely on retailers doing good business to ensure they make a profit. The personalised nature of these webs, their negotiability, and also their lack of interest payments regarded as haram in this mainly Muslim economy—means that they are unlikely to spiral out of control, unlike the credit and debt system in the global economy.

For Nasiib Fashions, Mohaa reckoned that in 2011 he and Siad had debts of about 150,000 Kenyan shillings to various wholesalers for goods advanced, debt that they paid off depending on their takings in a current period. At one wholesale shop in another mall the trader told me that Mohaa had a debt to them of goods worth 36,000 shillings. On that same day, Mohaa added to his debt by taking forty pairs of chino trousers from another wholesaler on credit, hoping to sell them himself at 1,400 shillings while returning the wholesaler 880 shillings, the rate they charged. This debt was not felt as especially burdensome by Mohaa, although wholesalers send staff round occasionally to chivvy him into repaying some. He has had several years' experience in the Eastleigh economy and knows many wholesalers personally, avoiding those who are too pushy in getting him to settle his debts. He thus chooses carefully those with whom he does business.

Wholesalers are usually positioned in larger shops in the basements of malls, selling their goods from Dubai, China, Turkey and other such hubs of the Global South. Some importers keep overheads extremely low by selling goods out of the containers in which they arrive.[26] It is to such wholesalers that retailers such as Mohaa venture when in need of stock, forming relationships not with one wholesaler alone but many. Some bring goods directly to retailers, however. Mohaa told me of a friend of his called Haji, known for being a mobile wholesaler. He is a Somalian who learnt the clothes trade early on in life. Nowadays he imports containers to Eastleigh, and visits hundreds of retailers individually to pass on his goods, while his wife runs a retail shop.

Every trader in the estate is flexible in where they source goods, and retailers themselves sometimes look beyond the estate and its web of wholesalers. Mohaa is constantly on the move, sometimes chasing down new stock from Eastleigh wholesalers, at others venturing elsewhere in Nairobi. For example, nearby Gikomba—the centre of Kenya's second-hand-clothes trade (mitumba)—is somewhere stock can be found, and Mohaa has bought mitumba clothes of a high quality there, pressing them to make them look crisp and new for Nasiib Fashions. At one stage he also sourced goods from a Chinese importer based in the Industrial Area of the city, and recently had a Somali friend in London send him cheap suits bought online. Shopkeepers are always poised to catch the latest news of bargains spreading through the malls. Word of high-quality jeans being imported to Kampala spread through Amal Plaza in 2012, and some Oromo retailers travelled there to obtain stock both to retail and wholesale.

Mohaa has also built up a portfolio of regular customers, in central Nairobi and in Isiolo, who often are in need of uniforms or business suits. When Eastleigh is slow, he touts for what he terms a 'deal' elsewhere (either by phone or in person), some of which are far more lucrative than standard trade at the shop, as these clients can put in large orders. Indeed, for Mohaa, Nasiib Fashions is his 'office', not just a shop. It allows him access to credit among Eastleigh's network of wholesalers, and his deals generally involve him acting as a middleman between the wholesalers of the estate and customers beyond: for example, in supplying suits to government departments one time, he was not selling his own stock, but sourced them directly from a wholesaler. In one instance, he sold eighteen suits to a government ministry, making a profit of 300 shillings per suit after he had paid off the wholesaler. Most retailers and wholesalers have regular customers too, both within Eastleigh and beyond. For such customers, having good relations with particular shopkeepers helps navigate the estate and save time in finding what they need.

In terms of sourcing stock, an Eastleigh mall resembles one large organism rather than a mass of atomised businesses. While there is competition between traders, there is also much cooperation, and the Eastleigh economy is highly collective. For example, if a trader secures a good source of stock, they may very well obtain it in large quantities on credit, distributing the stock amongst their fellow retailers, keeping only a small amount to sell themselves. Mohaa did this with sixty pairs of jeans he obtained from the Chinese importer he dealt with in the Industrial Area of Nairobi, keeping ten pairs for himself and distributing the rest. Also, if a customer cannot find exactly the right product in one shop, the trader dealing with the customer might well visit other retailers or wholesalers looking for exactly what the customer wants. If the product is found in another shop, the trader who made the 'deal'—as Mohaa terms it—will split the profit with whoever supplied it. Some shopkeepers tell customers that they need to go to 'their storeroom' to look for what is requested, giving the impression of a larger business: the 'storeroom' is in fact the whole mall. Some wholesalers will even sell individual items to retailers in need of a particular size or colour for a customer at only a small profit, so keen are they to clear their stock.

As to manning shops, within the malls there is something of a collective industry. Traders often have to leave their shops, sometimes on the trail of stock, visiting a restaurant for lunch, or visiting the mosque at prayer time. If no one is around, security shutters will be brought down; however, usually there are traders in neighbouring shops who will look after the shop, checking on security and reassuring customers that the shopkeeper will return soon. Eastleigh malls also see much socialising, so traders often have friends visiting who will happily take over: they often have spent time there and know the price of stock. This was certainly the case with Elias, who often helps out at Nasiib Fashions despite not being officially a member of staff; indeed, being trusted by many in Eastleigh allowed Elias to make small amounts of money here and there in his student years, helping him survive in the city while pursuing his university degree.

If a customer is not quite sure of a product, polished salespeople such as Mohaa can seal a deal with praise of the customer's appearance.

This might be done in concert with other workers, holding up a mirror for the customer while stressing how well the suit or shirt fits. Mohaa is perhaps not typical, his matatu background giving him a very forthright approach to bargaining. Though always playful, he is prepared to engage in much banter to secure the best price. Once he was bargaining with a lawyer who had been his customer since 2007 and was buying two suits. Both sides had ruses: Mohaa wrapping up the suits before the customer had agreed the price; the customer complaining of a sick relative who needed money. He also said that he had brought many customers to Mohaa, so deserved a discount. Mohaa at one stage told the man he should visit the wholesaler with him to be told the wholesale price, the customer asking me with incredulity if I had ever heard of such practice before. Both had fun, and Mohaa made decent money: one suit was obtained from another retailer, and he made 1,000 shillings on it, calling that money his 'commission'. The other suit was from stock at Nasiib Fashions that sold at 4,200 shillings, Mohaa having paid 3,000 shillings for it wholesale.

For other retailers—some of them women fully covered in Islamic garb—his sweet-talking style would seem out of place, and many do not have the linguistic competence in Kiswahili to engage Kenyan customers in this way. As goods are usually cheaper in the estate than

Plate 19: Elias and Mohaa, Nasiib Fashions, December 2014

town, initial prices stated by traders are often accepted with only a slight feigned reluctance. Customers generally feel they are getting a bargain compared with the pricier clothes of the city centre. Traders might throw in a *Wallahi* ('I swear') to emphasise that a certain price is just and that they are not trying to deceive. In dealings between wholesalers and retailers, however, prices seemed more or less accepted, and I witnessed little negotiation between them: this was mainly reserved for retail customers. At Nasiib Fashions, each garment had an ideal price that it would sell for, and a lowest price for if the customer complains too much (*akilia* in Kiswahili). I was given a beginner's course in pricing by one of a number of Mohaa's friends who would occasionally help out on the stall. For example, for high-quality trousers the starting price was 1,500 shillings, but *akilia* you can reduce to 1,200 shillings.

The price a customer is charged in Eastleigh partly depends upon their background. Sometimes wealthier or more naïve customers can provide a windfall. As in many markets without fixed prices, such windfalls can be significant for overall takings, as many other transactions might reap little profit.[27] Most shoppers in the estate are Kenyan, but many other nationalities can be seen. Some see diaspora Somalis as targets for high prices, but also Sudanese, who have a reputation for paying more than hard-bargaining Kenyans. Local Somali customers are generally seen as difficult, as they are likely to either know the going price for an item—preventing any extra profit—or might ask for credit or a discount. Social closeness is sometimes not good when dealing with customers.

Traders are always looking to make extra shillings where they can, and again Mohaa was exemplary in this regard. Much of his stock consists of football jerseys, and he realised that some people were making good money by printing names on the backs of shirts. Not many people had the machine required to do this, but Mohaa managed to source one from a contact in Nairobi. He could charge customers per letter and number affixed to the shirt, and made extra money sourcing machines for other traders.

Mohaa recently started M-Pesa at Nasiib Fashions, though gave up on this after losing the 70,000 Kenyan shillings mentioned above, and now reckons that shops offering M-Pesa are especially targeted by thieves. Another trader supplemented income from his tailoring shop

Plate 20: Mohaa and his name-affixing machine

in Bangkok Mall by charging the shop next door 4,000 shillings each month for using his electricity supply to power sewing machines. The bill for his electricity is usually much less, however, giving him a profit.

With so much credit and debt, traders—whether wholesalers or retailers—have to keep track of all their transactions. While most have good memories, all generally note down transactions in lo-fi exercise books or ledgers. Mohaa had his own page in the accounts of various wholesalers, where how much stock he had taken and how much money he had returned was noted. In turn, however, he keeps records of all his transactions, debts and turnover in an exercise book turned into a ledger with the addition of hand-drawn columns representing buying and selling prices and profit. The book also shows Mohaa's conception of his profit being underpinned by the grace of Allah: every page in the book is headed with *Bismillah Rahman Rahim*.[28] Religious faith runs strongly through Eastleigh, as we will discuss in the next chapter. Mohaa let me look over his account-book entries for a few days in 2012. These demonstrate how income fluctuates day by day: on the first two days he made 10,000 shillings and 5,000 shillings, figures dropping to 1,000 shillings and 1,500 shillings on the next two days recorded. The accounts also show how profitable suits are for him, as most of his profit on 11 March came from the sale of two suits, one of the major products sold by Nasiib Fashions, and something for which Eastleigh is famous.

His account book may be lo-fi, but it helps Mohaa calculate how near to meeting his targets he is, and like most Eastleigh traders, these are very clear. Mohaa allows himself 500 shillings per day—when trade is good—for what he calls his 'daily bread', paying for meals and so forth. He also attempts to pay off his house rents and the monthly rent he pays to Amal Plaza (9,400 shillings), and expenses related to his family in the first ten days of a month. Then, in the next twenty or so days, he attempts to save as much as he can in a bank account. The main target he must hit with those savings is the 'goodwill' paid yearly to the owner of the 'key', and the extra goodwill he now pays to the mall management after the terms of his arrangement were renegotiated, around 200,000 shillings in total. When he pays back sums owed to wholesalers depends on how close to meeting these targets he is. Days when large deals are struck are often when wholesalers are at least part paid off, maintaining good relations and keeping the goods on credit flowing Mohaa's way.

Lo-fi account books are perhaps symbolic of much of the Eastleigh economy and its informality. Formal accounts are not needed in an economy run mainly through personalised relations. As we will discuss in chapter 7, the Kenya government—like governments the world over—is keen to capture the informal economy and tap into its ever-growing worth. While Eastleigh contributes a vast amount of revenue to the Kenya Revenue Authority (KRA) and Nairobi County Government—in particular through its more formal banking, service and retail industries—the malls themselves remain partially untapped. The Eastleigh Business Association over the years has played a key role in trying to normalise relations between the estate and the state, encouraging the replacement of VAT with a turnover tax of 3 per cent for small to medium-scale businesses (that have a turnover above 500,000 shillings but below 5 million shillings per year) which was applied in 2006.[29] Such a turnover tax is reckoned better suited in its simplicity for informal traders.

How much tax is raised on commerce within the malls is difficult to say, although large-scale wholesalers are reckoned to contribute much to the coffers of the KRA. The shopping malls themselves have arrangements with the KRA to pay a certain amount in tax (a proportion of monthly rents from shopkeepers going towards this). However, in the future more might be captured as the KRA hopes to introduce electronic tax registers,[30] and the shops within the Eastleigh malls would be targets in this regard. The encroachment of the KRA in Eastleigh is symbolised by the recent opening of a KRA tax clinic in the estate—although it seemed to have very few visitors. This encroachment might just grow in strength in the next few years, and perhaps this increasing formalisation of the estate's economy will see the likes of Mohaa moving from lo-fi account books to tax registers, linking shops like Nasiib Fashions into the heart of Kenya's formal economy.

Yaum Asal, Yaum Basal

Eastleigh is not somewhere where fortunes are guaranteed, and while many experience good times, there are bad times too: *yaum basal* as Mohaa would phrase it—'onion times'. Business fluctuates greatly, even day by day. Mohaa told me how the view of First Avenue from the steps of Amal reveals how good a day it will be: some days the street teems, on others the estate seems eerily quiet. When the streets are quiet, so are the malls. However, there is a predictability regarding Eastleigh's *yaum asal* and *yaum basal*. The run-up to Christmas and Eid are extremely sweet: at such times traders can usually find enough passing customers to make decent returns, and if their stock is well chosen it can even be cleared. At other times they struggle to make their daily bread, especially after Christmas when people have spent much of their savings.

Traders are also at the mercy of less predictable factors. The recent roadworks made it hard for customers to access the malls, while currency fluctuations are also felt keenly in an economy reliant on the dollar, another way in which Eastleigh is affected by the global economy. The tense politics revolving around Somali identity in Kenya—especially in the wake of the Westgate attack—also makes the Eastleigh economy susceptible to dips in trade. Grenade attacks in the estate—

Plate 21: A busy First Avenue—*yaum asal* for Mohaa (photo credit: Kimo Quaintance)

which have become tragically frequent since late 2012—raise security fears among shoppers. The April 2014 Operation Usalama Watch by the army and police (see chapter 7) also dented customer numbers as road-blocks and identity checks were imposed. Trade became so bad for Mohaa in September 2014 that he gave up filling in his account book for that month, writing 'we call September the worst'. Such difficult times are often survived with the help of others, and in this regard the malls themselves often generate networks of mutual help: for example, shopkeepers facing difficult times might be made the beneficiary of a fundraising drive. This happened to Mohaa after losing the 70,000 shillings in the M-Pesa fraud. His landing raised 40,000 shillings to help defray his losses.

In recent times Eastleigh's economy has at times appeared to slow down in general. People complained of how there are too many 'copycats' in the Eastleigh economy, who simply imitate what is already popular, a trait also attributed to diaspora investors in Hargeisa, keen to invest in a sector that is thriving while not diversifying the economy.[31] Thus, investors filled the estate's retail space with people all selling the same goods. Traders spoke of declining profits due to competition, including a larger-scale trader mentioned by Kantai, who spoke of making up to $2,000 a day in the 1990s as clients from throughout East and Central Africa would be waiting in a line outside his shop for goods sourced by his cousin in Java. Now everyone sells the same thing: there is increased competition, but 'no diversity'.[32] Perhaps Eastleigh's economy is a bubble at risk of bursting through such saturation?

However, new mall developments that sprang up in 2015 had little difficulty filling their shops, and Eastleigh is busy once more with both customers and traders. Thus, despite fluctuations in trade, the opportunities the estate offers for wealth generation, or at least a basic livelihood, continue to draw people to this land of opportunity: whether Somalis in the diaspora, refugees in the camps, or Eastlands residents willing to pull a mkokoteni. Its economy is hardly egalitarian, however, and even traders within its petty bourgeoisie sometimes lament how they in effect work for those to whom they pay so much in goodwill and rent, as well as for wholesalers, to whom retailers are often bound by debt. Indeed, those who own property or control the flow of goods are those best positioned to become successful in Eastleigh. Yet Eastleigh has given Mohaa—and thousands like him—a decent and meaningful business and an important sense of autonomy, while helping many vulnerable people survive, and making a lucky few rich indeed. In a world of economic and social volatility, where formal and secure employment is ever more elusive, economies such as Eastleigh—while hardly perfect—offer hope to many that hard work can pay off in these hard times.

5

TRUST AND THE EASTLEIGH ENTREPRENEUR

Eastleigh Entrepreneurs Reach for the Sky!

Burhan, 2012.

Their business prowess—so evident in the transformation of Eastleigh—has gained Somalis a strong reputation for entrepreneurship within Africa and beyond. The online magazine *Modern Ghana* recently published a list of 'Africa's most entrepreneurial ethnic groups', focusing on the likes of the Igbo, the Kikuyu, the Chagga and the Akan.[1] Somalis also feature on this list, success in transnational business contrasted with the failures of governance within Somalia itself. Somali entrepreneurship is also praised far from Africa, their economic success in the 'Little Mogadishu' of Minneapolis prompting another online article to debate what other businesspeople in Minnesota might learn from them.[2] Academia too has developed a fascination for Somali trade and its flourishing in spite of—and, some might argue, partially because of—the statelessness of the homeland, Little's *Economy Without State* now being a classic study of this theme.[3] This reputation for business and entrepreneurship is something that Somalis themselves take seriously and in which they take pride, especially in a hub such as Eastleigh. For many, their entrepreneurship is a positive story to tell in the midst of ongoing strife at home. Indeed, for some, *ganacsi*—'business' in Somali—has been etched onto Somali self-identity, and it is therefore unsurprising that in explaining the transformation of Eastleigh, Somalis—and non-Somalis—emphasise their entrepreneurialism as being key.

This chapter explores Somali entrepreneurship and how it is imagined in Eastleigh and beyond. In particular, it looks at two facets emphasised in discourse: a willingness to take risks, and a willingness to trust other Somalis. In this way, daring in business is embedded in a mutuality reinforced by Somali culture and social structure, as well as by Islam. We examine the dynamics and functions of business in an estate where deceit and mistrust are more common than the emphasis on trust might suggest, and explore what might account for the emphasis on 'trust', arguing that this is in some ways a normative rather than descriptive discourse. As noted in the literature on entrepreneurship,[4] 'culturalist' explanations of business success by particular ethnic or national groups often obscure other social factors underpinning success. Nonetheless, these idealised notions of Somali entrepreneurship play a role in supporting an economy built as much on mutuality as self-interest, and encouraging the flow of goods and capital that have made Eastleigh into what it is today.

The Risk-Taking Entrepreneur

The epigraph that began this chapter was my friend Burhan's title for an Eastleighwood event he wanted to host in Eastleigh, a promotional evening that would give businesses and their proprietors publicity, and would enhance the reputation of Eastleigh by showcasing its commerce and success, as opposed to its standard portrayal in the media as a place of dubious money and terrorists. This event was not to be, as Burhan became sidetracked by other projects, but the idea behind it neatly introduces entrepreneurial identity and values evident in Eastleigh. Whether computer-literate graduates with college diplomas like Burhan or the likes of Yasmin of Garissa Lodge fame with little or no formal training in business, Eastleigh's businesspeople are seen by many as embodying an enterprising spirit, one that resonates both with 'neoliberal' notions of entrepreneurialism and self-invention,[5] and with age-old stereotypes of the pastoralist Somali, encapsulated in Burton's description of them as a 'fierce and turbulent race of Republicans'.[6]

Burhan himself certainly embodies an entrepreneurial spirit, as his many different initiatives demonstrate; he is a man of great energy, and

I would often tease him that whenever I met him he was working on at least four new business ideas. After studying for a diploma course in information technology (with modules in business administration), he worked at a forex bureau in central Nairobi, before his mother—who lives in California—helped him with the capital to start up an electronics shop in Jamia Mall, (the Somali-owned mall next to Jamia Mosque, also in the city centre). After that enterprise he started both a cybercafé and his Iman e-Business in Eastleigh, renting a shop on Jam Street for the former, and an office in Garissa Lodge for the latter, a company that helped businesses promote themselves in the estate through advertising. The two businesses had a symbiosis, as Iman e-Business made use of the cybercafé for printing promotional material, and for establishing and maintaining its website.

While running Iman e-Business, Burhan also established a media company called Waaberi Media Limited, which produced a number of magazines designed especially for the Somali diaspora: Burhan and his

Plate 22: Burhan (second from left): Eastleigh entrepreneur and impresario

team of Somali youth told me they hoped the magazine would prove popular from 'Mogadishu to Minneapolis'. The articles in the magazine had a very Kenyan focus, however: the first issue included an interview with the founder of the Eastleigh Business Association on the history of Eastleigh. At Garissa Lodge, Burhan found his office becoming something of a social club for a number of young Somalis, including some talented singers. This led him and his entourage to the idea for Eastleighwood, the youth group which aims to harness these talents through music, films and Eastleighwood Youth Forum, a non-profit spin-off registered as an NGO in Kenya.

In fashionable terminology, Burhan would probably be classed as a 'social entrepreneur' in his Eastleighwood initiative, as while it has given him the chance to establish himself as an impresario for Eastleigh talents, and as an events manager, the organisation does fulfil a drive of Burhan's to make a difference, a drive he links to the influence of his late uncle, Ali Sharmarke. He was a Canadian Somali who returned to Mogadishu from Ottawa to co-found HornAfrik, a radio station in Mogadishu that was targeted by Islamist militants, leading to his murder in 2007. This family link to someone so touched by conflict in Somalia has left a strong mark on Burhan, especially as he respected his uncle greatly. Burhan often speaks of securing his 'legacy' and doing good for Somali society: that he sold up his businesses in 2011 to move temporarily to Somalia to establish an Eastleighwood office there is testament to his bravery. Upon his return, Burhan and his team secured international backers for Eastleighwood, receiving funding and equipment, now used on a number of productions, and organising anti-radicalisation events in the estate.

It is interesting to trace Burhan's entrepreneurial influences. He relates that what he sees as essential ingredients of business success—risk taking and hard work—are values emphasised strongly by Somali culture. Regarding the latter, he told me of a Somali saying *nin aan shaqeeysan shaah macabo*, meaning 'a man who does not work will not drink tea', suggesting that work is needed to enjoy life. A young friend of Burhan's—a Kenyan Somali from Mandera and fellow Eastleighwood pioneer—told me how his father—now in Sweden—instilled a work ethic in him, demanding that he succeed at school. While his father used to send him money from Sweden, he now insists that his son works hard in Nairobi to contribute to his family's well-being in Mandera. Much of Burhan's inspiration comes from beyond Somali culture, however. He is very fond of quotations drawn from his heroes from the world of business, including Bill Gates and Robert Kiyosaki, the American self-help author whose work includes the *Rich Dad* series of books. There is a quotation from Kiyosaki that he has posted on the Eastleighwood website that resonates with Somali business values and the praise of risk: 'Don't let the fear of losing be greater than the excitement of winning.' The work of Kiyosaki graces many a bookshop and roadside textbook traders' stall in Kenya, as the promise such books offer of riches draws in many would-be entrepreneurs. Of course, these are not limited to East Africa, but are common throughout the world. Indeed, the spread of such self-help books in Kenya mirrors the growth in self-help magazines in the post-Soviet world designed to help people become 'neoliberal subjects' and thrive in the new economy.[7]

Burhan is especially fond of Kiyosaki's 'cashflow quadrant',[8] whereby employees and small businesspeople are contrasted with investors and large-scale businesspeople. While the former two seek security, true freedom and wealth come for the latter, who allow their money to work for them. Burhan compared this with what he described as a Somali dislike of working for others: a Somali always wants to be her or his own boss.[9] As another Somali put it: 'The main problem with Somalis is that they all want to give orders but none want to follow.' Burhan felt that even some of his own Somali employees resented him for having power over them and curtailing their freedom. There is cultural depth to such notions, and Simons argues that the pastoralist heritage of Somalis has made them contemptuous of 'dirty' work such as agricultural labour, giving them a 'preference for management over production or hands-on maintenance',[10] a preference the thousands of shops of Eastleigh have allowed many to realise, as discussed in chapter 4.

This notion of freedom resonates strongly in Eastleigh, and elsewhere in the Somali world, as do other 'neoliberal' values.[11] This connects with the embrace of capitalism worldwide by those operating in the 'low-end' global circuits, of which Eastleigh is a part: as Mathews et al. state, 'those who practice globalization from below don't seek to destroy capitalism, but to benefit from it'.[12] A contention that the state should not be relied upon, but rather hard work and an enterprising spirit, is quite common throughout the Somali diaspora: some even embrace the suspicion of the welfare state promoted by the likes of the British Conservative party.[13] The notion that welfare benefits can stifle self-reliance was even mentioned in Eastleigh by an informant who stated that Somalis there prefer their families to be resettled in the USA where they have less welfare and more impetus to work hard as a consequence.[14] Furthermore, an apparent Somali ability to thrive in an 'economy without state' both within Somalia and in such apparently state-neglected places as Eastleigh means that some see the state as a hindrance to creative entrepreneurship rather than a potential provider of security and infrastructure that could enhance such entrepreneurship.[15] The very adoption of the word 'entrepreneur' also speaks of this embrace of business in a stateless era, one mirroring the promotion of entrepreneurial subjectivities in Eastern Europe in the post-socialist years: there too the self-made entrepreneur—'Me, Inc' in the phrase of Makovicky—was promoted, by some at least, as the remedy to discredited state economies.[16]

However, other influences bear on how businesspeople in Eastleigh present themselves, including, in the case of males, the hip-hop-infused cultural figure of the 'hustler'. The 'hustler' image is embraced by many young men, and is a common cultural reference throughout Kenya, being found in Kenyan music influenced by the likes of 50 Cent,[17] and even on a bus plying the Isiolo–Wamba route that is named Jungle Hustler. The term was used by *The Standard* newspaper to refer to Kenyan students studying in the USA who had to take on numerous extra jobs to survive,[18] while there is a recent organisation in Kenya called the Movement of Hustlers and Sufferers that campaigns for the lowering of experience requirements for employment, which they argue discriminates against the young and those lacking formal qualifications.[19] Politicians too are not averse to the allure of the hustler image: Deputy President William Ruto has embraced the nickname of the 'Grand Hustler'.[20]

'Hustling' to make a living through one's wit and ingenuity is imbued with daring and 'cool', but is also seen as a necessity in straitened times. In this sense, it has the same resonance as it has in the USA, where Wacquant describes the 'social art of hustling' as 'a field of activities that have in common the fact they require mastery of a particular type of symbolic capital, namely, the ability to manipulate others, to inveigle and deceive, if need be by joining violence to chicanery and charm, in the pursuit of immediate pecuniary gain'.[21] In Eastleigh the term is much used. A Kenyan Somali I met who referred to himself using the term had come to the estate after falling on hard times in Isiolo where he had 'hustled' tourists to buy the brass bracelets and other tourist merchandise sold in that town. In Nairobi he was hoping to get work as a security guard, having heard about opportunities with G4S, but in the meantime was surviving by making small amounts of money here and there, helping out the likes of Mohaa, whom he knew from their time together in Isiolo. The last time I met him he was barely making enough to subsist, hanging out on Second Avenue with some friends, living the life of a 'street hustler'.

The term also has negative connotations, and being 'hustled' is seen as unpleasant. A Somali woman told me how she was 'hustled' by smartly dressed young Somali men in Nairobi city centre who approach people like her asking for money; if she refused or only gave a little, the 'hustlers' would let everyone around know how mean she was. It is not just people scraping a living on the bottom rungs of the Eastleigh economy who like the 'hustler' image, but even politicians. In the by-election of 2011 one candidate told a friend of mine how if elected he would 'hustle for the people of Eastleigh'. This annoyed my friend—a Kenyan Somali who had lived in Canada—and she thought a politician aspiring to be a 'hustler' hardly inspires confidence in their professionalism.

For some male entrepreneurs, however, 'hustler' was an attractive image. Another Eastleighwood friend—born in Somalia but to a Kenyan Somali father—had co-founded alongside Luo and Kalenjin partners a company offering professional cleaning services: he described himself and his team as 'hustlers', as they had started with only 1,000 shillings capital but quickly grew the business to a monthly turnover of 60,000 shillings thanks to their hustling. Another businessman keen on the term is Mohaa himself. A conversation between us on WhatsApp went as follows:

> Neil: Unajiita 'entrepreneur'? [Do you call yourself an 'entrepreneur'?]
> Mohaa: Weka jina ingine sxb [Put down a different name, my friend].
> Mohaa, after a pause: 'Hustler.'

When pushed to clarify the meaning of the term, he replied: 'According to me a hustler is a person in business determined to succeed.'

'Hustler' is not a term everyone in the estate embraces—particularly women and more conservative men—but in its suggestion of daring it does resonate with what are considered characteristic Somali traits that underpin the Eastleigh success. As one Somali expressed it in a media article about the estate, this success owes much to *inda adheeg*: 'audacity'.[22] Indeed, being prepared to risk is reckoned to set apart Somali business from that practised by others, as is a willingness to cope with hardship on the road to success. This readiness of Somalis to take risks was emphasised by many—Somali and non-Somali—as a key explanation for the dynamic nature of the Eastleigh economy. Beyond Eastleigh too, Somali risk taking is well attested. Perhaps this is most evident in the many who travel into the unknown in search of greener pastures, putting their lives in the hands of people-smugglers in the process. Steinberg's evocation of the life of Asad and his tortuous journey from Somalia to South Africa is eloquent testimony to the drive for something better that compels such journeys.[23] Of course, this is not just a Somali trait, as demonstrated by the many thousands of other migrants who pay great sums and endure much hardship to enter richer countries the world over.[24] However, in the last two decades Somalis have certainly risked much the world over, many doing well for themselves in the process. Furthermore, some link this capacity to take risks to the traditional Somali pastoralism of the Horn of Africa, where a precarious environment can impel risk taking, and where audacity is valued in a context of competition over grazing, water and trade.

While there are examples of Somalis who fail in the Eastleigh economy, there is usually no shortage of people prepared to back a venture with at least some chance of success, and to do so quickly. The willingness to close deals swiftly when buying real estate, even paying over the odds to do so, was used by Somalis to suggest a key difference in their business compared with others in Kenya: paying a large sum initially added to the risk of losses should a venture fail, but Somalis were willing to take on the risk, as by paying more they could sooner start building and reaping in returns. Were the situation reversed, it was suggested that other Kenyans would bargain long and hard to secure the best deal. However, not all Somalis were seen as so relaxed about taking risks. A Kenyan Somali friend suggested that risk taking was especially pronounced among Somalians, Kenyan Somalis being more cautious: a function, perhaps, of the stability and legal security of Kenyan Somalis, who have less need to take risks for survival. He also asked me whether I would consider investing in an opportunity he had heard about. My reluctance was for him a sign of a very different and cautious worldview from that of the risk-embracing Somali. Similarly, Elias gently chided me for not investing in the venture of a Somali friend of his who was establishing a supermarket in Nairobi's Kibera estate. My cautious reluctance—seen by him as characteristic of a *mzungu* (European)—made me miss out on a good return, as his friend had already doubled his money.

Being impatient to enter a profitable economy has been documented among Somalis in Minnesota too: 'There is a universal belief among Somali entrepreneurs in the Twin Cities that they can become rich very quickly; therefore, they need to hurry up and start their business so they can get to the Promised Land and strike a fortune in the process.'[25] The same is also said of diaspora Somalis investing in Hargeisa, as Hansen suggests, and in Eastleigh the risk of missing out has no doubt been a factor in persuading some in the diaspora to invest.[26] And risks are very real in the Eastleigh and Kenyan economy in general, from theft, deceit, corruption, increased competition and fluctuations in the market. However, such risks do not necessarily correlate with the degree of risk taking emphasised in the discourse on Somali entrepreneurship. In fact, some argue that much Somali business in places such as Eastleigh is actually rather conservative, as there is much 'copycattism', reflected in the standard model of the malls (a model that some are moving away from, however) and in the typical goods that traders there sell. Furthermore, Somali support networks provide a degree of security underpinning risk, meaning that even when risking capital in large ventures, well-connected Somalis have much social capital to fall back on if things do not work out as planned.

However, risk taking is emphasised so strongly and the economic boom so compelling that taking risks in business is valued highly: in the Somali displacement economy many have profited, and the danger of missing out through caution is more compelling for many than the risk of trying. As Mohaa stated in Kiswahili, *mambo ya biashara ni mbili: kufaidika au kuhasirika*,[27] which he paraphrased in English as: 'get rich or die trying'.

In Somalis we Trust

If Somali businesspeople are risk-taking entrepreneurs, they also appreciate the value of strong social ties:[28] 'Me, Inc.' is embedded in 'Lineage, Inc.' and even 'Somali, Inc.' Obligations and bonds that tie together Somalis are commonly described as crucial for Somali trade, allowing better-connected individuals access to support networks now stretching across the globe. And it is even more commonly stated that underpinning all this mutuality is 'trust'.

In formulating the project from which this book emerged, trust was to be a major theme in analysis of the networks running through Eastleigh: I anticipated it as an etic concept that would link Eastleigh trade with a wider scholarly interest in the 'organizational role of social ties that shape economic behaviour outside the state through embedded relations of solidarity and trust'.[29] However, trust as an etic term with which to analyse the economy of Eastleigh is greatly overshadowed by the emic use of the term and its cognate Kiswahili and Somali terms within the estate. Indeed, whether the English word 'trust' itself is used, or the Kiswahili *amana* or Somali *aaminaad* (also translated as 'credibility' and 'confidence' in Zorc and Osman's Somali dictionary),[30] the concept is a key factor in how Eastleigh businesspeople—from shopkeepers to mall owners—present themselves to the outside world and to each other.

My field notes are saturated in 'trust'. In describing his growth as a businessman, Mohaa strongly emphasised the need to be perceived as trustworthy to succeed, while Mohamed Shakul—manager of Al-Bushra, a major property developer in the estate—told me that Somalis 'have an advantage in business because they trust each other'. Burhan also emphasised how trust between Somalis allows them to raise initial capital for enterprises, while the director of Garun Investments, another real-estate company, told me that 'Somalis, wherever or which clan they come from, can do business together as they trust each other'. The manager of Sunrise Mall told me that 'trust was the backbone of the

Eastleigh economy', and you had to hire people you could trust. Trust also permeates the branding of companies, Al-Bushra using the motto 'People You Can Trust' on its promotional material. The Garre owner of a shopping mall in the Nairobi city centre illustrated the capacity of Somalis to trust each other by relating how he was given a cheque for 1 million shillings by a wealthy Eastleigh businessman with no legally binding documentation to underpin the transaction. The notion that Somalis do not require legal contracts in such situations is also much remarked upon, almost as the corollary to 'Somalis trust each other'. All this emic usage is fascinating in itself, and we will return to trust as discourse later in the chapter. First, however, it is worth looking more deeply at the concept and its potential and limits in analysing Somali networks.

Trust and the Informal Economy

Many social scientists have tried to clarify and define trust,[31] and it became a key focus in academia and beyond, particularly in the 1990s when Fukuyama argued that the USA, Japan and other countries with high levels of generalised trust throughout society were more dynamic and successful than the likes of China, where transactions were said to be based instead upon restricted family-bound trust in the absence of reliable formal institutions.[32] A controversial thesis in many ways, not least given the contemporary economic power of China. Related to this, some linked different forms of trust with ideas of modernity, arguing that 'pre-modern societies' had little need for trust, being based on confidence in a 'very particular mode of social organisation based on ascriptive categories';[33] while modernity, formal law and other institutions were thought to reduce the need for personalised trust as people trusted systemically instead. However, 'late modernity' and globalisation, it is argued, have brought greater complexity, uncertainty and risk to social life, making the production of trust more problematic, increasing reliance once more on personal relations.[34] 'Trust becomes a more urgent and central concern in today's contingent, uncertain and global conditions.'[35] It has thus become a master-concept in understanding how people forge networks within a contemporary world said to be marked by uncertainty.

Within anthropology, however, the concept has a longer history, perhaps connected to the early interest anthropologists had in understanding informal economic networks. Anthropologists have focused on defining trust (for example, distinguishing it from faith and confidence)[36] and exploring the social 'stuff' of trust: the types of social ties that promote or impede it, so giving someone confidence in their reliability.[37] For example, its links to kinship are explored, as trust is reckoned stronger among kin,[38] although this is an ambiguous connection: for example, familial obligation might mean that someone has little option but to entrust something to another, even though they do not 'trust'. Others focus more on friendship as a foundation for trust where kin are few and uncertainty great, for example the Frafra migrants studied by Hart in Accra.[39] Here again there is ambiguity, as we might like someone but not necessarily trust them in trade. An asymmetry has been noted in how trusting relationships can take much work to be forged as the trust placed is validated over time through much repetition; one occasion of broken trust is all that it sometimes takes for suspicion to take over instead.[40]

Anthropologists have also examined how trust operates at distance in trade networks, even transnationally. Cohen's classic work on Hausa cattle traders in Nigeria shows how they form a 'trading diaspora' connected by shared 'values, language, a legal system, kinship ties and other forms of social solidarity' that allows trust to operate at long distance without formal contracts.[41] How ties are maintained in the transnational informal economy, for example between Congolese traders operating between Kinshasa and Paris, also rely heavily on the term in understanding how kin and associative ties offer advantages and disadvantages to traders.[42] Rosenfeld has analysed the bounds of trust for Lebanese and Beninese traders in the operation of the transnational used-car trade.[43] Theorists of transnational social networks emphasise 'bounded solidarity', a sense of unity amongst communities of migrants that is heightened compared to that felt at home due to the need for mutual support in an alien setting.[44] Such bounded solidarity generates enforceable trust, a mechanism that 'discourages wrongdoing by network members, who as part of a tightly bounded group must rely on one another for their mutual support and livelihoods'.[45] Whitehouse emphasises how this helps Soninke traders from Mali in Congo who have little faith that Congolese state institutions will help them in case of need.

Lineage, Inc.

Trust and its limits are much debated in regard to Somali political, social and economic life, especially in the wake of state collapse in Somalia. Then a deficit of trust in wider society and institutions generated a greater dependence on trust between those more closely related,[46] and lineage became a source of some certainty amidst great uncertainty. Indeed, if the standard trope in the literature on trust is the uncertainty of contemporary life,[47] then the contemporary story of Somalia and Somalis offers an especially compelling case study. In such a risky environment trust tends to be restricted to members of one's own lineage, and networks based on family and lineage therefore become key conduits for trade: 'Lineage, Inc.'.

Here the classic Somali segmentary lineage model, as described by Lewis, looms large analytically, as lineage and trade connect in what is seen as a 'continuation of the collective economic interests of agnates'.[48] Goldsmith expounds this view: 'members of the same *jilib*, subclan or sublineage units, retain especially strong reciprocal obligations to relatives, even if they are complete strangers who might share a common ancestor five or six generations removed',[49] and such reciprocal obligations allow strong trade networks to form while incubating trust. Bjork offers a processual view of these obligations, convincingly showing that they are not of a primordial form but have to instead be constantly reproduced through practice and discourse. However, she argues that clan and lineage remain important as 'social capital', and emphasises how Somalis 'manage transnational capital through clan networks'.[50]

Simons explains how people require rules that 'quickly, conveniently, and unequivocally tell them how they can expect others to act and what they should expect others to be (i.e., friend or foe, reliable or unreliable)'. She continues:

> Genealogy works perfectly as one such set of rules, mapping trustworthiness—by charting who has trusted whom in the past and where this has led in terms of thicker or thinner, and sustained or broken relationships. Or, turning this around and rethinking linear models: Breaks between lineages indicate breaks, or at least gaps, in trust.[51]

Lewis wrote of a negative corollary of trust between kin: 'the highly segmentary and exclusive character of the Somali political system makes it impossible, or at least extremely difficult, for one who is not a kinsman to be trusted'.[52] While in times of conflict the bounds of trust might be so constricted, at other times this claimed restriction of trust to kin is dubious: in Eastleigh, as we will see, trust expands beyond kin, while the classic emphasis on patrilineal lineage-based trust is blind to the advantages accruing to women who 'hold more "ambiguous" clan affiliation and maintain alternative forms of association based on solidarity and reciprocal support mechanisms that go beyond the family or the kin group'.[53]

Regarding the practicalities of living and trading transnationally for Somalis, trust also features in analysis. Key to Somali support and trade networks has of course been the hawala money-remitting companies that allow capital to flow transnationally, and have themselves become trusted institutions by Somalis, though not by authorities in the West, who suspect them of money-laundering (see chapter 2). The hawala system is said to have evolved through relationships of trust, whereby one agent could accept money for a client in one location and trust that another agent would release the remitted money in another location, the remittee often being identified through their place in the lineage structure. Even today, when hawala are multinational companies with franchises throughout the world, they are still said to recruit agents through clan networks, 'which helps ensure loyalty among staff and customers',[54] and money is still handed over at branches in Eastleigh to customers who identify themselves not with ID documents, but through their lineage.

Furthermore, even in more formal economies, informal relations of trust underpinned by kin and lineage are said to dominate business. For example, Samatar talks of a Somali restaurant in Minneapolis established by three partners who each put in $35,000, but also raised $300,000 from twenty others (family, friends and acquaintances):

> None of the investors signed any document describing the nature of their investment or the expected return on the investment. The investors completely trusted the three partners and believed that they would get their money back with a decent return at some point in the future.
>
> Actually, there was no written partnership agreement between the three main players in this deal either. No attorney was consulted on how to form a partnership agreement. Nothing was agreed upon on paper except to form a partnership and manage a restaurant.[55]

'Trust' can also be applied analytically to the networks running through Eastleigh and its 'openly informal economy'[56] where much business is indeed conducted unburdened by enforceable contracts. This is only a generalisation, however, as there are different scales and types of enterprises in Eastleigh (see chapters 4 and 4), some more intertwined with Kenya's formal system than others. Banks and larger-scale businesses are all integrated into the formal legal system, while Kenyan law permeates the estate in many ways. Even refugees treat Kenyan law as a resource, especially with the help of Kituo cha Sheria, the legal charity that in Eastleigh has helped many refugees fight against infringement of their legal rights. Indeed, a number of court cases are pending concerning Eastleigh businesses.

There is thus at least some systemic trust in Kenyan law by Somalis in Eastleigh, Kenya clearly offering more certainty in this regard than Somalia itself. In business disputes, while most refugees—and many Kenyans too—prefer to seek resolution through the mediation of elders, sheikhs or the Eastleigh Business Association, there are still those who turn to Kenyan state institutions at times of need. Eastleigh's Chief's Camp is always busy with people seeking redress. Nevertheless, many connections and agreements—in fact, most of the activity that happens between wholesalers and retailers, based as it is on credit—are made on a very informal basis with no written contracts. As we saw in chapter 4, a page in a wholesaler's notebook detailing how much stock has been advanced is the nearest one sees to a legally binding record of debt.

In this context, personalised relations dominate, and many businesses and networks are connected through kin and lineage. Indeed, social ties resulting from notions of relatedness are frequently translated into business enterprises, whether within Eastleigh, within Kenya or transnationally. Such connections are common between business partners, whether in small businesses or large malls, and family businesses, as we have seen, are common. Most clans of significant strength in Eastleigh—for example, Ogaden and Garre—have strong representation within Kenya, but also in the West, Middle East and in Asia, providing great opportunities for lineages within them to access capital, goods and credit. Thus, like the Lebanese diaspora written about by Rosenfeld, many Eastleigh Somalis have a constellation of related people around the world who can generally be trusted to honour obligations and business transactions, and whose reputation would be threatened among that constellation should they renege.[57]

Such bonds offer reassurance to participants in trade that their investments are safe, while the risk of default on debts within the groups is lowered through the threat of social ostracism and the loss of business reputation: the 'enforceable trust' described above. Anyone who fails to fulfil obligations can be pressurised through his or her relatives to make recompense, or relatives may even make reparations themselves to save the reputation of the wider social unit. Indeed, in an economy as dependent on credit as the Eastleigh economy, reputations have to be preserved so that one can be entrusted with goods and capital, and a good reputation is considered crucial by traders in the estate. Knowledge is a key component of this. Within lineages information can spread quickly about the trustworthiness of an individual, even transnationally, and as networks stretch globally, Somalis can place potential business partners within a social map whereby people who know the person in question can be consulted.

However, there is more to trust in Eastleigh than lineage, important though this may be. Indeed, networks of trust in the estate are not restricted to kin and family, but frequently stretch across clan boundaries, and business in Eastleigh would scarcely have become so dynamic if networks of trust were constrained completely by lineage and familial ties. Elliott describes this in relation to the camel-milk trade, where middlewomen in northern Kenya often send milk to kinswomen in Eastleigh, but where networks have expended to draw in 'actors from beyond their immediate families, garnering trust through more commercial relationships'.[58] Larger businesses—including some malls—are also operated by businesspeople from a range of clans.

Furthermore, business networks based on personalised trust also encompass non-Somalis: for example, credit is often extended cross-ethnically, and even across nationalities. Somali wholesalers in Eastleigh frequently do business with large-scale non-Somali traders from as far afield as Tanzania, giving goods on credit. Importers also report receiving goods on credit from Chinese factories keen on cementing an outlet for their stock. While small-scale traders buying wholesale in Eastleigh to sell elsewhere in Nairobi or around Kenya would be unlikely to get goods on credit (and traders such as Mohaa often prefer non-Somali customers in this regard, as they are less likely to ask for credit), those operating elsewhere on a large scale are a good resource for Eastleigh traders, and should be kept happy with credit. Indeed, giving out credit is a key way to build one's business. More than this, 'entrusting' credit to someone is not only something that is built on pre-existing social relationships, but also an action that itself builds social relationships: giving credit is a key ingredient of social ties within and beyond kin groups in Eastleigh and elsewhere, as Shipton has emphasised.[59] Sztompka writes of this as 'evocative trust': by trusting someone, one can create trust.[60]

Indeed, there are many ways that personalised trust is generated beyond lineage. Friendship can be key, and the estate forms a fertile environment where cross-clan and even cross-ethnic business relations can be forged, while commercial relationships can become friendships. Meru told me how the estate was a resource for them not just as a place where they could come and sell their commodity—khat—but also as a place where friendships with Somalis might lead to bigger things: when khat was legal in the UK, Somalis who were resettled there might get in touch with their Meru friends from Eastleigh to establish a khat-trading network. Furthermore, there are more concrete bases upon which trust is generated. If one has a shop, information about reliability and trustworthiness soon percolates throughout the mall and beyond, whether or not there are kinship or clan connections. For Mohaa, the very fact of having a shop can induce a wholesaler to give stock on credit: a shop shows a degree of permanence, and means you can be found when payment becomes due. It also means you have a valuable asset that can be cashed in to pay wholesalers if business goes especially badly. There is thus a materiality to trust in the estate. However, there is also a religious dimension to trust, evident in how Islam is emphasised as underpinning Eastleigh networks and pushing the bounds of trust beyond lineage, and even beyond Somali ethnicity.

In Islam we Trust

Both the Kiswahili and Somali words for trust are etymologically derived from the Arabic word *amana*, a term referring to the fulfilment of trust. The Arabic origin of this term is important, as it connects with the wider Islamic values that have always been prevalent in Eastleigh, but appear to be getting stronger. Indeed, Somali businesspeople in the estate are often quick to highlight the role of Islam in delineating the bounds of trust, and being a good Muslim is seen by many as a crucial component of someone who can be trusted in business. Of course, Islam has long featured prominently in trade, and indeed much of the spread of Islam through Africa and elsewhere can be linked to the spread of commercial networks through Muslim traders, as the history of the East African coast—of which the Somali coastline has always been an important part—and West Africa (where Arab traders introduced Islam from the tenth century onwards)[61] makes clear. Islamic brotherhoods have also been influential in organising and expanding trade in various urban centres, as Simone describes in an article about the 'worlding' of African cities.[62] The Prophet himself engaged in trade,[63] and the morality of Islam often links to the morality of doing business and making money. Also, as Osella and Osella describe for contemporary Malaysian Muslim entrepreneurs, economic success and piety are considered mutually reinforcing: as a Muslim you can both 'make good' and 'do good'.[64]

In Eastleigh many aspects of business revolve around Islam. Certainly the rhythm of business itself is strongly structured in this way, as Somalis and other Muslims punctuate their routines with prayer, many visiting mosques provided by the shopping malls to do so. It is not uncommon to see women at work in the malls erecting a curtain in front of a shop so that they can pray out of view inside. On Friday business comes to a halt for the congregational prayer (*salat al-jumu'a*), making this the quietest daytime period in Eastleigh as so many businesses close. Attending mosque is a crucial part of sociality and hence business in Eastleigh, bringing people and their networks together, while festivals such as Eid also play a similar function, enhancing solidarity among Muslims in the estate. Sermons in the mosque also influence businesses by emphasising the need for giving away charitable donations from profits, alms-giving known as *zakat* in Islam: this influence was especially strong in the drought of 2011 when businesses in the estate were urged by religious leaders to donate clothes, food and money to those in need.

However, Islam has become ever more central to business in Eastleigh, and to its entrepreneurship. As noted in chapter 3, Eastleigh has become a more overtly Islamic space over the last two decades, even if most Somali remain at least nominally Sufi rather than Salafist, and despite much of Eastleigh hardly conforming to conservative ideals. The stimulant substance khat (see chapter 6) is something of a barometer of religious change in Eastleigh, and feelings against it have hardened recently: for example, stories are reported of wealthy Eastleigh khat traders trying to make donations to mosques but having their money rejected for being sourced from something haram. Less conservative Somali friends of mine have suggested that this hardening of attitudes towards khat owes much to the increased influence of Salafi Islam.[65] Another indicator of the increasing religious influence on the Eastleigh economy concerns the practice of charging 'goodwill'. For some staunch Muslims in Eastleigh goodwill goes against Islamic principles: one Somali businessman I met categorised charging goodwill as similar to the charging of riba (interest), the similarity arising as they are both seen as money earned for little reason other than the exploitation of another. Some recent Islamised business ventures pride themselves on not being based on goodwill, for example the Al-Bushra-built properties Madina Mall and Mecca Plaza.[66] As Amal approached the tenth anniversary of its construction, the management had to decide whether to renew the goodwill arrangements on the shops (which were charged for a ten-year period). Amal traders told me that they expected the management to do away with goodwill under the influence of preachers at the mosque.[67] Thus two important elements of the Eastleigh economy have come to be held under much greater suspicion in the estate of today.

The increasing importance of Islam within the Eastleigh economy is further demonstrated by the rise of Islamic finance in the estate. Banks in the estate all offer Islamic accounts and loans, and there is now an Islamic insurance company called Takaful (an Arabic word referring to a system of reimbursement in case of loss) operating in the estate.[68] In an interview, the Takaful branch manager in Eastleigh (a young Kenyan Somali) claimed that the company would be revolutionary in an estate where many have suffered losses—for example, in the Garissa Lodge fire of 2001—without any recourse to insurance, although he did emphasise that Somalis had ayuuto (the money-go-round saving schemes) to fall back on. Standard insurance is seen as a form of gambling, and hence as un-Islamic; instead, with Takaful, losses and gains are said to be shared equitably between the company and the client. Many in Eastleigh still prefer to bank with hawala rather than formal banks, and few have taken up insurance, but there are certainly more formal options for the Muslim businessperson as regards financial institutions than there ever was before, options that might also bring more formalised forms of trust.

Islam is reckoned to underpin more personalised trade relations too; indeed, the spread of more Salafist forms of the religion in Eastleigh appears to owe much to its trade connections abroad. Here Aisha Ahmad, on the relation of Islam to Somali business in Mogadishu, is very useful.[69] She relates how, in the wake of state collapse in Somalia, businesses soon came to depend on tight, clan-based networks as trust between clans and sub-clans disintegrated, and numerous businesspeople were able to do well out of clan conflict, especially with the flow of aid money that was eagerly exploited. When aid money dried up in the mid-1990s with the withdrawal of UNISOM, the 'Mogadishu business community grew increasingly sensitive to the negative costs of tribalism to their business concerns'.[70] Instead, they increasingly turned to Islam. She continues:

> Aspiring and established businesspeople alike attempted to bolster their more universal Islamic identity over their more limiting clan identities, sometimes with a level of superficiality that appeared comical. Criminal bosses grew long beards and began wearing traditional clothing. They carried religious paraphernalia, such as prayer beads and took on the label of Sheikh, despite having no religious training to warrant the title. The head of a Mogadishu business school explained, 'Since there is no regulatory or law enforcement agency and everything is based on trust, this is where Islamists come in. Most companies are led by people who look like Sheikhs.' By the mid-1990s, Mogadishu experienced an overnight boom in its sheikh population, as the business community sought to gain from the social capital afforded by Islamic identity and association. While clan divisions didn't at all disappear, Islamic identity became an increasingly important reputational tool and mechanism for navigating clan divisions at home and securing international contracts abroad. Over the course of the civil war, clan identity simply became more costly and less useful to the business community than the Islamic alternative.[71]

Thus Islamic identity began to underpin trust, and this connection between trust and Islam is strong throughout the wider Somali world of business.[72] Worldwide Somali investment opportunities often stress Islamic credentials, as they do in Eastleigh itself. The estate's economy—as we have seen—is intertwined with that of Somalia and its diaspora, so what happens in one part of the Somali transnational economy soon affects another. In the case of business and Islamic identity, the fall of the UIC in 2006 had a great effect, as more businesspeople fled Mogadishu for Eastleigh, bringing a new wave of investment to the estate. While not wholly related to this group of refugees, Islamic identity and business have since become more interconnected, as several of the new developments—including Madina Mall and Mecca Plaza—bear a sharp Islamic imprint evident in their very names. The real-estate firm behind them consists of a number of sheikhs, and a pious-looking management team, some from Kenya, some from Somalia and some from the wider diaspora. To encourage investment in their enterprises, such companies highlight their piety, often relying on well-known Eastleigh sheikhs to help promote business. Takaful—the Islamic insurance company—also relies on such respected religious figures. As the Eastleigh branch manager related, for the company to sell insurance in an economy where such an intangible commodity had not previously featured required the influence of Islamic scholars. He emphasised how they had to rely on word-of mouth-campaigns based on 'trust' in Sharia scholars, chiefs and elders.

Key investors in such companies are drawn from a range of clans, and also from beyond Kenya. Islamic identity plays a role not just in overcoming deficits of trust between Somali clans and lineages, but also spatial distance. Advertisements on Somali cable TV channels for investments in Eastleigh, or elsewhere in the Somali constellation of business hubs, emphasise the Islamic credentials of the companies seeking investment, to make potential investors feel more secure. According to Ahmad's research, this emphasis on Islamic identity is effective in generating trust, as her surveys of the business community suggests that 80 per cent of businesspeople saw Islam as a sign of trustworthiness, while 'only 17% felt strongly that clan identity was a good measure of trust'.[73] This probably also reflects the negativity attached to clan identity and a fear of looking 'tribalist' or 'clannist' to others, and might not necessarily reflect how such businesspeople actually behave. Indeed, emphasising Islam is also a reaction against the global image of Somalia in the stateless era, as a place of conflict and distrust built on clan divisions: 'if Somalia carries an image of continuous war, refugees, misery, and the haven of terrorists, Islam as a global religion instead represents dignity, respect and morality'.[74]

Islamic identity also helps expand the bounds of trust, not just between people of different clans, but also between people of different ethnicities and nationalities. Ahmad shows how Islamic identity grew in significance as Somali businesspeople gradually built up trusting relationships with elite Salafi businesspeople in the Gulf, both by showing their reliability in fulfilling small business deals and by building upon their own Islamic identity, even adopting a Salafi identity. As she states, 'the largest and most well connected Somali businesspeople today have adopted a Salafi approach to Islam and are part of the Gulf business network', outplaying non-Salafi Somali businesspeople.[75] As she recounts:

> Several members of the Mogadishu business community explained that in the mid-1990s their contracts with Gulf partners were smaller, reflecting the level of trust between the parties. A Somali businessman might have an agreement worth no more than a few thousand dollars. Because there was no government to enforce these deals, there were no written contracts and parties relied entirely on verbal agreement. These early investments allowed Somali businesspeople to demonstrate their trustworthiness, with less dollar value risk to their Arab partners. Anyone who defected with the loot was out of the club for life, whereas those that demonstrated that they could be trusted gained incrementally larger contracts. Eventually, trust-based relationships translated into multi-million dollar loans from Gulf partners, with no enforcement mechanisms for repayment.[76]

Such powerful inter-ethnic networks mediated by Islam stretch to Eastleigh too, while Islam is also important in the generation of inter-ethnic trust within Eastleigh, as can be seen in networks that form between Muslim Oromo and Somalis in the estate. Indeed, a number of Oromo who arrived in Eastleigh more or less destitute told me how they obtained a foothold in the estate through gaining the trust of Somali shop-owners as fellow Muslims, sometimes initially communicating via Arabic, as Oromo are unlikely to know either Kiswahili or Somali when they first arrive. A number of Meru in the estate have also converted to Islam over the years, some finding that this helps ease business relations with Somalis in the khat trade.

Of course, it would be a highly materialist explanation of religious practice in Eastleigh to suggest that Islamic identity is simply assumed there to ease business relations and so make money, although that would fit with other research on the relation of religious conversion to strategies of accumulation.[77] There are those who do make that argument, particularly those who suspect that the trappings of Islamic identity hide a simple desire to become rich. Indeed, an article in the *Daily Nation* from 2012 reflects on accusations that Islamic practices of Somali businesspeople could be a charade:

> Some [sheikhs] even go on Somali satellite television stations and 'bless' certain projects, persuading tens of thousands that it is the best real estate development or business enterprise to invest in.

> 'There are definitely cases of businessmen masquerading as clerics who go around and use religion for their own purpose,' Mr Abdirizak Hassan, deputy managing director of Al-Bushra Properties, a real estate development company, said.[78]

Ahmad questioned the Chief Legal Counsel for the UIC about the sincerity of the religiosity of these businessmen: he 'held up his right hand, bent his index finger and said, "If I tie a string around this finger and leave it like this for 10 years, when I untie it, my finger will stay like this. The business community is the same. After years of pretending to be a Wahhabi, you become a Wahhabi"'.[79] In the case of Eastleigh, Abdirizak Hassan—the man quoted above in the *Daily Nation*—went on to deny the allegations that the Islam of the businesspeople was a pretence: 'Most of it, however, is a smear campaign that is being touted by competitors. It has no base at all. Actually, if you combine the Somali culture and the Islamic traditions in the community, you will have a very trustworthy system.'[80] As in all aspects of life, disaggregating self-interest from more moral motivations is a difficult task, while seeing religion as something that should be free from commerce reflects, as Coleman suggests, Western 'assumptions about proper religion' as something ideally ascetic and transcendental.[81] In Eastleigh and in the networks that run through it, religion can clearly be a resource, and Islam offers much help in navigating the economic landscape, as many newcomers, both Somali and Oromo, find; however, Islam's role as such a resource no doubt strengthens further the faith of those whom it benefits. Like trust itself, religion grows stronger through practice.

Talking Trust

In Eastleigh, as elsewhere, one soon comes up against the limits of trust in understanding economic relations and motivations. Trust has been criticised for its apparently apolitical implications as it can mask situations of asymmetrical relations where the allocation of trust becomes irrelevant; as Sayer puts it, 'what appears to indicate trust may be largely a consequence of domination, or simple mutual dependency'.[82] In Eastleigh, and the transnational field within which it is situated, there are many who have little choice but to entrust money and goods to certain people through economic and social pressures. This is evident in the literature on remittances, for example, where Somalis in the diaspora are sometimes portrayed as feeling they have little choice but to send hard-earned money to family in places such as Eastleigh.[83] Also, for all the talk of 'we Somalis trust each other', there are people more able to access this trust and the social capital that comes with it than others. At a conference focused on the estate in September 2014, a representative of the Somali Bantu in Kenya reported how these networks of trust can exclude those seen as 'lesser' Somali by the more powerful clans.[84]

Furthermore, the strong emphasis that 'we Somalis trust each other' appears disconnected from Somalia's history of the last few decades, where, instead of trust, suspicion and conflict have often prevailed. It is also disconnected from the far from deceit-free context of trade in Eastleigh. Indeed, that Mohaa and others stress the need to be trustworthy is born of the knowledge that there are many who are not, and there are cases of deceit that offer a salutary warning for traders not to be naïve and take the trust narrative at face value. In this distrustful context, reputation becomes ever more important. For Mohaa the risks of trusting were brought home in a saga of 2011 that generated what he and his friends refer to as Operation Linda Duka ('Operation Protect the Shop') named after Operation Linda Nchi ('Operation Protect the Nation', the name for the KDF's 2011 incursion into Somalia). The story goes thus:

A young man Mohaa had known from Isiolo had come to Eastleigh recently, and Mohaa gave him some work in Nasiib Fashions. He worked hard at first, bringing in good profits, but then the amount he was giving Mohaa started declining, and Mohaa began to suspect that he was keeping some profit for himself. He would say he could only sell at the lowest price. Thus, an operation was planned to 'catch a thief'. Mohaa stayed away for the day, leaving the young man to run the shop. Meanwhile, Mohaa gave a Sudanese woman 10,000 shillings and told her to buy shirts and trousers. When he returned and asked the young man how much he'd sold, the latter said he had only made a small profit. Mohaa then revealed that he knew how much he had really made, and the young man was given the sack, returning to Isiolo.

There are many other such examples of deceit, including the Trojan-Horse scam mentioned in the last chapter. As mentioned earlier in the book too, there are a number of ongoing court cases where ownership of plots of land is under dispute by different groups of Somalis. Also, Burhan was defrauded of a deposit for an apartment in a residential block in the estate which was never built—he turned to the Kenyan legal system to resolve this case, a threatening letter from a lawyer forcing the Somali-owned company to repay him his money.

Diaspora investors are seen as especially at risk from deceit in Eastleigh, especially if they have become used to the more formal systems of business in Europe and North America. The chance of riches has led some to invest without sufficient knowledge of how to navigate the social and economic landscape. The perils of this were evident in the story of Abdul, a US Somali who had saved up money through working as a taxi driver in Chicago. He worked hard enough to be able to buy a much-sought-after taxi 'medallion' required to operate a taxi business in the USA for $50,000. These medallions have soared in price, as they are limited in number, yet demand is high: so eventually he was able to sell it for $250,000. It was this money that he decided to invest into a business in Nairobi, joining a cousin living there in trading in sugar, a commodity that Somalis have traded much in recent years, obtaining cheap supplies from Brazil that are sold especially in northern Kenya after entering via Kismayu in Somalia. His business involved selling sugar to the Kenyan military. However, this was a chastening experience for him, as his cousin deceived him, giving him a fake cheque after a business deal and running off to South Africa with much of Abdul's hard-earned savings. Abdul—living in an Eastleigh hotel at the time—gave me this story as an example of how diaspora Somalis can be naïve when they come to Kenya to do business. Burhan too emphasised the dangers of investing for diaspora Somalis, and planned at one stage to open a business advice bureau for such investors.

Clearly therefore, the 'we Somalis trust each other' discourse is idealised, and operating a successful business in Eastleigh would scarcely be possible if a businessperson was so naïve as to believe it. The discourse of the trusting and trustworthy Somali entrepreneur is not so much a descriptive discourse as a normative one. Every time trust is emphasised within Eastleigh, the message is further spread that being trustworthy is the correct way to behave, and that one should be prepared to entrust goods and capital to someone else—especially if they are Somali. The same goes for the emphasis placed on proper Islamic conduct, which has also become normative. Such discourse lubricates the flow of capital and goods, providing reassurance that plenty of people have trusted before and done well from doing so. For someone worried about the lack of contracts and legal recourse, talk of 'we Somalis don't use contracts' might well be reassuring. For a diaspora Somali to enter the Eastleigh economy asking for legally binding contracts might suggest a distinct lack of trust, and some investors often have to adjust to these non-contract relations after becoming accustomed to formal business elsewhere.

Of course, these discourses of trust, Islam and entrepreneurship are not just an internal discourse within the world of Somali business, but are also designed for a wider audience. They feature often in newspaper accounts of the estate, forming a counterpoint to the negative articles rooting the Eastleigh boom within nefarious practices such as piracy and tax evasion. Moreover, just as an emphasis on Islam can be attractive as a way to distance oneself from clan, so this narrative of trust serves a wider purpose beyond business and trade in building a unifying vision of what Somali society should be, one that counters the common depiction of Somalia as a conflict-ridden place of little trust.

Entrepreneurship in a Boom Town

Thus, the idealised image of Somali entrepreneurship as brimming with risk taking and trust is exactly that: idealised. Like other 'culturalist' explanations of business failure or success it is rather blind to relations of power,[85] and elides away other underpinnings of Somali success in Eastleigh: for example, the vast diaspora created in recent history that provides many with transnational social capital and networks of support. Such transnational networks clearly put Somalis at an advantage compared with other ethnicities in Kenya. However, while notions of what constitutes Somali entrepreneurship are idealised in the discourse floating around and beyond Eastleigh, and sometimes more wishful thinking than an accurate description of business practices and values, they are still ideals to which many aspire, and they do play a role in encouraging mutuality and spurring investment. The discourse suggests to those with capital that they might miss out if they do not take a risk in trusting someone, while offering reassurance that there is a strong moral basis to the Eastleigh economy that will protect investments.

All these values combine with a commonly expressed view that hoarding capital is neither sensible nor moral: better financially and socially to let it fertilise other business ventures rather than stagnate in a bank or hawala account. There is a moral imperative to redistribute wealth. In all this too, the simple fact that the Eastleigh economy is highly successful should be remembered when considering the propensity to take risks and trust within its economy. There is a wider trust beyond that embedded in Somali businesspeople operating there: trust in the estate itself. It is a place of *bashbash iyo barwaaqo* (prosperity and abundance),[86] a Somali phrase referring to abundance that comes with the rains, and with abundance comes peace, as the saying *caano iyo nabad* (milk and peace) suggests. While connected to Somalia in many ways, its economy is a place where certainty is at less of a premium than in Somalia itself, despite the ups and downs experienced by Somalis living there. Many business ventures do work out well, further encouraging the allocation of risk and trust within its economy. *In Eastleigh we trust.*

Furthermore, the critical mass of its success creates its own compulsion to keep taking risks and to keep trusting. Many—even wealthier wholesalers and importers—are compelled to take risks and trust by the very goods that flow through the estate. There is a huge momentum in this flow that derives from the sheer scale of trade as trucks daily bring yet more containers to the estate. If one was too picky as an importer or wholesaler (regarding to whom these goods were entrusted on credit) then the estate's economy would seize up. The amount of money circulating in the estate generates a similar dynamic. In such an economy, educated risks have to be taken to prevent logjams, and Eastleigh's economy has boomed so much in the last two decades that these risks have been well rewarded for most traders. Indeed, in some ways the discourse of risk, trust and Islamic business practice serves to rationalise transactions impelled by the objects of exchange themselves. The following chapter looks more closely at the very demanding goods that flow through the estate and form this critical mass.

6

DEMANDING GOODS

Garissa Lodge ... the place in Africa where you can buy everything from Sony TVs to AK 47s to nuclear secrets thanks to Somalis.

(Contributor to the Somali.net online forum, 2010)

The epigraph above is testimony to the excess inherent in how Eastleigh and its economy are imagined. It is seen as a place not only where anything goes, but also where anything sells. An 'anything can be bought in Eastleigh' narrative further enhances its wild image in the eyes of outsiders, especially the claim that guns are easily available. Nuclear secrets are certainly not available in the estate, and guns are not an integral part of its true economy, although they are sometimes sold there;[1] but all these commodities—real and imagined—speak to the dynamic commerce in the estate, where even interviews with fake pirates can be bought and sold,[2] as can identity itself, in the form of fake passports and other identity documents, and resettlement abroad.[3] As this chapter will show, however, it is more mundane goods such as clothes and electronics that are central to the growth of the estate's economy, as they are in many similar places throughout Kenya, Africa and the world beyond.

This chapter takes a 'commodity-eye' view of the estate, looking at the meanings and values of certain goods for those who trade or buy them in the estate, and looking at how these goods have been hugely influential in the building of Eastleigh. Such an approach shows how they are made potent through the meanings ascribed to them, and in a sense are themselves agents in the Eastleigh commercial transformation as their momentum demands their efficient exchange along the networks running through the estate.[4] Indeed, Kenyan demand for such goods, combined with Somali control of the networks that bring them, is a key formula behind the Eastleigh success.

While classic commodity analyses in anthropology and other disciplines—for example the seminal work of Mintz[5] on the transformations wrought in the Atlantic region by the sugar trade—have tended to focus on one type of commodity, this chapter will focus on five different types of commodity that have helped effect its transformation. It will trace their histories and 'social lives', to use Appadurai's term, exploring their trajectories, the varying politics of their exchange,[6] and the varied cultural and social messages they convey.[7] However, while Mintz, Appadurai and others follow the transnational trajectories of goods to examine the systems of power they help generate, this chapter suggests how powerful their flow can be for a particular place. Eastleigh's commodities link the estate into many circuits of trade, telling a wider story of connection, but are also inscribed into its very landscape, shaping the estate and resonating throughout its streets and buildings. This chapter thus seeks a broad understanding of these goods from their points of production to points of consumption, and how their confluence upon Eastleigh has been critical in its transformation. We will consider Eastleigh and the khat trade, the sale of foodstuffs (camel milk in particular), gold and clothing. Paradoxically, however, the first type of commodity we consider is one not generally sold in the estate, but still of crucial importance to its economy: livestock.

Livestock

Indeed, animals are rarely seen in contemporary Eastleigh—with the exception of Eid, when large numbers of live goats are sold for the festivities. Of course, as an estate linked to pastoralist peoples, the products of livestock feature prominently in the diet of the estate, as meat and milk are consumed in its many restaurants. They feature culturally too, as the romance of pastoralism remains for Somalis: for example, the logo of Eastleighwood gives pride of place to a camel, as does that of the aptly named hotel: the Nomad Palace. Indeed, much work highlights the continued—and in some ways growing—importance of the 'camel complex' in northern Kenya among Somali, Gabra, Rendille, Sakuye and others,[8] an importance that filters into an estate so intimately connected to the north of the country. For many Somali groups, camels have long been one of the most culturally symbolic and valued of exchange items, vital in the inter-family and clan negotiations around bride-price, in the settlement of *diya* payments (paid in compensation for a death) and in livelihoods: they are thus central to Somali social reproduction. Camels have been a prominent theme in Somali poetry too.[9]

Despite this cultural significance, most livestock from northern Kenya and Somalia arrives in Kariobangi, a kilometre or two from Eastleigh, rather than in Eastleigh itself. However, the impact of the trade is strong in its transformed landscape: capital raised from the sale of cattle, camels, sheep and goats circulates through the estate, while livestock—together with buildings—remains an attractive investment for those making money in the estate. Historically, too, livestock have been important for the estate's economy. As we saw in chapter 1, Somalis in early colonial Kenya had grown relatively wealthy thanks to the livestock trade, and it was this wealth that allowed them to buy plots in Nairobi East township. For earlier generations of Somalis in Nairobi, the livestock trade bridged the rural–urban divide, connecting Nairobi to northern Kenya and elsewhere, and confusing the British, who saw their links to the pastoralist economy as evidence that they were not townspeople.[10] Furthermore, in earlier times livestock actually roamed Eastleigh: the land that is now the airbase previously provided pasture for Somali livestock.

It was not only Somalis who engaged in the livestock trade, however. Mzee Gulu—a man whose family originated in the Punjab and who still owns a restaurant business in the estate—told me how Abdul Aziz, an influential Indian and a prominent land owner in Eastleigh, dealt in livestock from northern Kenya. He would take *unga*—ground corn—to the north from Nairobi, bringing back cattle in return. This trade relied as much on trust as Somali-to-Somali networks, and also provided some capital for building in Eastleigh in its early days. Indeed,

Mzee Gulu's own great-grandfather engaged with this trade. Suppliers in the north would give him livestock on credit, not being paid in full until they themselves visited Nairobi. For his ancestor, this trust-based system worked well as it meant he often had a long period of time before the supplier came to Nairobi when he could invest the money raised from the sale of the livestock into other ventures, some of which centred on Eastleigh.

However, as with all aspects of the estate's economy, it is in the last two decades since the collapse of the Somali state that the importance of the livestock trade has become so enhanced for Eastleigh, and for a town to which it is intimately connected: Garissa. Peter Little emphasises how the livestock trade—like that of other commerce—has boomed in Somalia's stateless years, forming a key case study of the country's 'economy without state'.[11] At the same time as Somalia collapsed, Kenya's livestock industry was liberalised, opening up a large market for Somali-bred cattle, mainly routed through Garissa town:

> From 1989 to 2002, cattle sold annually at Garissa market increased from around 24,500 to more than 130,000. ... By the early 2000s, the pastoralist areas of stateless Somalia were supplying more than 65 per cent of the cattle sold at the Garissa market and about 16 percent of the beef consumed in Nairobi, Kenya, a city of 3.5 + million people.[12]

Indeed, ever-growing demand for meat in Nairobi and other Kenyan towns has long been a spur to the cross-border livestock trade with Somalia,[13] no doubt generating and cementing social networks used in the transport of other goods too.

Such trade was a major factor in a population surge in Garissa over the same period, and a major source of funding for Eastleigh developments. While many could earn enough from the sale of livestock to provide start-up capital for small shops—helping to construct the malls in the process through goodwill payments—for large-scale traders enough money could be raised to invest in more substantial ventures including hotels. Little provides some examples:

> Abdinoor, the owner of one of the largest hotels in Garissa, used profits from livestock trade to finance the establishment's construction. Despite his hotel and other investments, including in the Eastleigh neighbourhood of Nairobi, he remained active in livestock trade during the 2000s. ...

Abdullah, another prominent businessman and hotel owner in Garissa town, also amassed his initial capital through livestock trade and transport, and he also has investments and businesses in Eastleigh.[14]

Such linkages between trade in Somali livestock and Eastleigh businesses are common. Campbell relates how a Garissa cattle trader operates a shop in Eastleigh selling women's clothes (which he also sells in Garissa) in the dry season when cattle are more sedentary.[15] Little comments on this intriguing case of a male Muslim dealing in women's clothes and cattle: 'Such is the perplexing world of Somali businesses in Eastleigh, where a male Muslim trader imports and sells women's fashionable clothes, but also operates a cattle business with ties deep inside Somalia's rangelands.'[16] Many traders in Eastleigh have diversified portfolios of business interests, but owning livestock—still so culturally valued a commodity among Somalis—is one to which many in Eastleigh still turn. Indeed, many camels are thought to be owned by wealthy businesspeople in Eastleigh and beyond,[17] and so a place in some ways built through livestock is, in turn, leading to further investment in livestock.

Stimulating Development

While the livestock trade has played a crucial yet inconspicuous role in the development of the estate, another significant trade item is seen on almost every street corner: khat, more usually known as miraa in Kenya. This is the ever more controversial stimulant substance that consists of the stems and leaves of the tree *Catha edulis*, which we have already met on a number of occasions in the course of the book. It is hugely popular throughout Somalia and Kenya, both as a stimulant that aids nightwatchmen, truck drivers and others in their work, and as a sociable substance whose effects—known as *handas* in Kenya, and also as *mirqaan* by Somalis—can ease conversation in recreational contexts. It is also a demanding commodity, whose active compounds and palatability degrades rapidly after harvesting, necessitating swift transport and sale, increasing the momentum of its trade.[18]

It is viewed with great ambivalence wherever it is found (principally in the Horn of Africa, Yemen, East Africa and Madagascar), reflecting the ambiguities of its potential for harm; while moderate consumption is fairly innocuous, there are medical and social harms associated with

Plate 23: Mururu, an Eastleigh khat trader holding two bundles

excessive use; socially it can act to bring people together, but can also prove divisive; economically it earns much for producers and traders, yet can be a burden on household finances. In this ambiguity and ambivalence it resembles all stimulants and intoxicants, especially alcohol. In Kenya it has long been controversial, and the colonial state led an abortive attempt to prohibit the substance in the 1940s and 1950s, before changing tack after realising its economic worth.[19]

Meru are the principal growers and traders in Kenya, especially the Tigania and Igembe sub-groups of the Nyambene Hills district to the north-east of Mount Kenya, where it has probably been grown for centuries.[20] The twentieth century was a period of rapid growth for khat from this region: it spread throughout Kenya and East Africa as the road infrastructure was built (though proving especially popular in

Somali-populated parts of the country such as Eastleigh itself), and throughout the world, as demand followed the Somali diaspora in the 1990s and 2000s. Archival records show how Eastleigh was very much a centre of the trade by the early 1940s, Meru traders bringing the substance there for Somalis and others. By the late 1940s an Eastleigh Somali named Mohamed Hassan was one of the few licensed to trade the substance at the time, and for a while had a monopoly on its distribution in Nairobi, though other legal traders and smuggler soon joined the trade.[21]

As an item of consumption, khat was not just popular among Somalis in Eastleigh, but also among its Asian population, and Kenyan Asians remain a key market for khat traders. However, Somali consumption was such as to constrict supplies to others: an Arab trader in Pumwani complained that his customers could not get supplies in 1947 as the supply that reached the city mainly went to Somalis.[22] This growing consumption in Nairobi in the 1950s prompted some Somalis there to campaign against it,[23] opposition to khat having as long a history as its consumption. It remained so popular, despite this opposition, that hundreds of Meru traders have started businesses in the estate over the years (see chapter 3), selling the commodity supplied from their home district.

Today khat chewing forms one of the main Eastleigh pastimes, albeit one that many regard as not 'respectable'. Much consumption occurs in the evening as activity switches from the central shopping district of First Avenue to Second Avenue, a street containing more khat kiosks and restaurants than malls: khat in this way influences how space is used in the estate, especially in the evening. Khat kiosks stock up with fresh supplies from Meru in the afternoon, advertising this with a fresh banana leaf hanging from the door. A large proportion of Eastleigh's population buy khat from these traders, adjourning either to private rooms or, in the case of men, often to such public areas as Shaah Macaan. This means 'Sweet Tea' in Somali, and is a small area located on Thirteenth Street, near such Eastleigh landmarks as the Grand Royal. One can indeed buy sweet tea at Shaah Macaan as well as indulge in shisha, khat and, most importantly, chat. Shaah Macaan is not the most idyllic of spots. When I visited, the view out from the rather scruffy seating area was of a muddy road that required great care to traverse without falling (although this road has now been repaired), while the nearby fleet of buses bound for north-eastern Kenya continually punctured any semblance of tranquillity with blasts of their horns. The atmosphere is hardly healthy either, with dust, sewage and diesel fumes swirling around. Yet chewers do not seem to mind, and happily continue their consumption and conversation. This is one of khat's key appeals: it helps induce comfort and ease in such unprepossessing locations.

Some who frequent Shaah Macaan are diaspora Somalis visiting the estate on holiday, and chewing khat is a rare treat for such Somalis, many of whom live in Western countries where khat consumption is illegal and consequently expensive and risky: this now includes those from the UK, where it was only recently banned (see below). Many others are Kenyan Somalis and Somalians resident in the estate, some sealing business deals over a chew, or relaxing after a day's business. Some feel shy in admitting they chew, especially given the increasingly conservative nature of the Eastleigh economy in recent years: khat has long been subject to debate as to whether it is haram or *halal*. Chewers sometimes lament how the increasing Islamisation of the estate has encouraged some to only chew when elsewhere in the city where they will not be judged so harshly. While hostility to khat chewing is common among the religious, there are also others who lament its consumption, especially when chewed by those sustained through remittances from abroad. An Oromo trader emphasised to me how some of his co-ethnics become dependent and lazy when receiving remittances, getting up late, then spending cash sent from abroad on their chew. To chew in those circumstances, he said, is to be disrespectful to those working hard to earn the money abroad.

Khat consumption continues apace despite its dubious reputation among certain segments of Eastleigh society, and there are varieties sold to suit every pocket. There are high-quality bundles of *giza* and *kangeta*—two famous types—that can sell for up to 2,000 Kenyan shillings (about $20). Indeed, Meru traders can sell high-quality khat at higher rates in Eastleigh than in other parts of the country as there is so much money circulating in its economy. However, for those of lesser means there is cheap khat available, especially *mokokha*, a variety from Embu sold as handfuls of leaves rather than bundles of stems, which can fetch as little as 20 shillings for a retail unit. Mokokha has become a key commodity for Oromo (men and women) in the estate, providing a living for many that requires little start-up capital.

However, it is the international trade in the commodity to Somalia and the West that has played a key role in the Eastleigh transformation itself, a trade stymied by recent bans imposed by the UK and Netherlands. The trade to European and North American countries was another result of the spread of the Somali diaspora, creating far-away markets for Kenyan khat. The institution of the *mafrish*—khat-chewing venues—in the diaspora became key sites of sociality for some, despite the condemnation of khat consumption by others as an unproductive waste of time and money. The scale of demand was so great that by the end of the 2000s Kenya was supplying around 50 tonnes weekly to the UK.[24]

As well as being a site of khat consumption, Eastleigh has for over two decades formed the Nairobi hub for this trade, just as it was a hub for the growing national and regional trade in colonial times. A fleet of pick-ups brings large supplies of the commodity daily from Meru, in particular the town of Maua, itself transformed into something of a Somali enclave since the collapse of the Somali state.[25] For the now illegal UK and Netherlands markets, some of this was then processed at a number of establishments in the estate, being standardised into small bundles and boxed up ready for delivery to the airport. This reprocessing was another source of income for those trying to survive in the estate: before the European bans they were paid piecemeal rates, working for around forty export companies.[26]

A few became rich from the trade, especially those exporting large numbers of boxes, and some invested profits in malls and other businesses. It is reckoned that three malls in particular owe their construction, at least partially, to khat export. However, as we saw in the last chapter, money made from khat is reckoned tainted by the more religious as Eastleigh itself has become more overtly religious. For some traders, khat is something to move away from once established in business.

Khat's future is far from certain, especially given the recent prohibitions in the UK and Netherlands, which have sparked further calls in Kenya itself for a ban, especially from Somalis in the north-east. The loss of the legal UK market has affected Eastleigh's khat economy; indeed, reports already suggest that some of the UK khat is now flooding the national market, reducing prices in Nairobi. The flow of the commodity is lower, and many Meru who were processing it in the estate have returned to their home towns after losing their jobs: the expanding khat trade brought them to the estate, while its contraction has chased them away.

However, new markets are being opened up, including Mozambique, where there is a growing Somali population, while Somalia itself still offers Eastleigh exporters rich pickings. Also, khat has been illegal in most other European and North American countries for some time, but still finds its way there and sells for very high prices.[27] Prohibition has not stopped smugglers meeting demand, and consignments destined for illicit routes are also processed in the estate. Furthermore, khat consumption in Eastleigh itself is hardly likely to diminish any time soon, despite the hopes of those who see it as a vice. Khat is likely to remain a part of life there, whether through refugees chewing time away while hoping for resettlement, or businesspeople sealing deals over a bundle or two.

Eating and Drinking Culture

While not seen as an archetypal Eastleigh commodity, food is an important and valued aspect of the estate's social and economic life. As Caplan suggests, 'food is never "just food" and its significance can never be purely nutritional',[28] a sentiment with which many in Eastleigh would agree in relation to the value ascribed to various foodstuffs. More mundanely, Eastleigh's inhabitants need feeding, and selling food in the estate can be profitable; furthermore, foodstuffs are also sold there in large quantities as commodities destined for consumption elsewhere. Indeed, Eastleigh contains many small shops selling food-stuffs—especially cooking oil, rice, pasta, sugar and spices—as well as street stalls selling fruit and dates, and larger supermarkets selling a wider range of goods. Such supermarkets are mainly Somali run, and include a chain of shops run by a Somali family with a history of business in China. However, Eastleigh links into the wider Kenyan economy too as far as food shopping goes, as there is a branch of Tuskys, a major Kenyan supermarket chain, at Madina Mall.

Many foodstuffs sold in the estate are Kenyan, including tea, fruit and vegetables, bread and so forth. However, there are many imported items too, some linked to the contraband economy: for example, it is well known that much sugar circulating in Kenya is smuggled over the Somali border, having travelled the world from Brazil, through Dubai and Kismayu before entering Kenya. Eastleigh is not a major hub for this smuggled sugar—much of which is reckoned to be taken directly from Mandera to other towns in northern Kenya, as well as the Dadaab camps—but no doubt it is sold and consumed in the estate. Pakistani rice is also reckoned a key contraband of the cross-border trade, and another item sold in food shops and supermarkets in Eastleigh. Sugar and rice are particularly troublesome for Kenya as the country is itself a major producer of these commodities, so such cheap smuggled varieties can undermine local industry, especially in northern towns where Kenyan-produced equivalents are much more expensive.[29]

Much Eastleigh food has strong links to 'homes' elsewhere, as seems fitting in an estate with such a large refugee and diaspora population. The importance of food for recreating a sense of 'home' in contexts of migration has long been recognised, Sutton emphasising how food allows a sensory connection with a past elsewhere.[30] For those visiting from the West, supermarkets sell many familiar products, including Oreo biscuits, much to the delight of one dhaqan celin Somali teenager I met. Also, numerous restaurants cater for diaspora tastes by serving burgers and pizza, but with some hybridised Somali twists such as the use of camel meat as topping. For Ethiopian refugees many small shops stock popular foods from north of the border, for example the barley-grain snack known as *kolo*, while Ethiopian-style coffee is sold everywhere, sometimes by hawkers walking through the malls with their flasks. Such niche foods not only provide a taste of home, they also offer yet more opportunities for refugees to survive. The popularity of Ethiopian food with the wider Kenyan and Somali population has also meant that some have become relatively wealthy through running restaurants, including the Eritrean proprietors of the Big Mack restaurants that many visit for its *injera* (Ethiopian flatbread) and Ethiopian-style layered fruit drinks.

Of course, Somali food is available in profusion, especially meat and rice or pasta dishes. Camel meat is especially popular, and large dishes full of meat and fat from the animal are often shared. While camel meat is popular, perhaps the most interesting foodstuff—certainly in terms of its commoditisation—is camel milk, or *caano geel* as it is known in Somali. Hannah Elliott has studied the 'social life' of camel milk, including its incorporation into the survival strategies of women in Eastleigh, as well as its importance in narratives of a wider Somali identity.[31] Camel milk has become strongly resonant of *badia* (country-side) for urbanised and diaspora Somalis, a substance imbued as a consequence with 'Somaliness'.

Khat is steeped in ambivalence for Somalis, but not camel milk, a drink seen as highly healthy and even medicinal amongst Somalis, something they link to the trees and plants camels consume. In Eastleigh its popularity is evident everywhere, from the many restaurants in which it is sold, to the women selling it in yellow jerry cans around Seventh Street and Thirteenth Street. There is also a milk bar on Seventh Street selling glasses of camel milk. As Elliott reports,[32] camel-milk tea is more popular than cow's-milk tea among Somalis, and by early evening restaurants have often exhausted their supply.

Traditionally camel milk was seen as something for family consumption, not commoditisation: resorting to selling it was seen as a form of desperation. However, the collapse of the Somali state spurred the creation of a vibrant market in the product in Somalia and in hubs such as Eastleigh. In the case of Kenya, Elliott documents how Kenyan Somali women from Isiolo and Garissa became involved in the trade,[33] spotting its market potential in Nairobi. As more Somalis came to Eastleigh—from northern Kenya, Somalia and later from the wider diaspora—so commoditised camel milk became a trade item offering livelihood opportunities, both for those needing an economic activity in Eastleigh and for women able to leverage connections between suppliers in the north and urban sellers. Some of these intermediaries organised themselves into a cooperative to facilitate its transport on buses running between Eastleigh and the north. Garre women have been especially involved in the trade, able as they are to speak both Boran and Somali, and so communicate with camel herders from a number of different ethnicities (Somali, Boran, Sakuye and Gabra). As it was regarded as a petty trade, men generally left women to it, although there is an increasing formalisation of the trade: one company now markets processed camel milk derived from herds in ranches around Nanyuki.[34]

Thus, like khat, the popularity of camel milk in the estate has created an informal trade that many can enter as it requires so little start-up capital. As Elliott found, most women operating the trade in Eastleigh were Kenyan Somalis, although refugee women also are involved, and were seen as trustworthy even if they had only weak ties to other traders, partly because they had nowhere to go if they ran away without paying what they owed. Camel milk links many disparate groups together, from suppliers and middlewomen elsewhere in the country, to women from different backgrounds in Eastleigh itself, and despite its commodification it remains an item of consumption full of cultural and social—as well as economic—value for many in the estate. Like khat, it is also a perishable substance that must be traded and entrusted swiftly before spoiling, its material qualities once more generating momentum. It resembles khat in another way too, in being another part of the Eastleigh economy embedded within very Kenyan networks: in this case, like livestock, it is a key commodity linking the estate to the pastoral economy of northern Kenya. Also, both khat and camel milk are intimately related to the 'displacement economy' formed in the wake of the Somali civil war that prompted their expansion, albeit on different scales.[35]

Gold

The next commodity we consider is one that comes to Eastleigh after travelling much longer transnational distances, and one distinctly non-perishable: gold, or *dhahabu* as it is known in Kiswahili.[36] Gold was one of the first goods sold in the estate at the beginning of its transformation, and it is of great social significance within Somali society. It has also become ever more significant to the Eastleigh economy in the form of jewellery sourced from the Middle East, mostly from Dubai, although more recently sourced from Bahrain, Jeddah and Singapore. While the jewellery is bought in these places, it is hard to know where the source material itself originates. The quality of gold sold in Eastleigh varies greatly, though traders say that customers are only interested in 22- or 21-carat items: 18-carat items are sometimes bought by traders to return to Dubai where it can be mixed with other gold to make it 21 carat. Of course, many items sold are much cheaper gold-plated products. Retailers report that they test the purity of items bought from wholesalers using chemicals, although they say that their customers usually trust retailers and do not demand to see the gold tested.

Wholesaling and retailing gold jewellery in Eastleigh is mainly the preserve of Somali women, though there are men who sell gold from bigger shops, and some Somali retailers also buy from Asian and Swahili wholesalers. Women sellers can be seen at a number of malls, usually retailing from small stalls. At such locations—which require extra security—informal currency exchange also takes place, a trade operated almost entirely by young men, and a trade much needed in an estate where money itself—in several currencies—is a crucial commodity. This gendered division is striking, especially in a building known as Al-Kowther near Garissa Lodge, where women sell gold in one section, and men exchange money in another.

For Somali women, gold jewellery has, for a long time, been a key item received from a husband as *mehar*, the essential payment from a man or his kin to the bride herself (an Islamic practice known as *mahr* as transliterated from Arabic). It is seen as a form of insurance in case of divorce or difficult times, providing an independent resource that can be tapped when needed. As something that can hold its economic value in the long term, gold is especially well suited in this regard. Demands for gold jewellery can be seen as a burden by men, especially in the context of a transnational space such as Eastleigh where there is competition with diaspora men of means who can offer more wealth than most locals. However, the economic importance of gold in Eastleigh can be deduced from its socio-cultural importance: as a key item of exchange between men and women, there will always be demand for it from the estate's Somali residents (and most customers in the Eastleigh gold markets appear to be Somali).

Of course, it is not just Somalis for whom gold sourced in the Middle East has this significance: gold jewellery also has a long history in Indian and Pakistani dowries, and demand in these countries boosted the gold trade in Dubai from the 1940s. Also, towns along the Swahili coast—including ports such as Brava—have long been hubs for gold jewellery, some claiming that such jewellery represented the main source of financial power for women in pre-colonial times. In the words of Hecht:

> The official position of women was a poor one. Their social and economic security depended on marriage only. Divorce was easy (from the men's side), often only on the grounds of the fading beauty of the wife; men had

the sole right over the children; women were not entitled to learn or to practice a trade to make a living; the only way to gain economic and social security was a second marriage, and of course to extract from their husband(s) as much jewelry as possible, since her personal jewelry was the only property a woman had claim to in case of divorce.[37]

That women were as devoid of agency as this depiction suggests has been disputed by Mohamed in her analysis of the position of women in Brava.[38] However, the importance of jewellery as a store of value, and not just as objects of beauty, rings true with gold retailers in Eastleigh. For example, one had come recently from Toronto after living there since 1992: she came with her four children, reporting that the education they receive in Kenya is far superior. The retailer was divorced, and so came to Kenya without the father of her children. Needing to establish herself in business, she sold half her collection of 400 grams of gold jewellery, making $8,000, which she used for the start-up costs required for her business. She kept the other half of her collection in reserve, in case she needed more money in the future.

Gold sellers act as informal bankers within this gendered economy, and women's social networks are strengthened through various sorts of exchanges. For example, those with personal relations with gold sellers in Eastleigh can sometimes use them to get cash advances by leaving sets of jewellery with sellers on the proviso that they will not be sold until after a certain timeframe, rather like a pawnbroker system. One woman interviewed—Asli—had a large hospital bill to pay and no cash with which to do so. She had a large piece of jewellery, bought for a wedding, and took it to a friend of hers who sells gold. This friend gave her 100,000 Kenyan shillings[39] for the piece—actually rather more than it was worth—and Asli bought it back for the same price before the agreed two-month period elapsed. As they were friends, and Asli a regular customer, there was no payment, though some sellers might charge a fee of 1,000 shillings or so for this service. In purchasing desired items of jewellery, women sometimes also make use of personal relations with traders. Asli had another relationship with a trader whereby she could give her money in increments whenever she had some to spare, and these payments acted as a deposit for a certain piece or set of jewellery, the trader agreeing to set them aside until Asli had paid in full. In this way, Asli would not divert money she saved to other purposes.

Like other Eastleigh commodities, and Eastleigh trade in general, there is concern over how to ensure that the trade in gold meets Islamic moral standards. While there is doubt over how halal the trade in khat could ever be, gold is seen as a very respectable commodity, but one that must be traded according to certain rules derived from the sayings of the Prophet: in particular, a verse in the *Sahih Muslim* stipulates that no usury can be applied to gold for gold transactions (and transactions of other monetary instruments), and that transactions must be 'hand to hand'. There is debate as to exactly how to interpret these verses, but the stipulation 'hand to hand' is generally taken to mean the transaction must be completed in person at one time.[40] This interpretation is known among Somali gold traders and their customers, and, as a consequence, the usual form of trade relations based on trust and credit in Eastleigh is precluded. As a result, in theory retailers must buy their stock outright before they trade it, and so often buy from whoever is wholesaling gold at a decent price, rather than necessarily building long-term, trusting business relations. In practice, those with pre-existing relations of trust might bend the rules a little, perhaps giving a retailer gold to sell to be paid back the next day. Apparently gold sells so fast in Eastleigh that such arrangements of short-term credit are easy to manage.

Thus gold is another commodity bursting with cultural and social meaning, forming a crucial store of value among women's economic networks: it demonstrates strongly the interpenetration of social, cultural, moral and religious dimensions in the economic life of Eastleigh.

Clothing East Africa

While gold, camel milk and khat are commodities brought to the estate chiefly for Somali consumption, we now turn to those brought mainly to attract non-Somali customers, and which are fundamental to Eastleigh's transformation: clothes and textiles. Imported clothing is the Eastleigh commodity par excellence, being the most commonly sold item both in the earliest incarnation of Garissa Lodge and in the shopping malls of today. As a member of the Eastleigh Business Association told me, 'the clothes trade is the father of all Eastleigh business'. Indeed, clothes are powerful commodities: as Hansen describes in relation to the second-hand-clothes trade in Zambia, clothing mediates 'notions of self and society, which make this commodity different from any other in terms of indexing welfare and development. ... People in Zambia want well-dressed bodies.'[41] The same is very much the case in Kenya, and Eastleigh is a place where that desire can be satisfied cheaply.

A proportion of clothes sold in Eastleigh are Muslim-style dress mainly bought by Somalis and other Muslims, as well as feeding networks leading to other Somali trade hubs, including Eldoret, Kisumu and Kampala. International Islamic fashion is everywhere in the estate, as huge demand exists for such items as abaya and hijab for women, and *galabbiya* (long, loose robe) and *kufi* (skull cap) for men, increasing as the influence of more conservative forms of Islam grows.[42] These items clearly have much symbolic value, linking Somalis to the broader Islamic world, and also have a strong political significance, reflecting the increasing strength of Islam politically for Somalis since the 1970s. Indeed, items now common amongst Somalis—jilbaab for women and *macawis* (sarong-type garment) for men—became widespread under the influence of other Islamic societies in the last four decades, rather than reflecting pre-existing Somali styles of clothing.[43] Other items specifically appealing to Somalis are also common, including clothing designed with the Somali or Somaliland national colours, including football tops.

However, it is non-Islamic clothing, which appeals to a wider population in East Africa, that has been such a major catalyst of its transformation. These include jeans, T-shirts, football shirts, smart shirts, shoes of all types, dresses (often tailor made from fabric sold in the estate), underwear and suits; almost all of these products sold in the estate are exemplars of the goods sold through 'low-end globalisation', to use Mathews' term.[44] Other items sold in Eastleigh also form part of this phenomenon of goods manufactured cheaply in factories in China, Thailand, India and elsewhere that are often traded in South–South networks—especially electronics, perfumes and cosmetics.[45] These commodities form the key connection between manufacturers and agents in Dubai, Hong Kong and most recently Turkey, wholesalers and retailers in Eastleigh, and the East African customers keen to buy them, some to wear themselves, others to retail elsewhere in markets throughout the region.

Eastleigh imported clothes cater for both men and women. Indeed, most shops specialise in either menswear or womenswear, aside from some bigger shops that have separate sections for each. For men, suits in particular are a prime reason to visit Eastleigh: while other trade hubs such as Kampala now offer items such as jeans at cheaper prices than Eastleigh (and as a consequence, Eastleigh traders travel to Kampala to import them), Eastleigh appears to have a monopoly on cheap suits in East Africa, and people from Kampala and elsewhere travel in the other direction to obtain them. While Eastleigh menswear shops stock a variety of items from shoes to casual sports attire, most—including Nasiib Fashions—rely mainly on suits. Despite the high profit possible from suits, some reckon that in general more money can be made from women's clothes. Indeed, most shoppers seen in malls such as Amal are women, and while some look for clothes for male relatives, mostly they shop for themselves. Womenswear in the estate is very varied, from ready-made dresses, skirts and jeans, to underwear, shoes and accessories. Mohaa sometimes wistfully considers moving into womenswear (there are Somali men in malls selling women's clothes) as he considers it much more profitable, though all his experience and connections lie in menswear.

These typical Eastleigh clothes are also worn by Somalis themselves: women often wear non-Islamic clothes under their abaya or at home, while Somali men in the estate are often sharply dressed in suits. Diaspora Somalis also shop in Eastleigh to buy clothes to take back to the West: one woman I met there was from the UK and bought several football shirts from Mohaa with her relatives' names printed on them for a far cheaper price than would be possible in the UK. However, most of the Eastleigh stock is worn all over Nairobi, Kenya and the wider region, being bought in the estate directly by customers, or sourced there wholesale to be sold elsewhere. Indeed, many items of clothing sold in shops in central Nairobi, as well as Marsabit, Dadaab, Kampala and elsewhere, will have been sourced in Eastleigh.

This centrality of Eastleigh to clothing Kenya and East Africa arose because the estate provided new clothes at such cheap prices. Indeed, price is key, and Eastleigh traders have long sought out ways to reduce costs. As discussed in chapter 2, networks through which smuggled clothes and other consumables were brought into Kenya were recentred on the estate with the Garissa Lodge revolution in the early 1990s, providing intense competition to the more expensive Indian shops in town. Smuggling was a source of comparative advantage early on, though as Somali networks and infrastructure solidified it was their ability to source in bulk and ship cheaply from such hubs as Dubai that became a major reason why these clothes could be sold so cheaply. Of course, there are other factors behind the cheap prices, including lower business overheads in the estate, and, crucially, the fact that much of the clothing consists of items manufactured cheaply abroad, items that could be imported in larger quantities thanks to the trade liberalisation of the early 1990s.

Indeed, the very affordable nature of the clothes that Somali networks began to bring in at the time of liberalisation has been a key part of Eastleigh's success, success that parallels that of another post-liberalisation clothing boom in East Africa: mitumba, the Kiswahili term for second-hand clothes, many sent to Africa from Europe and North America along elaborate networks. As trade tariffs designed to protect Kenya's own manufacturing industries were dropped, imports of both mitumba and new, cheap clothes increased dramatically. While these new clothes helped transform the landscape of Eastleigh, mitumba led to the expansion of Gikomba market, now a major centre for the trade, and located only a couple of kilometres away from Eastleigh.[46] While blamed by some for the decline of the Kenyan textile industry, mitumba—like the clothes of Eastleigh—generates much business and informal employment throughout the country, from wealthy importers to more lowly street hawkers, and is seen by others as a genuine source of poverty alleviation. The sudden availability of such cheap goods at Eastleigh and Gikomba allowed a flourishing of Kenyan consumerism, affordable goods allowing more than just the rich to indulge in the purchase of great quantities of clothing, and to follow fashions more avidly: Eastleigh and Gikomba goods both provide affordable ways towards the 'well-dressed body' so evocative of development.[47]

One might assume that the clothes and shoes sold in Eastleigh would be more prized than mitumba, being new items rather than cast-offs. However, many Kenyans I have spoken to—even wealthier ones—expressed the view that Gikomba clothes were often far more desirable. Mohaa himself wears mitumba clothes rather than those he himself stocks, being especially partial to jeans and shoes from Gikomba. This links to the often-perceived inferior quality of the goods sold in Eastleigh—many reckoned to be poor copies of fashionable brands—but also to the many desired brands that find their way into mitumba markets. Indeed, mitumba comes in a wide range of qualities, some shops and stalls specialising in items in good condition branded as Nike, Adidas and so forth. Mitumba clothes are imported in bulky bales, and wholesalers allow buyers to choose clothes from the bales in distinct rounds known as *camera*; those of the highest quality go in the first round, while third-round goods are often sold in bulk for the lowest prices, being destined to be worn by those with the smallest wallets.[48]

Such is the potential quality of mitumba that media reports in Kenya describe how the affluent enjoy searching for its bargains, and hold fashion events revolving around mitumba. There are also shops in central Nairobi (and in other cities such as Kampala) that specialise in high-quality mitumba, resembling the trade in 'vintage' clothes in the UK and elsewhere. However, like shopping in charity shops in the West, Kenyans appear to appreciate the uniqueness of mitumba goods. It is said that in Eastleigh you might buy a shirt then see another ten people on the street wearing it, while with mitumba you can have something exclusive to you.[49] Thus, commodities that start out their 'social lives' as mass-produced goods become sources of individuality when filtered through the mitumba network.

Some mitumba goods are sold in Eastleigh by hawkers. However, Eastleigh clothes are generally new and come directly from Asian factories, often through Dubai, Hong Kong and other such hubs.[50] Most customers are aware of this origin, and can be quite sceptical about their quality as a consequence. Although so many high-end goods are now manufactured in China—including fashionable electronic brands such as Apple—there is a widespread notion in Kenya, as elsewhere, that 'made in China' equals low-quality, shoddy goods. Some even joke that the many roads built by Chinese contractors in Kenya will have only a short lifespan as they are 'made in China'. It is hard to generalise too much about the quality of Eastleigh goods, as there are many different gradations of quality sold: not all could be dubbed low-end global products. For example, tailor shops stock a wide range of fabrics, from high-end material to use for wealthy weddings, to cheap synthetics used to make dresses and other items for the lower end of the market, some sellers telling me that such material is usually bought by Kenyans coming from more rural parts of the country.

While people may be more concerned about buying cheap electronics or phones, which can prove unreliable, even the cheapest Eastleigh clothes have their uses, especially for school uniforms, where a functional look and feel are more important than designer-fashioned elegance, or suits which do not vary much in design (although certain colours seem more in fashion at particular times). Nevertheless, many customers want clothing resembling the high-end fashions seen in the media, and especially in music videos. The way Eastleigh networks are set up allows for swift imports of new styles, as wholesalers in the estate—either in person or through agents—can order in popular lines, some even made specifically for that purpose at Asian factories. Information on what is selling well in this way flows from Eastleigh retailers to wholesalers to Dubai, China and elsewhere. Indeed, while

Plate 24: Handmade dresses for sale, Eastleigh

clothes are not as rapidly perishable as khat and camel milk,[51] it is essential that traders keep up to date with what is popular, otherwise one might be left with lots of old stock to be sold *harash* (at a discount price). However, as with fashion everywhere, what is old one week might be back in fashion the next. As Mohaa told me in a WhatsApp chat: on the one hand *kila siku design mpya iko* ('everyday there is a new style'), but on the other, *old stock iko na faida* ('old stock has profit'), sometimes even more than new. He recounted how back in 2007 Gucci-labelled jeans were popular, but now are hard to find in Eastleigh. He met someone recently who is prepared to pay up to 2,500 shillings a pair for the same jeans (double what they originally fetched, and much higher than normal jeans, which sell around 1,000 shillings).

As well as offering obscurely branded goods, Eastleigh offers many brand names that satisfy customers' desires to be part of wider global fashions: labels reading Lacoste, Polo, Gucci (as with the above jeans) and the like are sold on many items of clothing, as well as bags and shoes. While some goods so labelled might be genuine, many of them— of course—are copies, part of the counterfeiting industry that has thrived in recent years, especially in China where such goods are known by the name *shanzai*. Lin suggests that such counterfeit goods can be categorised in the following three ways:

(1) Unauthorized use of a brand name or trademark (e.g. a leather bag with the letters L and V printed on it in a way that exactly replicates the Louis Vuitton logo, but without authorization from Louis Vuitton);

(2) Intentional resemblance of a brand name product (e.g. a pair of running shoes that are designed to look like a pair of Nike shoes, but have the name Vike and a checkmark rather than a swoosh);

(3) Unauthorized sale of unauthorized production or overstock (e.g. a pair of Nike running shoes or a Louis Vuitton leather bag, the sale of which is not authorized).[52]

The scale of the global trade in such goods (including electronics, medicines and so forth, as well as clothes) is enormous, reckoned by some estimates to be worth around $600 billion in annual sales.[53] It is also controversial, as some brands seek to use international property rights legislation to fight back against copies, while some see the copies as actually adding value to the genuine brands by raising awareness of their labels in markets such as China, India and Africa.[54]

Labels are certainly sought after in Eastleigh, even where there is awareness that a product is not a genuine Polo or Lacoste, and all three types of shanzai goods are probably circulating. With regard to suits, those sold as Dunhill and Marks and Spencer are very popular with men: so much so that if one has a suit with such a label, one often leaves the tag on the sleeve. Interestingly, Marks and Spencer is seen as especially good, which is odd as in the UK it is seen as fairly middle of the road. Such are the contrasting impressions of these globalised brands. Many shanzai goods in Eastleigh come under Lin's second category. As with watches and electronic items sold there—some of which rather than being Citizen or Panasonic are Citizien or Panasoanic—there are many more obvious 'knock-offs', the term used by Mathews for goods sold under slightly altered names.[55] Eastleigh suits display a good range of such brand names. Mohaa stocked a number of Hoog Boss blazers, as well as trousers and suits labelled Prada Milano that gave their fakeness away by describing themselves as 'Made in Lialy'. Another such label is the one featured in plate 25, referencing the UK's Marks & Spencer brand.

It is easy to dismiss the importance of such goods, given their often low quality, comical misspellings, and dubious relationship with the 'genuine' articles of the global fashion trade. As we have seen, many Kenyans too—especially those of at least moderate means—would rather seek out the 'authentic' in the mitumba stalls than wear the 'fake' of Eastleigh.[56] But for the vast majority of its shoppers, and those who buy the same items further along its distribution networks, most are not too concerned about their origins: for them it was the look and label that counted rather than authenticity. Only *fala* (Kenyan slang for 'fools' with a naïve, up-country connotation) are thought to believe such goods are genuine, though authenticity is sometimes ambiguous and difficult to gauge. Some will complain of goods that fade in the wash or quickly fall apart, but most clothes sold are better than that even if fake.

Moreover, being original does not necessarily mean being of higher quality: in the world of global fashion, few items are designed to be especially long lasting, either in style or ability to survive wear and

Plate 25: Mark Spencer suit for sale

tear, and so perhaps it is better to buy a cheap copy than pay the premium for a genuine brand stuck on a T-shirt of equal quality. Whatever the case, however, thanks to the types of goods sold in the estate, Kenyans and other East Africans of modest means can taste 'the fruits of globalization at prices they can afford'.[57] Furthermore, the cheap electronics sold in the estate—mobile phones and computers—play a crucial role in connecting East Africans to the wider world. The goods may in general be humble, but when sold in great quantities as a result of the great demand for them, money can be made and shopping malls can be built. In this way, the demand for such 'low-end' goods is a crucial part of the Eastleigh equation, as well as wider urban transformation in the Global South. From the manufacturing hubs of Yiwu and Guangzhou to the streets of Lagos, such goods have catalysed much social and economic change: while they have helped build a 'Little Mogadishu' in Nairobi, they have also built 'Little Africas' in China, as so many from Africa—including Somalis—now reside in China itself helping to facilitate their flow.[58]

In the latest round of mall-building in the estate, however, there appears to be a distinct move towards the high end, especially in the plans for the forthcoming Comesa Shopping Mall of General Waruingi Street. In design this mall much more resembles the huge new complexes emerging throughout Nairobi, and it will be home to a large Nakumatt (the Kenyan supermarket chain) as well as more Eastleigh-flavoured shops. Perhaps this mall will lead to more standard Kenyan and global brands coming to the estate, and a move towards high-end goods as well as high-end malls? Somali businesspeople in the estate—the elite at any rate—certainly have the means to import such goods, but whether they could find so ready a market for them remains to be seen.

Potent Goods

Livestock from northern Kenya and Somalia, khat from north-east of Mount Kenya, and clothes, textiles and electronics from Asia have all played a part in making Eastleigh what it is today. They are objects of desire and often necessity, filled with meanings that drive forward their trade even when—as in the case of khat—they are viewed with great ambivalence and no little alarm. Furthermore, whether khat, camel's milk or the latest fashion, the 'need for speed' in the sale of these items increases greatly the rhythms of commerce in the estate, further oiling the social networks along which they travel. Linking back to the theme of the previous chapter, the momentum of goods flowing through the estate can itself precipitate transactions, urging their entrustment to others. Eastleigh is the Nairobi crossroads for many of these goods, facilitating their arrival or expediting their dispatch to consumers or to other hubs, and many have grown wealthy as a consequence of controlling the pathways they take. Thus, while the nuclear weapons mentioned in the epigraph that started this chapter are not available in Eastleigh, the commodities that are have created their own shockwaves and been critical catalysts in the transformation of this urban landscape.

7

STATE OF SUSPICION

Eastleigh estate has been taken over and it is no longer regarded as part of Kenya. Indeed, many Kenyans rarely venture into Eastleigh because it is under siege from various Somali elements.

(Maurice Amutabi, *Daily Nation*, 18 July 2011)

Under Vision 2030, the government has identified Eastleigh as a future business and commercial hub.

(John Cheboi, Kenyan Urban Roads Authority, 2012)[1]

Such has been frustration at the running sore that was the Eastleigh infrastructure—long symbolised by the river of sewage that often was First Avenue—that in 2008 the Eastleigh Business Association suggested an innovative solution. They would collect the estate's tax themselves on behalf of the state and plough back much of it into repairing public services. This offer and its suggestion of subversion of state sovereignty is highly telling of the relationship that has developed between Eastleigh and the state within which it is, at least in theory, embedded. While Somalis poured money into private investment in the last two decades, many—including the Eastleigh Business Association— have long complained of a lack of matching public investment. Indeed, business people and residents lament the poor roads and the lack of security at a time of gang violence. For far too long the major mode of state engagement has appeared one of malign neglect symbolised by decrepit infrastructure, heaps of garbage and regular police swoops.

This neglect derives in part from the suspicion in which Eastleigh is held in Kenya, many viewing it not as an example of valuable economic growth, but of displaced development brought by an increasingly dangerous 'alien' other. Such a perception is only too common after a wave of terror attacks in Kenya linked to the Somali militant group Al-Shabaab, including that on the Westgate Mall in September 2013 and Garissa University College in April 2015. In this context, policy towards Eastleigh and Kenya's refugee population is ever more securitised and characterised by authoritarian measures that have led to increased mutual distrust.[2] Before this securitisation of policy, however, a more positive narrative of the estate's place in national development was strengthening to the point that Eastleigh had been incorporated into Kenya's high modernist blueprint for its future: 'Vision 2030'.[3]

This chapter explores this fraught relationship, one built on a wider history of the similar disjunction between the Kenyan state and its marginalised north where most of its Somali population lives. Eastleigh has increasingly become a stage where the Kenyan government can act the authoritarian state with apparent impunity, as it has been able to do in the north since independence. Understanding Eastleigh once more requires placing it into a much wider temporal and spatial context: its politics—like its economy—are constantly buffeted by historical and political forces. Moreover, people in Eastleigh—especially its Somalis—have been put into a state of suspicion and into a bind: they are themselves major victims of Al-Shabaab, yet also have become soft targets in the war against the militant group. Some have even departed for more welcoming places, pulling investment from Eastleigh. The chapter contrasts this fraught recent history with the renovation of the main roads in the estate and other forms of recent state engagement, suggesting that there is potential for a more positive and mutually beneficial relationship, one worth fighting for in Vision 2030.

Entering Vision 2030

While the concept and industry of 'development' is seen with growing suspicion by many, especially by those who see it as a front for distinctly Western interests and conceptions of what society should be,[4] the term remains potent in the contemporary world, not least in Kenya.[5] 'Development' permeates much Kenyan discourse, especially in the form of its Kiswahili equivalent: *maendeleo* ('progress'). This term is everywhere, and is used in the names of bars, cafés and shops, as well as being liberally plastered in the policy documents of the government. In this regard, 'development' in Kenya has undergone a great renaissance with the grand government plans of Vision 2030, a blueprint of large infrastructure projects (many targeting the previously neglected north of the country)[6] designed to turn Kenya in to a middle-income country.[7]

Given this emphasis on development and economic growth, one might think that Eastleigh's transformation would be a compelling example of what can be achieved through hard work, private investment and transnational trade. Indeed, Eastleigh has clearly brought economic growth, and Somali diaspora investment in Kenya in general has produced an influx of wealth. Frustratingly for its businesspeople longing to prove the true scale of Eastleigh's worth, accurate figures are not available. There is no separate tax band for Eastleigh, so exactly how much tax paid is uncertain: estimates abound, including the figure of $22.8 million annually.[8] Eastleigh is frequently said to trail only Westlands—where many upmarket malls are located—and the CBD in revenue collected by the KRA in Nairobi.[9] While individual shops in the malls may make only erratic and limited contributions, the larger-scale businesses—including the malls themselves, the banks, hotels and so forth—all contribute much to Kenya's revenue. It is not just tax either. The city council—now replaced through the new constitution by the Nairobi County Government—has collected large amounts of revenue in the form of rates and business permits in Eastleigh, from shops, restaurants, hotels and roadside stall operators.

Furthermore, another estimate suggests Somali investment and remittances bring around $780 million to Kenya each year, much through Eastleigh.[10] A large proportion is invested in the businesses and trade that provide Kenya with even greater rewards regarding employment and enterprise. Also, the commodities that flow through it have their own multiplier effects, creating yet more employment throughout Kenya, providing the means to start small enterprises requiring little initial capital from Kakamega to Marsabit. Meanwhile, demand for Kenyan commodities including khat and camel milk, in Eastleigh and beyond in the Somali diaspora, has had a significant impact on Kenyan rural economies.

In fact, there are many in Kenya who do positively appreciate Eastleigh as *development*. Despite the neglect and even hostility that is often perceived as being the state's main reaction to Eastleigh and its population, different sections of the state vary in how they treat it. The 'state', as always, needs disaggregating in this regard. States are not monolithic entities, but are 'replete with contradictions', as different parts have different outlooks and objectives.[11] In this regard, Eastleigh has a number of friends in high places. There are numerous Kenyan Somali politicians keen to promote Eastleigh, from Aden Duale— Majority Leader of the Kenya National Assembly—whose family have business interests in the estate, to Yusuf Hassan Abdi, the current MP for Kamukunji. His election as the first Somali MP in the city was something of a turning point for Kenyan Somalis in Nairobi. Other politicians are conspicuous in the estate, for example Yusuf Haji cutting the ribbon at the opening of Madina Mall in 2011 when he was Minister of Defence. These politicians often speak up for the estate in National Assembly debates. For example, Duale in December 2011 criticised the lack of attention to Eastleigh's infrastructure, whose decay have been a perennial symbol of state neglect:[12]

> Eastleigh is the third largest area in Nairobi after Westlands and Nairobi Central Business District, in terms of revenue collected by the Kenya Revenue Authority (KRA). I want the Assistant Minister to confirm whether it is deliberate effort by the Government, and more so in the Ministry of Roads, to neglect Eastleigh. The Government is doing the roads in Westlands and other places through out the country. … Could he confirm whether it is a deliberate attempt by his Ministry not to improve the roads and the sewer network in Eastleigh?

Non-Somalis in government have also been well disposed to Eastleigh, including Raila Odinga, Prime Minister during the Kibaki presidency. Odinga is no stranger to Eastleigh, campaigning there on behalf of Johnny Ibrahim—who lost to Yusuf Hassan in the by-election of 2011—and opening the Grand Royal Hotel the same year. Furthermore, his office was responsible for infrastructure planning, and his Infrastructure

Secretary, Sylvester Kasuku, was appointed chairman of a taskforce for the Eastleigh Business District Infrastructure Programme,[13] while the Kenya Urban Roads Authority (KURA) claimed that Eastleigh was a priority area for road renovation.

I met a KURA spokesman in 2012, and he was clear in expressing admiration for Eastleigh and the need to cement its position as a major business hub for Kenya through improved infrastructure. He praised the influence of Somalis on Eastleigh, and how they facilitated the development of a neglected estate while the government was too focused on the city centre; he declared himself impressed by how Somalis brought security, and how their 'trustworthiness' gave them great advantages in business. Growing awareness of revenue from the estate had been the factor that made the government take greater notice of it, he said, and convinced KURA to implement improvements. These included upgrading First and Second Avenues, as well as General Waruingi Road on the approach to Eastleigh. He claimed that not only would this enhance trade in the estate—giving it better access to ring roads for ease of transportation—but would also have a knock-on effect on the 'slum' estate of Mathare Valley as well as nearby Gikomba. With better infrastructure in and around Eastleigh, people would also put more money into Mathare, leading to its upgrading. As to be expected of someone in the business of improving roads, he claimed that 'roads bring development'.[14]

The KURA spokesman, like others at that time connected to the Office of the Prime Minister, emphasised that Eastleigh had become a focus of infrastructure investment as it was now targeted in Vision 2030 as a major commercial hub, giving it recognition for its economic importance to Kenya. Eastleigh seemed to be entering the Kenyan developmental mainstream.

Displaced Development

However, despite these moves, suspicion of Eastleigh within Kenyan government and wider society has remained strong. Indeed, it is perceived by many in Kenya as a dubious kind of development, especially given the suspicion that the Eastleigh economy was built on crime. Most cited in this regard are the alleged links to piracy and to terrorist financing, which came to the fore in the late 2000s and led the government to threaten an audit of property owned by Somalis to find out the source of its capital.[15] As discussed in chapter 2, there are far more compelling explanations for the Eastleigh boom than piracy. Indeed, a 2013 World Bank report—publicised in Kenya—stated bluntly that pirate money was not responsible for the real-estate boom in Kenya (suggesting that bank loans and diaspora investment were the chief sources of finance).[16] Nevertheless, suspicion remains in some quarters.

The types of commodities sold in Easteigh are also viewed as suspect. Guns and drugs are said to constitute some of the illicit flows into the estate, while there are frequent claims that its licit commodities are either smuggled over the Somali border or otherwise imported duty free through corruption. Allegations of tax and duty evasion—such as those aired in the KTN report on a Somali freight company mentioned in chapter 2—still generate the impression of Eastleigh continuing to supply contraband.[17] There is also much criticism of land-grabbing in Eastleigh. The disposal of public land in the estate has been much criticised by residents, but even state officials have found land sold from beneath them. Indeed, in 2009 the Eastleigh Chief's camp was moved when its old plot was sold to a Somali property developer. Embarrassingly the camp was downgraded into a shipping container a short distance from its old site. In a way this symbolised the state's tenuous hold on Eastleigh, as Somali development was close to shipping out the Kenyan state in constructing a Little Mogadishu. While it is common to see Eastleigh as marginalised *by* the state given its neglect, in this example and others, one can also see the marginalisation *of* the state.

But of course, in these regards Eastleigh's economy is hardly unique. Indeed, corrupt practices there are symptomatic of a wider culture of corruption in Kenya that permeates all sectors of its economy.[18] The estate came of age in the deeply corrupt latter years of the Moi regime. Kenya is putting effort into improving tax collecting and making better use of revenue raised, but while endemic corruption remains untamed at its ports it is only likely that importers and freight companies—of whatever ethnicity—will make use of this.[19] Furthermore, there is talk of lobbyists from the City of London arguing for Nairobi to be made an 'international finance centre', or, less euphemistically, a 'tax haven' for powerful corporations.[20] Such talk is symbolic of the tax evasion that occurs at far more elevated levels in economies throughout the world, and is likely to lead to far fewer benefits than that of Eastleigh, which clothes Kenya cheaply, while also providing thousands of employment opportunities. A Somali economics student suggested to me that corruption facilitating trade in Eastleigh might even be positive, so many multiplier effects does the import of its goods bring: this is Osterfeld's controversial 'beneficial corruption', corruption that encourages market forces.[21] Of course, how much Kenya gains and how much it loses in this regard would be impossible to calculate, and the overall social corrosion corruption brings surely outweighs benefits in the long term. Doubts about Eastleigh and tax also speak to global interest in 'capturing' the informal economy,[22] certainly something Kenya aims to do as it has pushed on with new tax regimes considered more appropriate for small to medium-scale businesses typical of those in Eastleigh. Land-grabbing is another practice all too common in wider Kenyan society, as the recent example of schoolchildren being tear-gassed when protesting the land-grab of their playground in Langata on the other side of Nairobi highlights.[23] Private capital in Kenya appears to be voraciously eating up public land.

However, the crucial factor in the case of Eastleigh is that its economy—built upon a displacement economy formed after state collapse in Somalia—is perceived by many to be development displaced. Corruption, tax evasion and land-grabbing may be extremely common throughout Kenya, but they are emphasised more in Eastleigh as its economy is associated with people many see as foreign, or as people who should be confined to refugee camps. Eastleigh offers a mirror onto wider Kenyan social and economic processes—some good, some ill—but the reflection of wider society is often ignored, and Eastleigh's economy is seen as peculiarly un-Kenyan. The resonance of the nickname 'Little Mogadishu' is strong here, reflecting the continued perception of the estate as a piece of the Somali Republic transported to Kenya as a result of civil war. While the estate shows the power of diaspora-led development to bring economic growth in Africa,[24] and in Kenya there is much talk of mobilising the diaspora to invest in the country,[25] the problem for Eastleigh is that all this development is seen as having been brought by someone else's diaspora.

Aliens and Alienation

Underlying all fears of Eastleigh as somewhere foreign is the ambiguous identity and citizenship of the people who live there—Muslim Somalis—and their contested place within the Kenyan nation at a time of increasing insecurity, for which the Kenyan state has scapegoated 'illegal aliens'. Somalis have long been seen as 'aliens'—not just refugees, but even those solidly Kenyan in background, who feel increasingly alienated in turn. In the securitised era of the 'war on terror', the Somali Muslim and the refugee become perceived ever more as a threat, while economic development linked to Somalis becomes seen as ever more dubious. In this regard, understanding how the Kenyan state interacts with Eastleigh requires understanding of a broader history of perceptions of and policy towards Somalis in Kenya and the north of the country in general.

'Alien' has long been a term applied to Somalis in Kenya, used in colonial times to refer to Isaaq and Harti Somalis settled in the country by the British. They were regarded as trouble-makers by some in the British administration, including Gerald Reece, who saw the 'Alien Somali' of Isiolo as constantly fomenting trouble.[26] The history of arbitrary border setting, as well as colonial neglect, isolation and militarisation of the northern region of Kenya—where most Kenyan Somalis live—has left its mark on perceptions of Somalis.[27] But it was the era around independence that set in train the notion of them all as an 'alien' presence in their own country of citizenship, and places where they live—northern Kenya and locations such as Eastleigh—as also being somehow alien.

Before independence in 1963 many Somalis in north-eastern Kenya wanted the region to join the Somali Republic, a desire expressed in a referendum carried out by the British. This wish was thwarted as the region remained part of newly independent Kenya. Anger at this among Somalis led to a campaign by the Northern Province People's Progressive Party to force secession, a campaign met with great repression by the Kenyan state, which labelled the secessionists as 'Shifta', a pejorative Ethiopian term for a 'bandit' designed to delegitimise the movement. This conflict became known as the Shifta War.[28] While the war officially ended in 1967, a militarised policy in the region remained dominant, as did suspicion that Somalis there maintained their wish to secede.

In consequence, the area has long suffered from policies restricting movement, as well as 'collective punishments' in response to incidents of insecurity. The most notorious—though tragically not unique—instance is the Wagalla Massacre carried out against Degodia Somalis in Wajir in 1984; they were treated as villains in an effort to disarm clans in the region after various security scares.[29] Five thousand Degodia men were taken to Wagalla airstrip for interrogation, and beaten and tortured over several days, leaving hundreds—some reckon thousands—dead.[30] Wagalla and other wrongs of the era were the subject of an investigation by Kenya's Truth, Justice and Reconciliation Commission charged with uncovering human rights abuses in Kenyan history. Its report was published in 2013,[31] prompting a pledge by the Wajir County Governor to sue the state for compensation for victims of the Wagalla massacre.[32] A feeling that little headway has been made in redressing these wrongs lingers.

The massacre occurred in an era where there were increasing concerns in the Moi government over the porosity of the Kenya–Somali border as Somali banditry spilled over into Kenya, while Moi himself was trying to impose his authority after the 1982 coup attempt.[33] This tense atmosphere was heightened further by the perceived clannism of Moi's trusty Somali allies, the brothers Major General Mahmoud Mohamed and Minister of State Maalim Mohamed. While their power shows that some Kenyan Somalis have long been part of the Kenyan political elite, Moi was able to use the tactic of 'divide and rule' in the north through their influence.[34] Wagalla is a key moment in time for Kenyan Somalis, and a recent Al Jazeera documentary entitled *Not Yet Kenyan* builds a wider story of Somali and northern Kenyan political and economic marginalisation around Wagalla.[35] *Not Yet Kenyan* has now become a hashtag slogan used by Somalis and other northern Kenyans to raise awareness of their marginality.

Such northern troubles were to have ramifications for Somalis throughout Kenya. This was most apparent in the late 1980s. By then, Somalis had become scapegoats for increasing insecurity and poaching in the country, highlighted dramatically by the death of George Adamson, killed by poachers in Kora National Reserve in 1989. Identity checks and surveillance were increased wherever there were Somalis, including in Eastleigh. What Lochery describes is all too familiar from more recent targeting of the neighbourhood by the security apparatus:

> In one raid in May 1989, police in Nairobi raided homes, businesses, hotels, restaurants, and *matatus* in Eastleigh and Pangani, checking for identity papers. Police surrounded a mosque in Eastleigh, arrested worshippers, and confiscated identity cards. Somali women married to Kenyan men were detained until a valid marriage certificate could be produced, a document many had never obtained. About 800 people subsequently appeared in court charged with holding forged or defaced identity cards, being in the country illegally, or disturbing the peace.[36]

This targeting evolved into the notorious screening exercise of 1989, whereby Somalis were forced to prove their Kenyan citizenship via a certificate verifying that their indigeneity to Kenya had been vouched for and confirmed by elders in their home locations. As Lochery describes, 'from the mid-1980s, the increase in Somali migration into Kenya and the spillover of conflict from Somalia had placed severe strain on the mechanisms used to control movement across the border and distinguish citizens from non-citizens'. The screening was designed both to distinguish Somalians from non-Somalis and to render differences between Kenyan Somalis more 'legible' to the state.[37] It further set the tone for how Somalis would be treated in Kenya, and was resisted strongly by many in Kenyan civil society and, of course, by Somalis themselves. Eastleigh was once again in the spotlight in this regard as young Somali men led a protest there, declaring that 'the screening was causing internal strife and fear in their community'.[38] After the protest the screening was intensified, and a camp set up at Embakasi to deal with those chosen for deportation, eerily echoing more recent events.[39] Indeed, the screening of that time set the pattern for how Somalis in Eastleigh have been dealt with ever since.

Urban refugees have long been most vulnerable in this regard. As concerns over the security of Kenya's north and its borders intensified—especially the flow of arms—urban refugees were often rounded up by police sweeps, especially in the latter years of the Moi presidency. Police operations in Eastleigh in 1998 and 1999—that did little to counter the insecurity—were accompanied by mass arrests, and reports of harassment and extortion.[40] Urban refugees and Eastleigh itself were soft targets for a government keen on looking tough and diverting attention from its own deep failings in securing the safety of its citizens and the integrity of its borders. In September 1999 1,000 heavily armed police and immigration officers raided Eastleigh and other estates at night. Urban refugees had also become soft targets for corrupt police keen on earning extra money by extorting cash from Somali refugees, exploiting their ambiguous legal status. A pattern of arresting refugees, detaining them at Pangani police station, then releasing them when relatives came to pay up became almost institutionalised. This continued throughout the 2000s.

However, the Kibaki era did bring some hope of a change in approach to urban refugees. After Kibaki came to power in 2002, strong efforts were put into enacting a refugee bill, which had been stalled throughout the 1990s. This came together in the Refugee Bill of 2006 which, as Betts states:

> formalized many of the policies that had existed since the 1990s, institutionalising much of the encampment policy. However, it was also the first and only refugee legislation in Africa to provide for prima facie recognition under the OAU [Organisation of African Unity] Refugee Convention, creating an extremely inclusive basis on which to recognize all Somalis as though they were refugees. The act also included provisions for the establishment of a Department of Refugee Affairs (DRA), which assumed administrative responsibilities for refugees in Kenya. The DRA has plans to eventually assume responsibility for aspects of refugee policy from UNHCR.[41]

The DRA, Betts suggests, established a 'pro-refugee voice in the government', but 'has been hampered as a result of being housed in the Ministry of State for Immigration and Registration of Persons, which is strongly influenced by concerns over internal security'.[42] While Betts perhaps gives a rather too sunny portrayal of the DRA, here again we should not essentialise what is meant by the 'state', as not all government departments or officials have been unsympathetic to the plight of refugees.

All this linked into a wider policy change by the UNHCR to offer more support to urban refugees. This was officially stated in a 2009 report for the organisation documenting how urban areas were growing in importance for refugees and consequently urging that protection be expanded to such areas.[43] In the early 2000s the UNHCR launched a Nairobi Initiative examining how best to work with refugees in the city, and improving medical and other services for those in need. Interest in the impressive economic endeavour of refugees in Eastleigh and elsewhere played a part in this new thinking. In 2011 when Campbell, Crisp and Kiragu were writing, elements of the Kenyan government were sympathetic to this new approach, and they noted 'a slow change of mindset [in the government] ... towards some form of acceptance of a growing urban refugee population'.[44] At the same time, progress was being made in outreach programmes working with police and others to sensitise them to the plight and rights of refugees. The legal charity Kituo cha Sheria was doing good work in this regard, and in 2011, staff there told me that arbitrary arrests were declining. This was at the same time as government officials were incorporating the estate into Vision 2030: an optimistic time indeed. Sadly, this was not to last: as Somalis and Eastleigh itself have become ever more the target of Kenya's 'war on terror', refugee policy in particular becoming ever more securitised as a result.[45]

Eastleigh and Kenya's War on Terror

While most attacks labelled as 'terrorist' in Kenya have occurred since 2010, the country has a longer history of being targeted by extremist groups—the Nairobi US embassy bombing of 1998 and the 2002 bombing of an Israeli-owned hotel in Mombasa being the most egregious. However, Kenya has become more vulnerable to attack since the coming to prominence of Al-Shabaab in Somalia following the collapse of the UIC in 2006. Kenya became alarmed in the late 2000s as there was much fear of Kenyan youth being recruited to fight for Al-Shabaab against the TFG. Recruiting disenfranchised youth in Kenya has apparently proven straightforward for Al-Shabaab, while radicalisation of wealthier young people has also occurred—witness the case of Abdirahim Abdullahi, the law-student son of a government official who played a key role in the 2015 attack on Garissa University.

Eastleigh has long been seen as a hub for such recruitment, especially through the Abubakar Mosque on Sixth Street, whose clerics had some initial sympathy with the 'Al-Shabaab-supported implementation of the Sharia'.[46] Such clerics—including the influential

Sheikh Mohamed Umal, a man much respected in the Eastleigh business community—soon rejected Al-Shabaab, and have preached against them in recent years. While Al-Shabaab attempted to fundraise and recruit in Kenya, there were also attempts to persuade young refugees to fight for the TFG in Dadaab and elsewhere, apparently supported by the Kenyan government.[47]

The real game changer would come in October 2011, however. Following further incidents—including an attack on a British couple (the husband was murdered and the wife kidnapped) on Kiwaiyu island near Lamu—and with talk of a Kenyan desire to establish a buffer zone in Jubaland in southern Somalia to prevent more such attacks, the KDF launched an incursion into Somalia: Operation Linda Nchi ('Protect the Nation'). Exactly why this was launched is still not clear. It appears that the incursion had been planned for some time, and the return of the hundreds of thousands of refugees in Kenya was probably part of the reasoning, especially after their numbers had swelled even more in 2011 after a fierce drought in Al-Shabaab territory caused more Somalis to flee.[48] The plans for developing infrastructure in northern Kenya as part of the multi-billion-dollar LAPSSET corridor project is also a major factor,[49] Kenya needing a more secure border to ensure the security of this project and encourage investment.[50]

Right from the start, Kenyan politicians linked 'Linda Nchi' to Eastleigh in no uncertain terms, perhaps unsurprisingly given allegations that it was a hub of Al-Shabaab activities. As the KDF began its operations in Somalia, the Assistant Minister of Internal Security, Orwa Ojode, promised that Nairobi itself would see the 'mother of all operations' against Al-Shabaab: he described Al-Shabaab 'as like a big animal with the tail in Somalia and the head of the animal is here in Eastleigh'.[51] This instantly raised fear among Kenyan Somali MPs that Kenyan Somalis were to be harassed yet again in the name of security.

While Al-Shabaab certainly has some connections with the estate, the great majority of Eastleigh's population are vehemently opposed to the group and the attacks it carries out, and fear the malign influence of radicalisation. Many in the estate came to Kenya precisely to flee the group, while during my time there was much youth activity in opposition to it, including a march against it in early October 2011, after a bomb attack in Mogadishu killed many students who had been queuing near the

Ministry of Education while waiting to hear about the awarding of scholarships to Turkey. During the protest march, Eastleigh youth described Al-Shabaab as an enemy of youth and students. Indeed, Somalis remain its main victims, as continuing attacks within Somalia attest.

However, Eastleigh was now portrayed as a battlefield in the war on terror within Kenya's own borders, and the Kenyan security forces began yet another sweep of the neighbourhood to root out 'aliens' without valid documents in Nairobi: while, as we have seen, police sweeps for 'illegal' residents have been common in the estate since the 1980s, now every 'illegal alien' is a suspected terrorist. Refugees—long scapegoated for insecurity threats—were elevated to key players in Kenya's 'war on terror', and Eastleigh and northern Kenya viewed as key battlefields.

This portrayal of Eastleigh as the centre of Kenya's war on terror would become worryingly accurate in the years to come—not as a centre of terrorist planning or financing, but as a target itself. As 'Linda Nchi' was claiming some successes in conventional warfare in Somalia—and would in 2012 take the key port of Kismayu, long a major source of Al-Shabaab funding—there were hopes that the capacity of Al-Shabaab to threaten Kenya would be diminished.[52] However, numerous attacks occurred that made Eastleigh in particular a very tense place.

In 2011 and early 2012 there were a number of fatal grenade attacks—targeting bus stations, churches and bars in particular—in central Nairobi, Mombasa, Garissa and Dadaab, all blamed on Al-Shabaab. Then in August the first attack on Eastleigh occurred when an explosion was detonated in the vicinity of the airbase.[53] Its reputation as a base for Al-Shabaab operatives was consolidated by the discovery of a cache of weapons and grenades in a residential property in the estate and the arrest of two Somalis for their possession.[54] Late 2012 saw more attacks on Eastleigh itself. A bomb attack on a matatu running down Second Avenue led to seven deaths and precipitated a riot, when youth from Mathare came to fight youth from Eastleigh, the former accusing the latter of sheltering terrorists.[55] Section I near Juja Road became the main battleground. In early December there was another bomb explosion in the same area, killing one person and injuring several others, while two days later another explosion at the Hidaya Mosque on Wood Street killed five and injured many, including Yusuf

Hassan, the area MP. On 19 December another attack targeted the Al-Amin Mosque towards the Juja Road side of the estate, injuring two more people.[56]

Why Eastleigh was being targeted in this way is still unclear, as the perpetrators were never apprehended. While some claim that Eastleigh was previously immune to attacks by Al-Shabaab, due to the presence of Somalis and as somewhere useful to the organisation, it was perhaps a relatively easy target for the militants, and a place where many non-Somalis live (the matatu targeted in November was mainly occupied by non-Somalis). Also, targeting the area MP might have seemed suitable retaliation for the support a number of Kenyan Somali politicians had given to Operation Linda Nchi. However, to some Eastleigh residents, Al-Shabaab targeting the estate made little sense, and given that Kenya was preparing for a general election in March 2013, some felt that local politics were behind the attacks, especially that which targeted Hassan (who thankfully survived and retained his Kamukunji seat at the 2013 election). Once more the estate and its Somali residents were subject to arrest, though little solid evidence seems to have been discovered by the Kenyan intelligence services.

All this insecurity—and failures to apprehend any suspects—led once more to the heightening of suspicion against all Somalis, especially refugees. The proposed solution was brutally simple in theory but nigh on impossible to implement in practice: send all urban refugees back to the camps. This came in a press release from the Department of Refugee Affairs, showing how hopes of putting into action the 2009 UNHCR approach to urban refugees in Kenya were dwindling:

DEPARTMENT OF REFUGEE AFFAIRS PRESS RELEASE

The Government of Kenya has decided to stop reception, registration and close down all registration centres in urban areas with immediate effect. All asylum seekers/refugees will be hosted at the refugee camps. All asylum seekers and refugees from Somalia should report to Dadaab refugee camps while asylum seekers from other countries should report to Kakuma refugee camp. UNHCR and other partners serving refugees are asked to stop providing direct services to asylum seekers and refugees in urban areas and transfer the same services to the refugee camps.

Signed
Ag. COMMISSIONER FOR REFUGEE AFFAIRS

More worryingly, government correspondence related to the case spoke of how plans were being made for the removals, involving 'rounding [up] the refugees and transporting them to Thika Municipal Stadium'; later this would be followed by closing the camps and returning refugees to their home countries. While Mogadishu was becoming more stable, this proposed measure—going against national and international law against *refoulement*—hardly took into account the continuing instability and conflict in much of Somalia. The directive was met with condemnation within Kenya and beyond. For many refugees who had built up businesses and lives in Eastleigh and other urban areas of Kenya, this represented a potentially devastating blow. The conflation of refugees and terrorism suspects spoke volumes of the inability of the Kenyan security services to get a real grip on the situation.

Kenyan civil society and its judicial system came to the rescue, as Kituo cha Sheria and various individuals petitioned the High Court of Kenya to quash the directive. Victory was decisive as the judge averred that the directive 'threatens the rights and fundamental freedoms of the petitioners and other refugees residing in urban areas and is a violation of the freedom of movement under Article 39, right to dignity under Article 28 and the right to fair and administrative action under Article 47(1) and violates the State's responsibility towards persons in vulnerable situations contrary to Article 21(3)'.[57] However, the insecurity continued, and the directive would be revisited.

The Westgate Attack and its Aftermath

Election day 2013—when attacks by Al-Shabaab were feared—went relatively peacefully, although the next day another explosion occurred on the Juja Road side of the estate. Afterwards, the estate remained calm for the following few months—though more attacks took place elsewhere in Kenya: 9 June saw coordinated grenade attacks on Eastleigh and Mombasa.[58] National and international media interest in such attacks dipped in the following months, until reawakened by a spectacular attack on 21 September 2013 on a very different mall to those of Eastleigh: the Westgate.

While Eastleigh and its malls and commodities demonstrate the potency of 'low-end globalisation' to transform cities and society,

Westgate was a glitzy example of the wealth on the other side of Nairobi society and the continued potency of 'high-end globalisation'. Rather than the small, cheap retail spaces of Eastleigh, it was filled with large shops, many selling designer goods at expensive prices, and restaurants attracting Nairobi's middle class, expatriates and many Kenyan Asians. Israeli owned, frequented by tourists and yet a relatively easy target given its limited security, it proved a highly symbolic target for the four Al-Shabaab operatives who stormed it that day in September, killing sixty-seven and wounding many more.

As the world watched the events unfold live, Eastleigh rapidly came into focus, especially as word spread that the perpetrators of the attack had spent time there. Fear that resentment against Somalis in wider Kenyan society—a palpable force since the riots of November 2012— would lead in the wake of the Westgate atrocity to more attacks or repressive policies in Eastleigh led members of the Eastleigh Business Association to take pre-emptive measures: they were vocal in condemnation of the attacks, and conspicuous in bringing water and food to the Westgate to support the security services in their efforts.

As suspicions grew over the ineptness of Kenya's intelligence services in failing to predict the attack, and as Kenya's soldiers fell from being heroes to looters (as revealed by CCTV footage), the government needed to show its strength on all security matters. This was not just related to Al-Shabaab, but also to home-grown radical groups such as Al-Hijra, a group affiliated to Al-Shabaab, associated with the Kenyan coast, but also operating in Majengo and Pumwani in Nairobi. Further attacks had also taken place since Westgate, including one in Likoni on 23 March. In this atmosphere, the Interior Cabinet Secretary Ole Lenku reprised the refugee directive, going against the ruling of 2013 and again ordering refugees to return to the camps.[59] Once more the ultimate plan seemed to be the return of Somalian refugees to Somalia.

In response to such measures and the ethnic profiling of Somalis in the 'war on terror', Eastleigh community leaders and Somali politicians including Yusuf Hassan, Aden Duale and Yusuf Haji—all allied to Kenyatta and Ruto through the Jubilee Alliance—met with Kenyatta at State House to discuss how Somalis in Eastleigh and elsewhere could assist the government and security forces to root out the terrorists. This meeting was greeted with some optimism that more measured and effective responses to the security situation might be taken.

Usalama Watch

However, further attacks killed more people in Eastleigh only two days later, prompting the government to launch the now infamous Operation Usalama Watch ('Peace Watch') in an attempt to apply the refugee directive with force. While Usalama Watch is the most commonly used name in the media for the operation (renamed 'Usama Watch' by some Somalis) alarmingly its Eastleigh component was officially labelled 'Operation Sanitization of Eastleigh'.[60]

Once more, refugee status was equated with the potential to terrorise—victims becoming security threats, in the words of Mogire[61]—and the government sought to push through a similar directive to that of 2012 as part of the operation. This time civil society organisations such as Kituo cha Sheria would be unable to shut the directive down through the High Court—the UNHCR, who fund their urban refugee programme, have been silent on the operation—and shocking scenes of truck-loads of Somalis, Ethiopians and others without Kenyan identity documents or valid visas would be broadcast throughout the world. Eastleigh was again the scene of international media attention, as it was the first target of the operation that commenced on 2 April 2014.

In an echo of the past, where sports stadia have been used, those arrested were taken to Kasarani Stadium. Police and security forces (including the KDF and General Service Unit), having encircled the estate with roadblocks, would sweep from apartment block to apartment block in search of 'aliens'. Elias and Mohaa were both visited: their experience was relatively hassle-free. As bona fide Kenyans—with fluent Kiswahili and the correct identity documents—they were soon left alone by their visitors. For those without such identity documents, treatment was very different. Some would suffer beatings and various indignities, while many would end up at the stadium for 'processing'. Some could rely on the corruptibility of officers to prevent their arrest or secure their release; those least able to do this faced longer stays at Kasarani, where conditions would become unbearable despite attempts by the government to manage media portrayals of the detention camp. Social media overwhelmed government spin, however, the hashtag *#kasaraniconcentrationcamp* just one to do the rounds.

Ole Lenku spoke of 4,000 arrests as the operation spread from Eastleigh to estates such as South C with large Somali populations, as well as Mombasa and other Kenyan towns and cities. Kenyan Somali political voices—and the UNHCR, reliant on the goodwill of the Kenyan government for its continued operations in the country—were soon muted, despite initial protests by Aden Duale, while the Somali ambassador to Nairobi lent support to the operation, which also involved the deportation of several plane-loads of Somalis to Mogadishu. The refugee camps—already under-resourced—were further overstretched, now holding people who had previously been self-sustaining in towns and cities and who had been contributing to the Kenyan economy.

It seemed that the Kenyan legal system might yet again come to the rescue of urban refugees and foil the directive. A group of ten Somali refugees—led by a trader from Eastleigh—petitioned the High Court, arguing the directive went against the precedent of the earlier 2013 ruling in the case brought by Kituo cha Sheria and others.[62] Initially it seemed that the court would stymie the directive, but in late June the judge upheld it, to the delight of Ole Lenku, who continued to press for the eventual closure of the camps, equating hosting refugees—and the camps in particular—to higher risks of terrorist attacks. Thus, being a refugee anywhere beyond the camps—without a valid travel pass—was illegal, while being a refugee in a camp also made one a dangerous alien in the eyes of the state.

The security situation did not improve either. Indeed, brazen and bloodthirsty attacks continued: attacks on Mpeketoni and its environs near the coastal town of Lamu cost over sixty lives in June 2014, and two attacks around Mandera in December that same year killed over seventy. The use of beheading in the latter attacks demonstrated the increasing influence of Syria's self-declared Islamic State on Al-Shabaab's modus operandi. This mounting death toll prompted the hurried promulgation of a new security bill to expand the powers of security agencies and the president, cap the number of refugees in the country, and generally erode human rights as well as the freedom of the media to criticise security measures.[63] This was Kenya's 'Patriot Act', and was signed into law by Uhuru Kenyatta despite a fraught parliamentary session where opposition politicians claimed that Kenya was becoming a police state and reverting to the era of Moi.[64] Tensions were so high that a physical fight broke out among MPs.

Al-Shabaab was far from finished. Garissa University was the next target, resulting in the merciless murder of 147 students in April 2015. Once more this sparked the usual government response of making arrests in Eastleigh and threatening to deport Somali refugees. Deputy President Ruto demanded that the UNHCR close the refugee camps and repatriate their hundreds of thousands of Somali inhabitants to Somalia, a move that would blatantly violate the principle of non-*refoulement*. The UNHCR was given the impossibly tiny timescale of three months to carry out this Herculean task.[65]

A new policy of naming eighty-six individuals and organisations suspected of links to terrorism—including Muslim human rights organisations, prominent clerics (including Sheikh Umal) and hawala companies such as Kaah and Dahabshiil—seemed a diversionary tactic. Their accounts were frozen, meaning that companies such as Dahabshiil—which have tightened their operations thoroughly enough over the years to allow them to operate in jurisdictions like the USA—could not operate, reducing access to the remittances that are the lifeline of so many. A further show of strength came with the announcement of the bombing by the Kenyan air force of Al-Shabaab 'bases' inside Somalia in the wake of the Garissa attack.

While the atrocities of Westgate, Mpeketoni and Garissa—not to mention the many smaller-scale attacks in Eastleigh itself—clearly demand action, it is hard to see how draconian security measures that seem to victimise particular communities could work in the long term, hindering intelligence work by creating much resentment among Somalis and other targeted groups. To be effective, operations such as Usalama Watch require security services to act with the utmost profes-sionalism, and the widely acknowledged corruption endemic in the Kenyan security services—seemingly institutionalised in their dealings with Somalis—makes it difficult to see any gains being made aside from to the wallets of these operatives. Indeed, Kenya's recently estab-lished Independent Policing Oversight Authority (IPOA), a civil-soci-ety institution that aims to build trust in the police service by making it more accountable, has been investigating the alleged abuses and cor-ruption frequently reported during Usalama Watch: it has commented strongly on how a major effect has been to erode trust yet further between Eastleigh residents and state security services, causing many to flee at the sight of police or their vehicles: 'This development is counterproductive to the spirit of community policing and may erode gains made in the public–police partnership in the fight against crime.'[66] The operation also violated the time limit of twenty-four hours before arraignment in court guaranteed by the constitution. The IPOA pulled no punches in its report, demonstrating its independence. While it recognised the need for enhanced security, given recent attacks, it concluded: 'In the end, the Operation was not conducted in compliance with the law, respect for the Rule of Law, democracy, human rights and fundamental freedoms.'[67]

For both current and earlier Kenyan governments, Eastleigh and Somali refugees have long had political value as easy targets for state theatrics, designed to show strength in the face of continuing insecurity and accusations of incompetence. Of course, the familiar state response instead shows weakness: the operation has been a blunt instrument that cannot hide the deficiencies in its security services. Eastleigh and the Somali population of Kenya could have far greater political value in curbing radicalisation if engaged, precisely because they themselves are victims of Al-Shabaab. Many Somalis courageously speak, write and sing against the group, including Waayaha Cusub, a band formed in Eastleigh by Somali refugees, and Eastleighwood, which has formed an anti-radicalisation campaign despite some hostility and threats from certain elements in the estate.[68] Such Somali forces for peace are foundations upon which a safer Kenya for all could be built.

Instead, the government is attempting to bolster security by building a wall along the Somali border, taking a leaf out of the Israeli school of anti-terrorism.[69] As it was revealed that all four attackers in the Garissa University tragedy were Kenyan—and not just ethnically Somali either—expelling refugees to a still highly unstable Somalia and conducting the knee-jerk sweeps of Eastleigh only helps Al-Shabaab, which uses Kenya's fraught history in places such as the north and Eastleigh for its propaganda. Such propaganda has become more slick, including a video of the Mpeketoni attack that shared much of the professional quality of those grim productions by Islamic State. Footage of round-ups and caged Somalis at Kasarani only help the militants' cause. While radicalisation is a global issue, affecting the UK and USA as well as Syria, Somalia and Nigeria, the Kenyan faces of the killers—

one revealed to be a law student and the son of a government official—suggest that many factors underpinning insecurity in Kenya lie on its side of the wall and cannot be simply fenced out.

Fear and Flight

While the government claims that Somalis were not being ethnically profiled, the way security operations are handled and the history of treating Kenya's Somalis as potentially dangerous aliens—*shifta* in an earlier era, *terrorists* today—means that few are likely to trust the government in this regard. Mistrust is on the rise. Recently a Boran friend of mine—Boran are sometimes mistaken for Somalis by wider Kenyan society—was travelling on a matatu in Nairobi and engaged in the following interaction with a woman passenger:

> Woman passenger: 'You look Somali.'
> Boran passenger: 'I could be …'
> WP: 'That's a big problem …'
> BP: 'What is??'

(Awkward silence)

Somalis themselves are not immune to suspecting those of their own ethnicity. A Kenyan Somali told me how he found himself suspicious of other Somalis on matatus, wondering what might be in their bags, and what might be their intention; however, he also feels himself an object of suspicion when he gets on board, and can sense that his presence makes people tense. In earlier times I had often been struck by how stoical the likes of Mohaa and Elias seemed despite all the apparent risks in the estate of grenade attacks, risks which seemed greater under the media spotlight: the momentum of business and life in Eastleigh kept them too busy to worry too much. Such very Kenyan 'Kenyan Somalis' were also too sure of their rights as citizens—and too conspicuously Kenyan—to fear encounters with the police. However, the scale of Usalama Watch and the arrests, and the frequency of recent attacks on the estate, meant that a state of fear had become much more common for all residents of Eastleigh, Kenyan or not.

For refugees, remaining in urban areas such as Eastleigh in Kenya clearly leaves them more vulnerable than ever. Usalama Watch itself wound down—and it would be hard to maintain its intensity given the resources it must consume—and only a small proportion of the earlier estimate of over 50,000 urban refugees have been returned to the camps. The UNHCR put the number of refugees relocated by the DRA since the start of the operation at 3,771 in mid-July 2014.[70] Many suspect Usalama Watch of being an attempt by the security apparatus in Kenya to look tough through such theatrics of violence rather than a sincere push for refugee repatriation. For Ole Lenku the operation was even unsuccessful in this regard, failing to regain him an air of competence, and losing him his job.[71]

However, the operation and its aftermath prompted many Somalians to consider their futures in Kenya, with Kampala and its more tolerant policies towards refugees—enshrined in law by a progressive Ugandan refugee act made law in 2008—proving a key draw.[72] The area of Kisenyi within Kampala in particular has become a budding 'Little Little Mogadishu'. Back in Eastleigh, the recent insecurity, the ongoing securitisation of refugees and the departure of many Somalis to the camps or elsewhere has not just had social but also economic implications. Media reports painted a bleak picture of decline. It is already reported that millions of shillings have been taken out of the estate by Somalis, to be moved to places such as Kampala. Usalama Watch and the removal of Somalis to camps also disrupted refugee-run businesses in Garissa, Nakuru and elsewhere, while traders in the camps themselves can no longer travel as easily to resupply in Nairobi. Furthermore, demand for apartments reportedly plummeted, causing a crash in rents; though as friends there have pointed out, it is mostly the area around the First Avenue/Jam Street junction—the epicentre of Eastleigh commerce—that has suffered in this regard. Custom in the estate was also said to have declined. Many Kenyans have always feared venturing into Eastleigh, especially the middle classes, happy to pay extra for the same goods from shops elsewhere in the city centre. Traders reported after Usalama Watch that business was down considerably in Eastleigh as more shoppers deserted the estate. Mohaa reckoned in August 2014 that business was around 60 per cent of normal capacity: *yaum basal*.

However, accounts of imminent collapse in the Eastleigh economy were overblown, especially accounts of empty shops. In truth, a saturation of retail space in the estate means that for some time there have been empty shops, especially in less desirable sections of malls. Also, business picked up again later in 2014. By December, Mohaa and his fellows were back to *yaum asal*, and the streets were heaving with hawkers and shoppers upon my visit that month, as Christmas loomed. Furthermore, as with much of the Eastleigh economy, the wealthier one is, the more insulation one has from these ups and downs. Informants reported that while smaller shopkeepers had suffered from the screening operation, for the wealthy it was business as usual. This was most clearly demonstrated through the under-construction Comesa Mall, the latest Eastleigh shopping mall being built by a group of elite Somali investors (see chapter 2): one much more Westgate-like, with larger shops and Kenyan chains, as well as more typical Eastleigh shops (all of which, apparently, have already been sold). At the lower end too more and more shops were opening. Talk of an exodus of Somalians appeared overblown.

What the operation has done, however, is highlight to many Somalis—even to some of those born and bred Kenyan—how precarious a 'home' Kenya can be, even as a surrogate one while their own state is struggling to rise from the ashes of two decades of civil war. In the wider Somali diaspora, Kenya has drawn much ire for its recourse to the blunt security measures of Usalama Watch. The sight of Somalis locked up at Kasarani Stadium in particular drew much media coverage on Somali cable TV channels, and much disgust. Such sentiments towards the Kenyan state are not new. While many Somalians in Kenya and abroad appreciate the difficulties faced by Kenya in coping with such a vast number of refugees—and many are grateful that Kenya offered them sanctuary—there has always been concern over police corruption and abuse. There have also long been voices doubting the wisdom of Somalis investing in a country not their own. The Somali-language entry of Wikipedia in 2011 suggested that 'people who visit Eastleigh are surprised at the poor thinking of the business people who are building in a country that is not theirs, from which they can be quickly chased away'.[73]

Given the current hopes for the stabilisation of Mogadishu, and the moral pressure many in the diaspora feel to rebuild 'home', combined with the perceived hostility of the Kenyan government to Somalis and their investment, it is no wonder that many Somalis also feel Eastleigh to be displaced development: development in a foreign land that should be redirected back to the real Mogadishu.

Recalibrating the Relationship

While this tragic recent period of deadly violence, suspicion and repression has been unfolding and casting a grave shadow not only upon Eastleigh but Kenya more broadly, Eastleigh finally saw the fulfilment of KURA's promise to renovate its main roads. First Avenue and Second Avenue now no longer resemble rivers or bomb craters. This development has come at a considerable cost to some—including those whose kiosks and homes built on the road reserve were torn down during the work, apparently with little warning,[74] leaving them displaced *by* development[75]—and many lament the disruption the roadworks caused. However, most Eastleigh residents and businesspeople have welcomed this example of more positive state engagement.

Given recent insecurity and hardening of mutual suspicion, a freshly laid road may seem somewhat trivial. However, it is a welcome echo of the more optimistic times of 2011 when Eastleigh was commonly spoken of as a part of Kenya's development masterplan of

Plate 26: First Avenue in September 2014

Vision 2030, and where there was hope that statehood would be realised through actually providing infrastructural improvements and meaningful security, rather than through tragically theatrical swoops and round-ups. Its economy, built out of the ashes of the collapse of the Somali state, has endured much neglect and outright hostility over the years from the Kenyan equivalent: the Eastleigh story is one of a dialectic between state absence and state presence. Although Eastleigh's booming commerce has often benefited from circumventing the state, many Eastleigh businesspeople and residents have long demanded benign government attention that can bring security and public amenities, and could justify the revenue derived from their commerce. Rather than police swoops on refugees, Eastleigh residents and businesspeople want police action against gangs such as the Superpowers that cause much insecurity in the estate. Those lower down the social ladder, including the Eastleigh hawkers, now appealing to the Governor of Nairobi over land-grabbing in the area that once formed the Eastleigh Market,[76] would be very appreciative of more state protection of public assets too. In these regards, there are murmurs of better things to come. March 2015 saw the announcement that Nairobi County Government was to construct a hawkers' market for the estate (hawkers have been establishing stalls in the newly built road due to lack of space, thus adding to congestion) as well as an upgraded police station. In this, the Eastleigh Business Association was to donate 15 million Kenyan shillings for police vehicles.[77] The hope clearly is that a community police force—one close to the local population—will bring a more benevolent form of state presence.

As a member of the Eastleigh Business Association told me, Eastleigh is like a *shamba* ('farm' in Kiswahili), and needs the 'fertiliser' of good governance to make it grow stronger. Better governance requires a recalibration of the relationship of state to Eastleigh, and especially to the people within it whose innovation and drive pioneered an economy that has not just benefited Somali refugees but thousands of Kenyans too. Sadly, the securitised prism through which some in the Kenyan government (and their counterparts in the US and UK governments) see Eastleigh and its residents—especially its Somalians—and the suspicion many feel towards the state and its development means that this recalibration is a long-term vision.

Of course, this recalibration would also require recalibration of a deeper sort that could bring improved governance in Nairobi and Kenya more broadly, as highlighted by a recent campaign to pressure Governor Kidero into tackling garbage currently piling up in Eastleigh. The campaign spread to encompass the whole city as its instigators realised that this was a problem affecting the whole city.[78] Pictures of mounds of detritus trended on Twitter as part of this campaign in December 2015, suggesting in vivid material form that Eastleigh is not alone in suffering from state neglect. As in several other ways, this estate, so often portrayed as a place of exception, in fact has much in common with other parts of contemporary Nairobi.

CONCLUSION

EASTLEIGH AND CITIES YET TO COME

No-one knows about tomorrow. Let it come.

Mohaa, April 2015.

Eastleigh can seem a peculiar place, full of apparent contradiction: a place deeply associated with refugees and social marginality, yet also a thriving and dynamic hub of trade; a place long associated with a decayed public infrastructure, yet a place of great private wealth. Such contradictions can make an enigma out of Eastleigh, an enigma enhanced by the sheer rapidity with which this former residential estate sprouted shopping malls and entered a global geography of commerce. Yet with attention to social and economic processes of various spatial and temporal dimensions, the story of this estate becomes understandable; all the more so as these processes are in the main far from unique to Eastleigh, but instead familiar in a world continually being transformed through the movement of people, goods and capital.

As we have discussed, in large part this is a story of a commercial hub catalysed by the global shockwaves of the collapse of the Somali state and its social and economic repercussions. In this regard, we explored how in the wake of Somalia's civil war Somali networks expanded to form a vast, socially tight diaspora that could mobilise capital and connections to some of the world's most significant trade hubs. These networks coalesced in Eastleigh as thousands of refugees fleeing the war moved to the estate. As networks established themselves, refugees began making a living from the cheap Dubai goods they brought, and as their trade became successful, so their lodgings were turned into shopping malls. Growth continued apace, as the Garissa Lodge model was copied while trade networks expanded ever further into the booming manufacturing districts of the East: soon the Eastleigh landscape was well and truly 'malled'.

Indeed, the current physical, cultural and demographic complexion of the estate owes much to the displacement wrought by the collapse of the Somali state. It is a dramatic example of a 'displacement economy' where people have grasped the opportunities derived from state collapse, civil war and forced migration with great skill and inda adheeg (audacity). It demonstrates strongly the economic power of refugees and the productive livelihoods they can generate, not just for themselves but for their host communities too: with opportunities to work and trade, refugees can become positive assets, not the 'burden' they are commonly portrayed to be. Eastleigh also links to wider stories of the Somali diaspora in the twenty-first century, as Somalis transform other urban spaces throughout the world through their economic activity, while also contributing much to the development in their home regions through remittances and business investment. Furthermore, it links to the urban effects of transnational migration more broadly, as witness developments throughout the world from cities such as Touba in Senegal, transformed through the migration of Mourides, to the super-diverse boroughs of London and New York. It is urban environments such as Eastleigh where such migration and its social and economic effects are most conspicuous. As discussed in the introduction, the city and neighbourhoods such as Eastleigh are key analytical scales for the study of migration.

But, as we have also explored, this tale of displacement and transnational trade and sociality is only part of the story. Also hugely significant for the growth of Eastleigh are the much more local and national processes and elements that make Eastleigh such fertile ground for these developing networks. Somali diasporic networks would not have coalesced in the estate in the first place had it not been for the long history of settlement there by earlier Somali migrants from Somaliland and Somali parts of Kenya, while its growth also owes much to the in-migration of other Kenyans, including Kikuyu, Kamba and Meru, many attracted to its booming economy and keen to fulfil their own 'Eastleigh dream'. Eastleigh's story of migration is not simply one of refugee inflows from Somalia and Ethiopia. Furthermore, it was built on capital from expanding demand for the Kenyan khat crop (demand also spurred by the growth of the Somali diaspora), while the Kenyan institution of goodwill allowed diaspora capital to be channelled into the small shops that became its signature retail form. Eastleigh has also become deeply integrated into Kenya's formal economy, especially its banking industry, and the Kenyan state has provided a bureaucratic apparatus malleable for those with means, and an environment conducive to business. Somali importers and freight companies have leveraged Kenyan trade policies to formalise the import of many of the goods flowing along their networks.

These goods themselves have been critical, and link the estate to a much wider story of global trade in which cheap products of such manufacturing hubs as Guangzhou in China are transforming consumption patterns, especially in the Global South, and transforming urban landscapes in the process as markets and malls spring up as hubs for their flow. These are the goods of 'low-end globalisation'. Eastleigh would be a very different place were it not for the Kenyan demand for these goods. The Eastleigh story is only one of many in this regard, witness other contemporary stories of trade and transformation occurring from Hong Kong to Lagos to London as people attempt to gain comparative advantage in a world of intensified interconnections. Eastleigh also shows clearly how economies built on the 'low end'—in terms of goods sold; the buildings constructed for their sale; and business practices—can evolve to something more 'high end', as witness Eastleigh's new Comesa Mall and its burgeoning financial sector. Marginal gains on the sale of millions of cheap imports can add up into something of immense value, and lead to further transformation.

As we have seen, all this urban transformation has hardly been greeted with unalloyed enthusiasm in Kenya. Indeed, while Eastleigh owes much to the willingness of those within its economy to trust each other with goods and capital, it is striking how much distrust and suspicion its economic growth has prompted beyond, and even within, its confines. Of course, the type of economic development witnessed in the estate is scarcely perfect, especially with regard to its long-term sustainability, the lack of legal protection for those involved in its economy (especially those not insulated by wealth and power), stark inequalities between those who thrive and those who survive in its economy, the swallowing up of public land, and the general reliance on cheap imported goods instead of local industrial growth. Like Chungking Mansions,[1] it is a place resonant with neoliberalism; despite calls for more state involvement in its economy, most traders there enjoy the advantages of its almost-free trade and embrace its capitalist ethos. It is not an economy that would please the more left-leaning amongst us: it is a place born out of the 'neoliberal' global economy rather than in resistance to it, as Eastleigh's reliance on trade liberalisation policies of the early 1990s suggests. Furthermore, Eastleigh's success on the back of cheap goods speaks to the vast global inequalities of our era, as so many people's taste of global connectedness comes from low-quality products that the wealthy minority would disdain. While I find Eastleigh an exhilarating place and see many positives in its vibrant economy—especially its great emphasis on mutuality and trust as economic ideals that temper its capitalism into a more human economy, the role of women in its rise, and in its creation of innumerable livelihoods both in the estate and beyond—genuine concern over its darker sides might hold others back from seeing it as positive 'development', although the same anxieties hold for Kenya and the Global South's vast informal sector more broadly.

Yet, as argued in this book, it is not such anxieties about Eastleigh's economic form that underlie its treatment as a place of exception. Instead, this is founded upon the perception that its development—as well as the people most associated with it—are displaced. To some, all this development should be taking place in Somalia itself, while those doing the developing should either be warehoused in refugee camps or repatriated to their homelands. In Eastleigh, anxieties are heightened further by the increasing securitisation of refugee policy in Kenya in the wake of fear of Al-Shabaab. In all this Eastleigh links to very familiar themes in debates about migration and Europe's current refugee crisis. In such debates there is awareness of migration's power to effect positive change, as well as perpetual fear that it is a burden and threat to host countries and is making us less secure. As a place formed through migration and reliant on transnational mobility, Eastleigh finds itself caught in a very contemporary global bind.

What's in a Name?

Thus, understanding the change wrought in Eastleigh (and similar commercial hubs throughout the world), and how this change is both embraced and resisted, requires a multi-dimensional approach. Its rise has been remarkable, yet understandable when considered in the context of local, national, regional and global dynamics. However, Eastleigh's development is also testament to the power of a particular place and how it is imagined. While much scholarly attention focuses on the power of transnational networks and diaspora, the importance of particular towns, cities and neighbourhoods—the nodes in these networks—should not be forgotten. Eastleigh is not just any place, but one with its own strong character and an uncanny knack of capturing the imagination.

How Eastleigh itself is imagined and represented—whether by the state, shoppers, refugees, 'diasporas' or the many researchers it has attracted—is of crucial significance in how people interact with it, and in how they imagine its future. Economically, Eastleigh might be similar to other transnational hubs around the world—and even parts of Nairobi city centre dominated by the informal economy—but how it is conceived of as a place of exception and excess makes it appear extraordinary, further generating an impression of somewhere fortunes can be made, and, for those fearful of what it represents, a place where the presence of pirates appears only too credible. The legendary Eastleigh of anything goes and anything sells—a legend this book has attempted to subvert—is certainly a social fact of some importance in the life of the estate. As Myers reflects regarding Mogadishu, 'representations of space have consequences', as the associations of that city with conflict lead it to be conceived of as 'exceptional', with people living outside what the West considers the 'normal social order'. Such representations of spatial exceptionalism can encourage exceptional measures to be taken against people.[2] In the case of Mogadishu, this has entailed various military interventions by the USA and its allies; in the case of Eastleigh, all the numerous round-ups, sweeps and other euphemisms for the harassment of its residents.

In all this, the name 'Little Mogadishu' itself plays a role in how the estate is imagined. The emphasis placed in this book on just how Kenyan much of the estate's population and economy actually is, suggests that a name like 'Little Mogadishu' is in many ways a distortion. It is also quite possibly a dangerous one. Naming urban estates associated with particular groups of migrants by diminutives of names from elsewhere is itself seen by some as an act of symbolic violence, a way of denigrating the minority inhabitants of such enclaves.[3] More particularly in the case of Eastleigh, 'Little Mogadishu' further identifies the estate and its residents with foreignness and alien identities; this is not exactly helpful in the context of the fraught history of Somali identity in Kenya. Furthermore, given how some portray the estate as a place of violence and danger, linking it by name to a city known in recent decades for conflict also does not help in demystifying Eastleigh and its economy. In this regard, this book has performed the uncomfortable feat of picking apart its own title.

Yet in a number of ways the name is appropriate. Eastleigh's commercial revolution was catalysed by the influx of Somalians in the wake of civil war, many with previous trade experience in Mogadishu itself, and it is host to a significant population of people originally from that city or linked to it through family. Furthermore, as a hub for the Somali diaspora, and as a place symbolic of the Somali experience of the last decades, Eastleigh does function economically and socially as a 'Little Mogadishu', subsuming much activity that would previously have been centred on Mogadishu itself. Indeed, the identity of Eastleigh for the Somali diaspora transcends the Kenyan nation-state in which it is physically located. This geographical transcendence is strongly seen in the name *Eastleighwood*, the youth group with whom I spent time. The name not only links to Eastleigh as a physical place where its members are based, but also to the wider experience of Somalis since the collapse of the Somali state two decades ago. Eastleigh grew as Somalia collapsed, and thus symbolises the Somali experience of being a nation diffused throughout the world.

Moreover, 'Little Mogadishu' as a name can be reclaimed as a positive, as Mogadishu itself was for many centuries a highly cosmopolitan port and trading centre, linking inland Somalia with the wider Indian Ocean trade networks and broader global circuits. In this sense,

CONCLUSION

Eastleigh, with its diverse population, and links to vast trade networks, shares much in common with pre-war Mogadishu. Tragically, the actual Mogadishu lost much of this cosmopolitanism with the civil war, as Nuruddin Farah emphasises with his lament for 'Tamarind Market', a cosmopolitan space ransacked in the civil war, and replaced with Bakaara Market, which he sees as a space of clannism rather than cosmopolitanism.[4] Yet Mogadishu's proud history as a peaceful and inclusive place of vibrant commerce remains, offering a vision of what we all hope it is becoming once more. When seen in this light, as a reference to Mogadishu's great commercial past and a hopeful future, 'Little Mogadishu' is a much more appealing name for this Nairobi estate.

Anticipated Futures

What of Eastleigh's own future? Certainly, different visions of what it should become are being promoted at an ambiguous historical juncture. Businesspeople, including the influential Eastleigh Business Association, are busy imagining an ever more formalised future for the estate, where public infrastructure and security are tended to by a more benign state. They want Eastleigh to become a twenty-four-hour economy, in which the upcoming Comesa Mall and its 'high-end' shops might signify the next stage of the Eastleigh story. Meanwhile, some Kenyan politicians are also imagining an ambitious future in their Vision 2030, in which Eastleigh is becoming integrated as a key commercial hub. The place in such a 'gentrified' Eastleigh of the lower strata of traders—especially the hawkers whose presence many in the malls resent for clogging up thoroughfares—would become a pressing issue, as it is in upmarket parts of Nairobi in general. An estate built out of commerce from below should surely not forget its humble roots.

Of course, the turmoil of recent years in the wake of increasing insecurity and securitised policy—acted out most dramatically on the stage provided by Eastleigh—threatens grand future visions. The all-too-familiar police swoops and round-ups of Usalama Watch emphasised to Somalis in Kenya and throughout the diaspora that their presence in Kenya is always likely to be precarious. Some with mobility and mobile capital have looked elsewhere, to other parts of the East Africa, for investment opportunities—the more welcoming embrace of Somalis

(and refugees in general)[5] by Uganda suggesting that Kisenyi's importance as a Little Mogadishu might grow. Somali interests in petroleum,
freight and transport means that they have many opportunities for investment in the East African economy beyond Eastleigh and Kenya.

For those lacking the financial and social capital to leave Kenya, the
estate, despite the security prism through which it is seen and acted
upon by the state, is likely to remain a crucial place both to reside and
gain a living. The threatened closure of refugee camps in Kenya and
plans to repatriate their residents is likely to force dramatic decisions
on those Somalians in the lower levels of the Eastleigh economy.
Whether they tough it out in the estate, despite an ever increasing
precariousness to their situation, decide to be repatriated to Somalia,
or move to yet other pastures new, will depend on a multitude of factors. Key will be the future directions taken by the Kenyan state in its
refugee policy, as well as Kenyan policy and practices towards its
Somali population in general. Much will also depend on the Somalian
state currently on a difficult road to recovery.

While Eastleigh's development has very much been a story linked to
state collapse in Somalia and all its human consequences, hope for the
future of Somalia—vividly illustrated by the debates around the
hashtag *#somaliarising*—may yet encourage some in Eastleigh to contemplate moving back to a home that many miss. The very anticipation
of future security and development—as well as various steps in that
direction—have led some in the wider diaspora to return (albeit with
a foot still in more certain places), both to taste home and to help
rebuild it.[6] Of course, with the protracted nature of the civil war, there
are young Somalians in Eastleigh who feel more attachment to Kenya
than to a country some have never seen, despite how ambivalently
some views their presence. However, there are Somalis in Eastleigh
whose future in Little Mogadishu depends very much on the future of
Big Mogadishu the other side of the border.

Yet whatever happens in Somalia and in other nodes of the Somali
transnational world, it is very unlikely that Eastleigh itself is going to
decline. Eastleigh and the key actors in its economy have become too
powerful for the estate to fade away any time soon, despite the predic-
tions of such a decline in the wake of Usalama Watch. While the lower
rungs of Eastleigh's refugee economy have suffered, those with wealth—

CONCLUSION

Kenyan Somalis and Somalians—continue to prosper, benefiting from strategic links with key figures in Kenyan politics. Somali society has invested much in Eastleigh, and will certainly be loath to give up on it. A commercial hub such as Eastleigh with access to many millions of East African consumers is a prize worth keeping.

Furthermore, the benefits that Eastleigh's growth has brought the Kenyan economy in terms of employment and investment, as well as access to its sought-after global goods, means that many in wider Kenyan society would also not wish them to leave. As the still-busy shops, malls and streets of the estate demonstrate, many Kenyans (and Congolese, Burundis, Tanzanians, Sudanese …) continue to show their support for its economy by voting with their feet.

Finally, what future for Mohaa, our Kenyan Somali guide to the estate whose enterprise and drive is representative of many living the Eastleigh Dream? He himself is reluctant to predict the future. While proactive in business and always trying out new things, his Islam-infused philosophy on life is soaked in fatalism. When I asked about his future he told me, 'No one knows about tomorrow. Let it come…' However, as a man torn between life in Nairobi and its opportunities and his family in Isiolo, it may well be that his long-term future involves a return to northern Kenya, a place itself seen as a hub of development in Kenya's Vision 2030 and hence as a place of anticipated development and investment. Isiolo is billed as the site for a resort city along the lines of South Africa's Sun City. While very much at home within Eastleigh and its economy, Mohaa is a Texas Ranger—the name for an Isioloan derived from its nickname of Texas—and this changing town and its prospects might well draw him back on a more permanent basis. He is also only too aware of the heightened opportunities that can come through transnational mobility, as Eastleigh retailers such as he learn from wealthy importers and wholesalers with expanded horizons encompassing Dubai, China, Europe and elsewhere. He came to Eastleigh seeking, in his words, 'greener pastures', and may leave once more if other more verdant pastures become accessible.

However, while he may one day leave behind his life there, Eastleigh has been the making of Mohaa as a businessman, giving him a true education in entrepreneurship at the sharp end of the global economy. While this book has been a story of the transformation of a place,

Eastleigh is also a story of the transformation of selves, as people learn to become canny entrepreneurs (or *hustlers*, as Mohaa would no doubt prefer) in an estate whose life-blood is now business and commerce. There may be *yaum asal* and *basal* in this remarkable trading hub, but an Eastleigh education in surviving and thriving in times of economic and political uncertainty is valuable indeed.

NOTES

INTRODUCTION: WELCOME TO EASTLEIGH

1. As this book will discuss both Somalis originating in Somalia itself and Somalis with Kenyan citizenship, it will use the following terms for the sake of clarity: (1) 'Somali' refers to ethnicity (as well as language) and can be used for all ethnic Somalis in the Somali peninsula and beyond. (2) 'Somalian' refers to nationality and is used exclusively for the citizens of Somalia whether of Somali, Bantu or Arab heritage.
2. See chapter 7. It is commonly said by advocates for the estate that Eastleigh is the third most valuable sub-economy of Nairobi, after the Central Business District and Westlands (where a number of high-end malls are located).
3. See chapter 7.
4. Anderson and McKnight 2015.
5. Betts 2015.
6. On the industry that has developed around policing migration see Andersson 2014.
7. Sheikh and Healy 2009.
8. The three durable solutions of the UNHCR are resettlement, local integration and repatriation.
9. On the securitisation of refugee policy in East Africa see Kibreab 2014.
10. Hammar 2014.
11. Pérouse de Montclos and Kagwanja 2000.
12. IOM World Migration Report 2015.
13. Glick Schiller and Caglar 2010.
14. For an overview of literature on ethnic enclaves see Waldinger 1993.
15. Hanna and Hanna (1971) provide a broad overview of earlier research into African urbanisation, including a focus on migration.

16. For a recent ethnography of West African migrants in Brazzaville see Whitehouse 2012.
17. See the literature on Africans in China, for example Lee 2014; Bodomo 2012. Stoller 2001 offers a fine ethnography of West African migrants in New York.
18. For example, see Haugen and Carling 2005 on Chinese migrants in Cape Verde. The role of individual Chinese migrants and entrepreneurs in Africa links to the current debates on China in Africa: see Wang and Elliot 2014.
19. Bakewell and Jonsson 2011, 10.
20. Cohen 2008; Van Hear 1998; Page and Mercer 2010.
21. Laakso and Hautaniemi 2014, 2.
22. On the migration–entrepreneur nexus in southern America see DeHart 2010, especially chapter 3.
23. For a critical take see Raghuram 2009.
24. Bakewell 2007 and 2012.
25. Sheikh and Healy 2009.
26. Hammond 2015. See also Hansen 2014.
27. Sheikh and Healy 2009, 11.
28. Thanks to Kari Dahlgren for her input on these issues.
29. See Mathews 2011a and Mathews, Ribeiro and Vega 2012.
30. Mathews, Dan Lin and Yang 2014, 219; Mathews, Ribeiro and Vega 2012.
31. Lee 2014.
32. Mathews 2011a.
33. Mathews and Yang 2012.
34. On women traders in the informal economy, and their transformations of retail space in Nairobi linked to the trade of these goods, see Kinyanjui 2014.
35. Sassen 2005.
36. See Grant and Nijman 2004; Myers 2011, 5.
37. Glick Schiller and Caglar 2010.
38. Tsing 2005.
39. On economic reform in Africa from an anthropological perspective see Little 2013.
40. Glick Schiller and Caglar 2010, 3–4.
41. Brettell 2003, 7.
42. For example, De Soto 1989; for a popular account see Neuwirth 2012.
43. Meagher 2010, 20–6.
44. See chapter 7.
45. See Geschiere 2009 on autochthony in Cameroon and the Netherlands.

46. For a thorough discussion of refugees and their portrayal as passive recipients of humanitarian assistance in camps see Besteman 2016, chapter 2.
47. Vertovec 2007; Meissner and Vertovec 2015
48. See chapter 5.
49. See, for example, Tiwari 1964 and 1972.
50. E.g. Goldsmith 1997; Martin 1998.
51. E.g. Campbell 2005 and 2006; Horst 2006a.
52. E.g. Murunga 2009 and 2012.
53. E.g. Peter, Wandera and Jansen 2013; Jacobsen 2011.
54. E.g. Little 2013; Elliott 2014.
55. Lindley 2010a.
56. E.g. Elliott 2012; Campbell, Crisp and Kiragu 2011; Abdulsamed 2011.
57. For my research on khat see Carrier 2007.
58. The programme's website is found at http://www.migration.ox.ac.uk/odp/
59. http://www.migration.ox.ac.uk/odp/diasporas-trade-trust.shtml
60. On multi-sited ethnography see Marcus 1995. On the khat project see Carrier 2007.
61. Tsuda, Tapias and Escandell 2014, 124.
62. Mathews, Ribeiro and Vega 2012.
63. Steinberg 2014.
64. Privately owned minibuses that serve as Kenya's main form of passenger transport.
65. Gupta and Ferguson 1997.
66. Mathews 2011a.
67. 'Ethnoscape' is Appadurai's term (1996) that tries to capture the contemporary complexity of flows of people and ethnic identity.
68. Scott 2012, chapter 4.

1. FROM NAIROBI EAST TO LITTLE MOGADISHU

1. Otiso 2005, 80.
2. For histories of early Nairobi see Hake 1977; Nevanlinna 1996; Lonsdale 2002; Anderson 2005; Murunga 2012; Robertson 1997.
3. Cited in Robertson 1997, 12.
4. Ibid., 13.
5. Ibid.
6. Campbell 1999, 169.
7. 'G.E.A.' standing for German East Africa.
8. Annual Report, Nairobi Township, 1909, Kenya National Archives (microfilm).

9. Robertson 1997, 13. See also Otiso 2005, 73–4.
10. Murunga 2012.
11. Murunga 2009, 99.
12. Myers 2003, 36.
13. Ibid., 36–7.
14. Burton 2005, 22.
15. Myers 2003, 36.
16. Nevanlinna 1996, 109.
17. Oonk 2013, 83.
18. Loc. cit.
19. Parker 1948, 68.
20. Hake 1977, 36.
21. Nevanlinna 1996, 116.
22. Hake 1977, 255, footnote 6.
23. Parker 1948, 68, footnote 2.
24. Letter from Town Clerk to J. S. Macartney, Esquire, Minister of Local Government, Health and Town Planning (c. 1953), Kenya National Archives file KNA RN/6/31.
25. Hake 1977, 255.
26. This is a reproduction by Sebastian Ballard of an original plan of the estate found in the Kenya National Archives.
27. Parker 1948, 68.
28. Murunga 2012.
29. Parker 1948, 68.
30. Nairobi Sanitary Commission 1913, 48.
31. Statement by Principal Medical Officer, Kenya Legislative Council Debate, 17 April 1925.
32. Nairobi Sanitary Commission 1913, 48.
33. Parker 1948, 68, footnote 2.
34. Loc. cit.
35. There are various spellings of this name, including 'Isaq' and 'Issack'.
36. See chapter 3.
37. Turton 1974.
38. Whitehouse 2012, 39. The term 'auxiliary diaspora' is Robin Cohen's (2008, 84).
39. Turton 1974, 326.
40. Ibid. 325–6.
41. In this regard they resemble the Soninke of Mali, whose long use of transnational mobility as a livelihood strategy and source of power also challenges the idea of African transnationalism as new. See, for example, Jonsson 2008; Whitehouse 2012.
42. Quarles van Ufford and Zaal 2004, 128–9.

43. Nairobi District Annual Report 1912–13, Kenya National Archives (microfilm).
44. Tiwari 1964, 42.
45. The campaign in the 1930s to cement their higher status would become a famous example of early Somali diaspora mobilisation, as Isaaq in the UK lobbied on behalf of those in East Africa. See Turton 1974.
46. Turton 1974, 327.
47. Aims declared by Ahamed Nur and M. H. Mattan, members of the Isaq Association, cited in Turton 1974, 327. This campaign was headquartered in Eastleigh.
48. Weitzberg 2013.
49. Tiwari (1964, 50) gives Pangani as the location for one of the Somali villages.
50. Letter from C. H. Campbell, Assistant Land Officer, to the Crown Advocate, Mombasa, 13 February 1908, Kenya National Archives file KNA AG/19/127.
51. Letter from D. C. Hamilton to Chief Secretary U.F.S., The P.C., Nairobi, 24 September 1913, Kenya National Archives file KNA AG/19/127.
52. Annual Report 1913–14, Nairobi District.
53. Murunga 2012, 474.
54. Ukamba Province Annual Report, March 1917, Kenya National Archives (microfilm).
55. Telegram to Colonial Office No. 345, 19 September 1916, Kenya National Archives file KNA MOH/1/3932, 'Removal of Nairobi East Township'.
56. See Whittaker 2015. On the wider history of East African townspeople see Lonsdale 2002.
57. Telegram to Colonial Office No. 345, 19 September 1916, Kenya National Archives file KNA MOH/1/3932, 'Removal of Nairobi East Township'.
58. Letter, Principal Sanitation Officer to Medical Department, Head Office, 1 June 1918, Kenya National Archives file KNA MOH/1/3932, 'Removal of Nairobi East Township'.
59. Blixen 1980, 23–4. This description, though undated in *Out of Africa*, was certainly of Nairobi East rather than the earlier Somali Village at Ngara, as in a letter of September 1917 she talks of visiting the 'Somali town', by which point the Somalis had moved to Nairobi East (Blixen 1982, 54).
60. On this cultural institution see Tiilikainen 2011. *Dhaqan celin* is a verb form meaning 'to return to culture', *dhaqan celis* used as a noun to refer to someone sent to return to their culture.

61. *Kenya Gazette*, 19 January 1921, Proclamation no. 6, 33.

62. Hake 1977, 255, footnote 6.

63. Kirby 1968, 120.

64. Kenya National Archives (KNA) file BAA/1/17 (Eastleigh Township—Municipality), letter from Governor Edward Northey to Viscount Milner, Secretary of State for the Colonies, London, 29 January 1921.

65. Tiwari 1964, 116.

66. See Kenya Legislative Council debate, 17 April 1925, 232–5.

67. Letter, 5 August 1927, to Sir Edward Denham, Acting Governor and Commander in Chief, Colony and Protectorate of Kenya, Nairobi. From petition of Eastleigh residents, Kenya National Archives file KNA BN/7/14 Nairobi East Township, Eastleigh.

68. Nevanlinna 1996, 140.

69. See Legislative Council debates of 13 May 1927, 1 November 1927 and 19 May 1928.

70. The cutting up of plots in Eastleigh in this way was lamented in the Kenya Legislative Council debate, 17 April 1925.

71. Tiwari 1964, 119.

72. Parker 1948.

73. Wealthier Asians preferred the Ngara Road and Parklands areas (Morgan 1967, 106). Tiwari suggested the lower economic power of the Eastleigh Asians in stating that those living in Pangani and Eastleigh 'do not usually employ a full time servant' (1964, 97).

74. Halliman and Morgan 1967, 107.

75. Tiwari 1964, 116.

76. Correspondence in Kenya National Archives file KNA: LND 29/1/1/1/54 1932, Transfer between parties of different races, European to Asiatic, Mr. D. W. Noble to Kaniz Fatuma, Plot no. 79 Egerton Township.

77. Nevanlinna 1996, 281.

78. Vertovec 2007.

79. Campbell 1999, 192.

80. Tiwari 1964, 117.

81. Willem Jansen, personal communication.

82. Mervyn Maciel, personal communication.

83. R. C. Tiwari, quoted in Hake 1977, 101.

84. Tiwari 1969, 145–7; Tiwari 1964, 117.

85. Hake 1977, 101.

86. Oded 2000, 79. On the Shifta War see Whittaker 2014.

87. On a Somaliland town called Sheikh, split between two Isaaq clans, see Lewis 1994, 118–19.

88. Interview conducted with Mzee Dekow by Elias Isaac, Section III, Eastleigh, April 2014.

89. Kresse 2007, 40.
90. A population remembered by current MP Yusuf Hassan, personal communication.
91. Burton 2005.
92. The source material for this section is file BN/30/105 in the Kenya National Archives, which contains much correspondence on the topic of Thuku's purchase of the plot from February to April 1932.
93. According to Hake (1977, 101), Thuku was still trying to buy a plot in Section III in 1938.
94. Letter to Colonial Secretary, 21 March 1932, Kenya National Archives file KNA BN/30/105.
95. Parker 1948, 89.
96. Ibid., 97.
97. White 1990, 201. The opening of RAF Eastleigh in 1940 also increased demand for prostitutes in the area (ibid., 162).
98. Ibid., 202.
99. Ibid., 203.
100. Anderson 2001, 144.
101. Kenya Legislative Council Debate, October 1961, 113.
102. Oonk 2013, 212 ff.
103. Hake 1977, 101.
104. Tiwari 1964, 119.
105. Hake 1977, 102.
106. Tiwari 1972, 49. Tiwari reports that the overall population of Eastleigh ward rose to 73,400 in the same period, but much of that rise was due to African settlement of Mathare to the north of Eastleigh, which was included in these figures.
107. Ibid., 50.
108. Yusuf Hassan, personal communication. His first name was actually Kipanga.
109. McCormick 1998, 16.
110. Annah 2013, 48–9.
111. Another member of the Arr family—Hussein Mohamed Arr—was also a key Somali presence in the estate in this era, with a number of business interests including a lodge. He would later become a senior member of the Eastleigh Business Association, an organisation we shall encounter much in this book.
112. Trillo 1987, 82.
113. Goldsmith 2008.
114. The name translates as 'Suffering without hatred'.
115. A trip to the establishments is recounted here: http://www.eastafricanmusic.com/busines2.htm (accessed January 2015).

116. See Trillo 1993, 109.
117. Asoka, Thuo and Bunyasi 2013, 44; Anderson, Elliott, Kochore and Lochery 2012, 386. Elliott 2014. On the pressures faced in recent decades by East African pastoralists see Fratkin 2001.
118. Kagwanja 1998. Matatus are the minibus passenger services operating throughout Kenya.
119. Pérouse de Montclos 1998, 20.
120. Kapteijns 2013, 2.
121. Lindley 2010a, 95–6.
122. Ibid.
123. Hyndman and Nylund 1998.
124. On life for Somali refugees in the camps see Horst 2006a; Pérouse de Montclos and Kagwanja 2000.
125. Kagwanja 2000.
126. See Turner 2015 on Burundian refugees in Kenya rejecting the camps for the uncertainties of Nairobi.
127. Though the camps are important centres for business in their own right, and much trade occurs within and through them. Recently a university has been opened in Dadaab.
128. Pérouse de Montclos 1998, 5.
129. Some even in advance of actual compulsion, so called 'anticipatory refugees'. See, for example, Van Hear 1998, 44–5.
130. Lindley 2010a, 97–8.
131. Steinberg 2014, 44.
132. Goldsmith 1997, 470.
133. Pérouse de Montclos 1998, 12.
134. Pérouse de Montclos 1998, 12–13.
135. Asoka, Thuo and Bunyasi 2013, 43. Eastleigh is divided administratively into Eastleigh North and South, these are combined figures for both districts.
136. The first reference to the use of the term 'Little Mogadishu' in relation to Eastleigh that I have found comes from 1998 (Katola 1998, 146).

2. URBAN TRANSFORMATION

1. Hammar 2014, 25; see also Elliott 2014.
2. Mathews 2011a.
3. Crawford 1992.
4. For analysis of the mall in Cairo see Abaza 2001.
5. See Ochiel 2015.
6. The name Comesa emerges from the acronym COMESA (Common

Market for Eastern and Southern Africa) and is said to refer to the many visitors coming to Eastleigh from Rwanda, Tanzania and elsewhere. See Njanja 2015.

7. Cassanelli 2010, 139.
8. Feyissa and Hoehne 2010.
9. Trillo 1987, 322.
10. On Somali migration to the Gulf see Abdi 2015.
11. Bredeloup 2013, 203.
12. Carrier and Lochery 2013.
13. Elliott and Lochery 2011.
14. Hoehne 2015a, 795. For an account of life among the Reer Hamar in Mogadishu see Kapteijns and Boqor 2009.
15. Marchal 1996, 102.
16. Marchal 2002, 74.
17. Martin 1998.
18. Ibid., 43.
19. Ibid., 45.
20. Loc. cit.
21. Similarly, Mathews, Dan and Yang (2014, 226) note how African businesspeople in China rely on leasing stores indirectly through local Chinese to circumvent immigration hurdles.
22. See Mung'ou 2000; Siringi 2000.
23. Ahmad 2012, chapter 5.
24. On Bangkok's African traders see Bredeloup 2013, 204.
25. Mathews 2011a, 187–9.
26. Carrier and Lochery 2013.
27. Morrison 2015.
28. On Yiwu and its connections to North Africa through 'globalisation from below' see Pliez 2012.
29. For an introduction to African traders in Guangzhou see Lee 2014. See also Bodomo 2012; Bredeloup 2013.
30. Campbell 2005, 26.
31. Menkhaus 2005, 32.
32. Little 2013, 172.
33. Ibid., 182.
34. Herz 2012, 200.
35. Loc cit.
36. Geertz 1978.
37. Alexander 1992, 80.
38. Abey 2013, 56.
39. Lindley 2010a: 99, 4.
40. See Wambugu 2012.

41. Annah 2013.
42. Asoka, Thuo and Bunyasi 2013.
43. Ibid., 48.
44. Nairobi City Council became the Nairobi County Government following Kenya's adoption of devolved government in 2013.
45. See Abdikarim 2010.
46. Wells 2001, 273.
47. Property 24 website: http://www.property24.co.ke/vacant-land-plot-for-sale-in-eastleigh-103191220 (accessed December 2015).
48. Hass Property Index 2015. Available online at: http://www.hassconsult.co.ke/images/Q22015/HasslandIndexQ2.2015.pdf (accessed December 2015)
49. Paynter 2010.
50. Wadhams 2010.
51. See his website for this analysis: https://kimoquaintance.com/2011/08/11/did-pirates-finance-your-local-shopping-mall/ (accessed April 2016).
52. Abdulsamed 2011.
53. For a history of Kenyan economic policy and liberalisation see Gertz 2008. See Hansen 2000, 87 ff. on the effects of liberalisation on the Zambian second-hand trade.
54. Little 2003.
55. Ibid., 17.
56. Rono 2002, 88–9; Campbell 2006; Kinyanjui 2014.
57. Kinyanjui 2014.
58. Burbidge 2015.
59. D. J. Smith 2008.
60. For example, see NTV report of 3 February 2016. Available online at: https://www.youtube.com/watch?v=gMv-5COQ-AI (accessed February 2016).
61. See Manji 2012 and 2015.
62. 'Inside Story: Port of Impunity', KTN. Available at https://www.youtube.com/watch?v=JoQuEAXS4WA (accessed March 2015).
63. Jacob Rasmussen, personal communication.
64. Mathews, Dan and Yang 2014, 226.
65. Burbidge 2015.
66. Abdi 2015, chapter 3.
67. Carrier and Lochery 2013.
68. Kiberenge 2009.
69. There are also some shops that fetch no goodwill, but are simply rented out by the mall ownership: in some cases these are in less desirable locations within malls, while in others the mall ownership

charge no goodwill on the grounds that such payments are unethical and even un-Islamic (see chapter 5).

70. Martin 1998, 45.
71. Civil suit 80 of 2012. Available on the Kenya Law website: http://kenyalaw.org/caselaw/cases/view/84627 (accessed January 2016).
72. See Jacobsen 2005 on the economic agency and capacity of refugees.
73. Abdulsamed 2011, 10.
74. We will explore individual stories of raising capital in chapter 4.
75. See chapter 4.
76. Kinyanjui 2014, chapter 7.
77. This is of course true of operators in the wider informal economy in Kenya. See Kinyanjui 2014, chapters 5 and 7 on the 'solidarity economy' of women traders in Nairobi.
78. Laakso and Hautaniemi 2014; Lindley 2010a.
79. Myers 2011, 163–4; Sheikh and Healy 2009.
80. It should be highlighted too that a number of hawala companies have not just acted as a channel for remittance money coming into the Eastleigh economy, but have themselves invested in its developments. Thus, Amal Plaza—while it did seek goodwill for the construction of the mall—is linked to the Amal Express remittance company. With access to so much capital, such companies can finance the securing of plots and facilitate construction.
81. See Marchal 2004 on the closure of a Somali remittance company in the wake of 9/11. See Buggenhagen 2010 on hawala and Senegalese transnational networks.
82. Manson 2011.
83. Horst 2006a.
84. Lindley 2010a, 105–7.
85. Abdulsamed 2011, 7.
86. Available online: http://www.pontusmarine.com (accessed April 2016).
87. Portes, Castells and Benton 1989; Myers 2011, chapter 3.
88. Bop 2005, 1106.
89. Mathews, Dan Lin and Yang 2014, 229. A similar argument could be made for the lax enforcement of immigration laws in Eastleigh, despite the occasional conspicuous round-ups of 'illegal aliens' designed to demonstrate state power (see chapter 7).
90. Hart 2015, 33.
91. Campbell 2005.
92. A case was brought by the owners to stop the bank auctioning the mall. The case notes are available online at http://kenyalaw.org/caselaw/cases/view/102629/ (accessed April 2016).

93. Crawford 1992.
94. Mathews 2011a.
95. Kinyanjui 2014.
96. Kiminza 2010.
97. Kinyanjui 2014, 67.
98. See her photo-essay available online at http://www.migration.ox.ac. uk/odp/johannesburgs-ethiopian-district-photo-essay.shtml#& panel1–1 (accessed April 2016).
99. Abdi 2015, 201 ff.
100. Abdulsamed 2011, 10.

3. MORE THAN LITTLE MOGADISHU

1. Baumann 1996, 10.
2. Horst 2006a, 45; Laitin and Samatar 1987.
3. See the exchange between Lewis and Catherine Besteman in *Cultural Anthropology* over 'traditionalist'—clan-based—interpretations of Somali society and the collapse of the Somali state, versus those more linked to class (Besteman 1996; Lewis 1998; Besteman 1998). Also see Kapteijns 2004. Cawo Abdi's recent ethnography of Somali migration (2015, 24–5) describes her reluctance to ask her informants about clan and to use it in her analysis, and is a good example of how Somali society—especially in the diaspora—is increasingly studied through lenses other than clan. A recent movement known as Cadaan Studies ('white studies'), critical of how non-Somali voices dominate debates about Somali society and the colonial legacy in Somali studies, targets the role of anthropology in constructing the notion of the 'clannish Somali', and the real-life implications this has had (for a summary of Cadaan Studies see Aidid 2015 and Hoehne 2015b).
4. Kapteijns 2013.
5. Bjork 2007, 136.
6. Al-Sharmani 2007, 72.
7. For example, there were some reports of refugees accusing Kenyan Somalis of aiding the police in the swoops during Operation Usalama Watch. Bjork (2007, 152) makes an interesting argument that where there is strong state support—for example, in Finland—clan identities maintain a strong salience as there is little need for wider unity; whereas where they face harsher conditions and limited rights—for example, in Egypt—a more nationalist identity is promoted.
8. Portes and Zhou 1992, 514.
9. On Garre–Degodia conflict see Carrier and Kochore 2014.
10. Horst 2006a, 134–5.

11. Eastleigh is within Kamukunji constitutency.
12. Eno 2005, 334.
13. Sadouni (2009, 240) describes how Islamic identity appears to have gained greater significance than clan in the context of Somali migration to South Africa.
14. Jacobsen 2011, 44.
15. Ibid., 45.
16. Menkhaus 2002, 111.
17. Jacobsen 2011., 42.
18. Abdi 2007, 183.
19. Ahmad 2012.
20. The 2009 population census controversially gave a population for Kenyan Somalis of 2,385,572, a much higher figure than was projected from the 1999 census. Some results—including those from Mandera—were cancelled as a result of anomalies, resulting in a lack of faith in the figures (see Jerven 2013, chapter 3).
21. For information about LAPSSET see http://www.mipakani.net/ (accessed April 2016).
22. Goldsmith 1997, 472. The term is even used in Hargeisa, Somaliland (Hansen 2014, 151).
23. There are Ogaden from Ethiopia in the estate too.
24. Getachew 1996, 114 ff.
25. Af-Maay Maay—or Af-Rahanweyn—is as different from standard Somali as French is from Italian.
26. Schlee 2007.
27. 'Garri' is an alternative spelling of Garre.
28. The Garri Nation is available online: https://garagarri.wordpress.com/about/ (accessed April 2016).
29. See blog post by Dadaab resident and author Asad Husein for *Sahan Journal*, 16 April 2015. Available online: http://sahanjournal.com/call-dadaab-home/#.VS-GTpTF-nT (accessed April 2016).
30. Bakewell 2008, 440. On the construction of the 'refugee' and all the ideology and politics of the term and the industry behind it see Gatrell 2013.
31. Betts 2013, 140.
32. Lambo 2012.
33. On the 'Somali Bantu' see Eno and Eno 2007; Menkhaus 2010; Besteman 2016.
34. Horst 2006a, 140.
35. UNHCR and the Danish Refugee Council 2012, 17.
36. Lowe 2015.
37. Refugee Consortium of Kenya 2008, 17.

38. UNHCR and the Danish Refugee Council 2012, 17.
39. Ibid., 18.
40. Human Rights Watch 2013; Pavanello, Elhawary and Pantuliano 2010.
41. Steinberg 2014, 38 ff.
42. Ibid., 178.
43. Lindley 2010a, chapter 4.
44. Bosire 2006.
45. See also Kibreab 2014 on the securitisation of refugee policy in East Africa.
46. Campbell, Crisp and Kiragu 2011.
47. Ibid., 9.
48. Loc. cit.
49. Campbell 2015, 106.
50. Pavanello, Elhawary and Pantuliano 2010, 17.
51. Human Rights Watch 2013.
52. Sturge 2014, 12–13.
53. Hyndman 1999, 111.
54. Horst 2006a, 190–6.
55. Lochery 2012.
56. Campbell 2005, 12.
57. See the Passport Index: http://www.passportindex.org/byRank.php (accessed April 2016).
58. Horst 2006a, 190 ff.
59. Lindley 2010a, 111.
60. Horst 2006a, 195.
61. Ibid., 191.
62. Abdi 2015, 233–4.
63. In the past there were some notorious instances of corruption by UNHCR staff in charge of resettlement in Nairobi (United Nations 2001; Elliott 2012, 25).
64. Elliott 2012.
65. Horst 2006a; Horst 2006b.
66. Bhui et al. 2006.
67. Horst 2006b.
68. Ferguson 2006; for the Somali case see Abdi 2015.
69. Jacobsen 2011, 191.
70. Lindley 2010a, 111.
71. Abdi 2015, chapter 4.
72. Hammond 2015, 51.
73. The question of whether communities of African migrants within Africa can be classed as 'diasporas' has been asked by, among others, Bakewell (2008).

74. See Tiilikainen 2011.
75. Jacobsen 2011, 91–9.
76. Akou 2011.
77. Abdulsamed 2011.
78. Hansen 2008.
79. Ibid., 151.
80. Ibid., 150.
81. Warner 2013.
82. Hansen 2008, 153.
83. Abdi 2015, chapter 4.
84. Hansen 2014, 155.
85. Baxter, Hultin and Triulzi 1996.
86. UNHCR 2012.
87. There are Christian Oromo too: they were said to mostly stay in the Ngong Road area of the city where there is a Coptic church.
88. Baxter 1978, 284.
89. Material for this section owes much to Hassan Kochore.
90. For an in-depth history of the *longue durée* of being Oromo in Ethiopia see Hassen 1990 and 2015. Also see the edited collection *Being and Becoming Oromo* by Baxter, Hultin and Triulzi (1996).
91. Elliott 2012.
92. See Besteman 2016, chapter 3, on how the need to adapt to a trope of 'trauma' in resettlement processes guides many refugees in crafting narratives.
93. Oromo Relief Association 2011.
94. Malkki 1995.
95. Haneke 2002, 136.
96. Oromo Relief Association 2011.
97. Carrier and Kochore 2014.
98. Long and Crisp 2011, 6.
99. Chhatbar 2012.
100. Elliott 2012, 16–17.
101. Areas such as Kiambiu are also technically within Eastleigh, and also dominated by non-Somali.
102. For the literature on the Meru see Bernardi 1959; Peatrik 1999; Carrier 2007.
103. Goldsmith 1994; Carrier 2007.
104. Carrier 2007, chapter 4.
105. Ahmed 1995, 47.
106. Peter, Wandera and Jansen 2013.

4. LIVING THE EASTLEIGH DREAM

1. On refugees as cheap labour see Campbell, Crisp and Kiragu 2011, 35–6.
2. See Abdi 2015, chapter 4, on gender relations and their transformation for Somalis in the USA.
3. Jacobsen 2011, 31.
4. Ingiriis and Hoehne 2013, 325 ff.
5. Abdi 2007; Ritchie 2014, 33–4.
6. On the protection enclosed retail space offers women in the wider Kenyan informal economy see Kinyanjui 2014, chapter 7.
7. Horst 2006a, 146.
8. Kenyan privately owned public service vehicles. See Mutongi 2006 for a discussion of the industry.
9. On the earlier history of this route see Kagwanja 1998.
10. On the mkokoteni as micro-enterprise see Seierup 2001.
11. Lindley 2010a; Horst 2006a, 144 ff. See chapter 2.
12. Campbell 2005, 22.
13. Horst 2006a, 144 ff.
14. See Lowe 2015 on maternity clinics in the estate.
15. White 1990.
16. Omwenga 2014.
17. Kenya Citizen report, available at https://www.youtube.com/watch?v=0URGwS2L0OY (accessed April 2016).
18. See report by Mohammed in *The Star*, 3 January 2012. Available online at: http://www.the-star.co.ke/news/article-35736/how-notorious-criminal-gangs-rule-eastleigh (accessed March 2015).
19. Kinyanjui 2014, 35.
20. Scott 2012, 85.
21. See chapter 2.
22. Barawa in Somalia has long been famous for its weaving.
23. Goldsmith 2008.
24. Profit-sharing arrangements like this are common in Eastleigh, and such arrangements have long played a role in finance in the Islamic world in the place of interest-bearing investments (see Graeber 2011, 276).
25. See Graeber 2011.
26. Abdulsamed 2011, 9.
27. See Alexander 1992.
28. 'In the name of God, most gracious, most compassionate.'
29. See interview with Hussein Mohamed Arr (former Vice-Chairman of the EBC) in *Waaberi Magazine*, February 2011 issue. Also see the Kenya

Revenue Authority description of turnover tax: http://www.kra. go.ke/notices/pdf2011/Brochures/TURNOVER-TAX.pdf (accessed April 2015)

30. See the KRA website: http://www.kra.go.ke/notices/noticeetrs270 905.html (accessed April 2016).
31. Hansen 2014.
32. Kantai 2012.

5. TRUST AND THE EASTLEIGH ENTREPRENEUR

1. Anonymous 2013.
2. O'Neill 2013.
3. Little 2003.
4. Meagher 2012; Whitehouse 2012.
5. I sympathise with Laidlaw and Mair's position in a recent debate on the usage of the term 'neoliberal' in anthropology, that the term is overused and its meanings ever more blurred (Eriksen et al. 2015). As shorthand for the impact of types of economic policy—including the structural adjustment policies of recent decades—it is a powerful concept, but as a master-explanation for all sorts of contemporary phenomena, it can easily be overstretched.
6. Burton 1894, 122. Lewis also emphasises this individualistic image of the Somali in the very opening of his classic *A Pastoral Democracy* (1961, 1).
7. On such magazines in Russia see Yurchak 2003.
8. Kiyosaki 2011.
9. Kinyanjui highlights similar a similar desire for autonomy amongst Kikuyus in Nairobi's informal economy (2014, 86)—clearly it is not unique to Somalis.
10. Simons 1995, 110–11.
11. As Laidlaw argues, there is a danger that in linking such values to neo-liberalism one might miss how such ideas have been around for mil-lennia in various traditions (Eriksen et al. 2015, 913). Further research would be needed to investigate the history of such values among Somalis, a people long absorbed into various trade circuits in the Horn of Africa and beyond. Islam is certainly a factor in this regard, and Graeber (2011) highlights the free-market values present in Islam since its earliest days.
12. Mathews, Ribeiro and Vega 2012, 8.
13. A number of Somalis in the UK have in recent years embraced the Conservative Party, including a number of anti-khat campaigners drawn initially to the party after it promised to ban the stimulant in the UK (see chapter 6).

14. A report for the UK's Refugee Council suggested that such an anti-welfare sentiment is shared by non-Somali refugees too, on the grounds that welfare can make people lazy (Crawley 2010, 41).
15. Though see chapter 7 on how the state is involved in various ways in—and crucial to—the Eastleigh economy; also see Carrier and Lochery 2013. For the Somali 'economy without state' see Little 2003.
16. Makovicky 2014, 1–13.
17. Eisenberg (2012) describes hip-hop music and its influences on the Kenyan coast, including a song called 'Street Hustlers'.
18. See Baraka 2013.
19. Members of the group appeared on Kenyan TV to promote their cause: clip available at https://www.youtube.com/watch?v=Mv4AbBAaKws (accessed April 2016).
20. See this video clip from KTN: http://www.standardmedia.co.ke/ktn/video/watch/2000080912/-juu-ya-mawe-na-grand-hustler-william-ruto-hapa-kule-news (accessed April 2016).
21. Wacquant 1998, 3. On 'hustling' in the informal economy of Addis Ababa see Di Nunzio 2012.
22. Dahir 2010.
23. Steinberg 2014.
24. See DeHart 2010 on the notion that migrants are natural risk takers and entrepreneurs, and contemporary attempts by development agencies to capture this assumed entrepreneurialism in helping develop homelands.
25. Samatar 2008, 78.
26. Hansen 2014.
27. Literally: 'There are two things in matters of business: to make profit or to decay'.
28. Compare Umbres 2014 on self-interest and mutuality in post-socialist Romania.
29. Meagher 2010, 11.
30. Zorc and Osman 1993.
31. For overviews of trust see Gambetta 1988; Misztal 1996; Sztompka 1999.
32. Fukuyama 1995; see Harriss 2003 for an anthropological overview.
33. Seligman 1997, 37.
34. Harriss 2003, 758.
35. Misztal 1996, 9.
36. Hart 1988.
37. See Ensminger 2001 for an insightful article about the underpinnings of trust and trustworthiness among Orma herders of Kenya.
38. Umbres 2014.

39. Hart 1988.
40. See Carrier 2007, chapter 5.
41. Cohen 1971, 60.
42. MacGaffey and Bazenguissa-Ganga 2000.
43. Rosenfeld 2012.
44. Portes and Sensenbrenner 1993. See chapter 3 in this book on bounded solidarity among Somalis and Oromo in Eastleigh.
45. Whitehouse 2012, 76.
46. Little 2003, 10–13.
47. The trope of uncertainty is one that resonates in particular in accounts of contemporary Africa, as Cooper and Pratten discuss (2015).
48. Lewis 1994, 126.
49. Goldsmith 1997, 469.
50. Bjork 2007, 152.
51. Simons 1995, 139.
52. Lewis 1961, 30.
53. Nori et al. 2006, 20.
54. Lindley 2010a, 38.
55. Samatar 2008, 80.
56. Little 2003, 164.
57. Rosenfeld 2012. See Ensminger 2001 on the importance of reputation for trust among the Orma.
58. Elliott 2014, 137.
59. Shipton 1995.
60. Sztompka 1999, 28.
61. Whitehouse 2012, 95 ff.
62. Simone 2001.
63. See Graeber (2011, 271 ff.) on the positive valuation of trade and even profit in Islam.
64. Osella and Osella 2009.
65. This is not to say that negative opinions about khat are necessarily derived from Islam.
66. Of course their very names are suggestive of the Islamisation of the Eastleigh economy.
67. However, malls continue to be built on the goodwill principle (see chapter 2), and goodwill seems to hover in a very ambiguous moral space.
68. See Maurer 2005 for an anthropological look at Islamic banking.
69. Ahmad 2012.
70. Ibid., 196.
71. Ibid., 196–7.
72. See Abdi 2015 on how Islam helps Somalis form trusting relations

with other Muslims not just in the Gulf, but also in South Africa, where the Indian Muslim population has helped them by providing trade goods on credit.

73. Ahmad 2012., 199.
74. Tiilikainen 2003, 65.
75. Ahmad 2012, 201.
76. Ibid., 200–1.
77. The literature on conversion and accumulation tends to focus on how the former allows escape from social obligations that can hinder the latter: see Parkin 1972 on Giriama accumulation on the Kenyan coast and conversion to Islam; see also van Dijk 2002 on Pentecostalism among the Ghanaian diaspora.
78. Dahir 2012.
79. Ahmad 2012, 201–2.
80. Dahir 2012.
81. Coleman 2013, 206.
82. Sayer 2001, 699.
83. Lindley 2010a.
84. See also Sadouni 2009 on the felt exclusion of some Somalis in South Africa from networks of trust.
85. Meagher 2012.
86. Lewis 1961, 43.

6. DEMANDING GOODS

1. http://www.hrw.org/reports/2002/kenya/Kenya0502-03.htm. On arms smuggling in Kenya in general see Mkutu 2008.
2. See http://www.channel4.com/news/somali-pirates-journalists-jamal-osman-time-magazine-kenya report by Jamal Osman. He was tracing so-called 'pirates' interviewed in Eastleigh by various Western media who claimed to have fled from places such as Puntland. Osman as a Somali was able to tell that these 'pirates' were actually Kenyan Somalis exploiting the credulity of some Western journalists.
3. See chapter 3.
4. The agency of things and materiality in general has become a key focus in recent anthropology, for example Miller 2005. This focus is very much associated with the work of Bruno Latour (e.g. 1993).
5. Mintz 1986.
6. Appadurai 1986.
7. Haugerud, Stone and Little 2000.
8. Schlee 1989; Anderson et al. 2012.
9. Abokor 1987.

10. See chapter 1; also Whittaker 2015.
11. Little 2003.
12. Ibid., 170.
13. Cassanelli 2010, 143.
14. Little 2013, 172.
15. Campbell 2006, 24–5.
16. Little 2013, 178.
17. Hannah Elliott, personal communication.
18. Carrier 2005.
19. Anderson and Carrier 2009; Carrier 2014.
20. Carrier 2014.
21. See file in the Kenya National Archives: KNA—VQ/11/4.
22. See file in the Kenya National Archives: KNA—VQ/11/4.
23. Anonymous 1955.
24. Anderson and Carrier 2011.
25. Carrier 2007.
26. Ibid., chapter 5.
27. Anderson and Carrier 2011.
28. Caplan 1997, 3.
29. Jubat 2013.
30. Sutton 2001, 86.
31. Elliott 2014; see also Anderson, Elliott, Lochery and Kochore 2012.
32. Elliott 2014, 127.
33. Ibid., 135 ff.
34. Anderson, Elliott, Lochery and Kochore 2011.
35. Hammar 2014; Elliott 2014.
36. Thanks to Hannah Elliott for conducting the research on the Eastleigh gold trade upon which much of this section is based.
37. Hecht 1987, 6.
38. Mohamed 2013.
39. Around $1,000.
40. Such intricacies are much queried and debated online. For example, see this response to a query about whether gold can be bought on credit: http://en.islamtoday.net/quesshow-39–1042.htm
41. Hansen 2000, 90.
42. There are other Islamic commodities sold in the estate, including religious books, alcohol-free perfume, prayer mats and so forth.
43. Akou 2011, 75–6.
44. Mathews 2011a.
45. Shoes tend to come through different circuits, many pairs being brought from Ethiopia by Garre and others who live or have contacts in Moyale.

46. Gikomba has not escaped the insecurity that has affected Eastleigh, as witness a bombing in May 2014.
47. Hansen 2000, 91.
48. Perhaps because they are good enough to be photographed.
49. Hansen recounts a similar appreciation of second-hand clothes in Zambia (2000, 245–7).
50. Mitumba clothes also often originate in Asian factories, but their circuits take them first to the West. Further demonstrating the intricacy of such networks, the raw materials such as cotton used to make these clothes are often grown in the USA.
51. Though some complain Eastleigh clothes are indeed perishable, falling apart too quickly.
52. Lin 2011, 5.
53. Ibid., 7.
54. Ibid., chapter 3.
55. Mathews 2011a, 114.
56. On the resonances of the terms 'fake' and 'original' for imported goods in Nigeria post-structural-adjustment see Guyer 2004, chapter 5.
57. Mathews 2011b, 165.
58. On Africans in China see Lee 2014, chapter 2.

7. STATE OF SUSPICION

1. Statement made in *The Star* newspaper, 4 January 2012 in an article available online at http://www.the-star.co.ke/news/article-35468/eastleigh-dual-carriage-tender-finally-advertised (accessed February 2015).
2. Kibreab 2014.
3. On Vision 2030 see Fourie 2014.
4. For critiques of development see the work of such 'post-development' thinkers as Escobar (1995) and Sachs (1992).
5. J.H. Smith 2008.
6. Whittaker 2014, 152–3.
7. The main website is: http://www.vision2030.go.ke/ (accessed February 2015).
8. A figure given by the Eastleigh Business Association. See Patinkin 2014.
9. As argued in parliament by Aden Duale: Kenya National Assembly Record, December 2011, p. 23.
10. Barnes 2014.
11. Chalfin 2010, 44.
12. Kenya National Assembly Debates (Hansard), 8 December 2011, 23.
13. See Sangira 2012.

14. Roads are often key infrastructural symbols of development, material signs that the state takes somewhere seriously enough to bring it good connections to elsewhere (see Harvey and Knox 2012). Similar discourse of roads bringing development are commonly heard, including with regard to the Isiolo–Moyale road in northern Kenya, the main connection between Ethiopia and Kenya that is finally being tarmacked after years of neglect (see Kochore forthcoming).
15. Jamah 2009.
16. World Bank 2013.
17. 'Inside Story: Port of Impunity', KTN. Available at https://www.youtube.com/watch?v=JoQuEAXS4WA (accessed March 2015).
18. See Burbidge 2015 and his argument that perception of widespread corruption in Kenya acts as a self-fulfilling prophecy that induces yet more corruption.
19. Anyanzwa 2014.
20. Blessol and Kirk 2013.
21. Osterfeld 1988.
22. Joshi, Prichard and Heady 2014.
23. Kirkpatrick 2015.
24. Laakso and Hautaniemi 2014.
25. See, for example, Muraya 2015.
26. Anderson and Carrier 2009.
27. The colonial administration of the Northern Frontier District has been referred to as 'Garrison Government' (Anderson 2014).
28. On the Shifta War see Whittaker 2014.
29. Lochery 2012.
30. Sheikh 2007.
31. Kenya Transitional Justice Network 2013.
32. See Mohamed 2015.
33. For a full account of the Moi era and its repressions see Branch 2011, chapters 4–7.
34. Anderson 2014, 662.
35. Ibid., 2; Mohamed 2015.
36. Lochery2012, 625.
37. Lochery 2012, following Scott 1999.
38. Lochery 2012, 631.
39. Ibid., 632.
40. See reports in *The Sunday Nation* (6 December 1998). Also, reports in the *Daily Nation*, 3 September 1999.
41. Betts 2013.
42. Ibid.
43. UNHCR 2009.

44. Campbell, Crisp and Kiragu 2011. 10.
45. Kibreab 2014.
46. Hansen 2013, 58.
47. Human Rights Watch 2009.
48. Seal and Bailey 2013.
49. Browne 2015.
50. Anderson and McKnight 2015, 7.
51. Mureithi 2011.
52. What progress is being made by the KDF in Somalia is very hazy indeed, with little reporting on the operation. There are alarming reports of Kenyan service personnel profiting from Kismayu and its imports and exports just as Al-Shabaab did. See Journalists for Justice 2015.
53. Anonymous 2012a.
54. Limo 2012.
55. Anonymous 2012b.
56. Anonymous 2012c.
57. See the Human Rights Watch report, available online at http://www. hrw.org/sites/default/files/related_material/PETITION%20115%20 AND%2019%20OF%202013%20JUDGMENT(FINAL).pdf (accessed February 2015).
58. Mwakio and Ombati 2013.
59. Human Rights Watch 2014a.
60. See Independent Policing Oversight Authority 2014.
61. Mogire 2011.
62. Kenya Law 2014.
63. Human Rights Watch 2014b.
64. See BBC 2014.
65. The UNHCR protested this demand in a statement available online: see UNHCR 2015.
66. Independent PoliceOversight Agency 2014., 7.
67. Ibid., 19.
68. See Eastleighwood 2014.
69. Gitau 2015.
70. UNHCR 2014.
71. Anonymous 2014,
72. Iazzolino 2014.
73. A translation by Dahir Hirey of the following article: http:// so.wikipedia.org/wiki/Eastliegh_somali_section (accessed April 2016).
74. Achuka 2014.
75. How development projects can lead to displacement for the economically marginalised has been much studied (see, for example, de Wet 2005).

76. See NTV report of 3 February 2016. Available online: https://www.
youtube.com/watch?v=gMv-5COQ-AI (accessed April 2016).
77. Nairobi County Government 2015.
78. Wachira 2015.

CONCLUSION: EASTLEIGH AND CITIES YET TO COME

1. Mathews 2011a, 211 ff.
2. Myers 2011, 160.
3. Laguerre 1999.
4. Farah 2002.
5. On Uganda and the advantages of its refugee policy both for refugees
and the host country itself see Betts et al. 2014.
6. How development is anticipated is a growing theme in the anthropology of development, suggesting the productivity and social ramifications
in the present of dreams of the future. See, for example, Cross 2014
and Weskalnys 2014.

BIBLIOGRAPHY

Abaza, M. 2001. 'Shopping Malls, Consumer Culture and the Reshaping of Public Space in Egypt', *Theory, Culture and Society* 18 (5): 97–122.

Abdi, C. 2007. 'Convergence of Civil War and the Religious Right: Re-imagining Somali Women', *Signs: Journal of Women in Culture and Society* 33 (1): 183–207.

———— 2015. *Elusive Jannah: The Somali Diaspora and a Borderless Muslim Identity*. Minneapolis: University of Minnesota Press.

Abdikarim, A. M. 2010. 'City Council of Nairobi Stopped from Collecting Rates from Eastleigh Traders', *Network Al Shahid*. Available online: http://english.alshahid.net/archives/7950 (accessed April 2016).

Abdulsamed, F. 2011. *Somali Investment in Kenya*, Chatham House Briefing Paper. Available online: http://www.chathamhouse.org/sites/default/files/public/Research/Africa/bp0311_abdulsamed.pdf (accessed April 2016).

Abey, A. H. 2013. 'Economic Effects of Urban Refugees on Host Community: Case of Somali Refugees in Eastleigh, 1991–2012'. MA thesis, University of Nairobi.

Abokor, A. C. 1987. *The Camel in Somali Oral Traditions*. Uppsala: Scandinavian Institute of African Studies.

Achuka, V. 2014. 'Hundreds Left Homeless in Road Reserve Demolitions', *Nairobi News*, 18 May 2014. Available online: http://nairobinews.nation.co.ke/news/hundreds-left-homeless-in-road-reserve-demolitions/ (accessed April 2016).

Ahmad, A. S. 2012. 'Between the Mosque and the Market: An Economic Explanation of State Failure and State Formation in the Modern Muslim World'. Ph.D. thesis, Department of Political Science, McGill University.

Ahmed, A. J. (ed.). 1995. *The Invention of Somalia*. Trenton, NJ: Red Sea Press.

Aidid, S. 2015. 'The New Somali Studies', *The New Inquiry*. Available online:

279

BIBLIOGRAPHY

http://thenewinquiry.com/essays/the-new-somali-studies/ (accessed April 2016).

Akou, H. M. 2011. *The Politics of Dress in Somali Culture*. Bloomington: Indiana University Press.

Alexander, P. 1992. 'What's in a Price?' In R. Dilley (ed.), *Contesting Markets: Analyses of Ideology, Discourse and Practice*. Edinburgh: Edinburgh University Press.

Anderson, D. M. 2001. 'Corruption at City Hall: African Housing and Urban Development in Colonial Nairobi', *Azania* 36–37 (1): 138–54.

———— 2005. *Histories of the Hanged: Britain's Dirty War in Kenya and the End of Empire*. London: Weidenfeld & Nicolson.

———— 2014. 'Remembering Wagalla: State Violence in Northern Kenya, 1962–91', *Journal of Eastern African Studies* 8 (4): 658–76.

Anderson, D. M. and Carrier, N. C. M. 2009. 'Khat in Colonial Kenya: A History of Prohibition and Control', *Journal of African History* 50 (3): 377–97.

———— 2011. *Khat: Social Harms and Legislation: A Literature Review*. London: Home Office Occasional Paper 95.

Anderson, D. M., Elliott, H. R., Kochore, H. H. and Lochery, E. 2012. 'Camel Herders, Middlewomen, and Urban Milk Bars: The Commodification of Camel Milk in Kenya', *Journal of Eastern African Studies* 6 (3): 383–404.

Anderson, D. M. and McKnight, J. 2015. 'Kenya at War: Al-Shabaab and its Enemies in Eastern Africa', *African Affairs* 114 (454): 1–27.

Andersson, R. 2014. *Illegality, Inc: Clandestine Migration and the Business of Bordering Europe*. Oakland: University of California Press.

Annah, M. T. 2013. 'Urban Planning and Development of Eastleigh District Commercial Centre in Nairobi'. Master of Architecture thesis, University of Nairobi.

Anonymous 1955. 'Increase in Drug Taking Alleged', *East African Standard*, 19 September.

———— 2012a. 'One Killed in Nairobi Explosion', *Standard Digital*, 3 August 2012. Available online: http://www.standardmedia.co.ke/?articleID= 2000063288 (accessed April 2016).

———— 2012b. 'More Rioting in Eastleigh Following Matatu Bomb Attack', *Kenya Forum*, 19 November 2012. Available online: http://www.kenyaforum.net/2012/11/19/more-rioting-in-eastleigh-following-matatu-bomb-attack/ (accessed April 2016).

———— 2012c. 'Two Injured in Kenya Explosions', Al Jazeera, 19 December 2012. Available online: http://www.aljazeera.com/news/africa/2012/12/20121219172758769966.html (accessed April 2016).

———— 2013. 'Africa's Most Entrepreneurial Ethnic Groups', *Modern Ghana*,

BIBLIOGRAPHY

30 March. Available online: http://www.modernghana.com/news/455846/1/africas-most-entrepreneurial-ethnic-groups.html (accessed April 2016).

———— 2014. 'Interior Cabinet Secretary Joseph Ole Lenku Fired as Inspector of Police David Kimaiyo Resigns', *Standard Digital*, 2 December 2014. Available online: http://www.standardmedia.co.ke/article/200014 3316/interior-cs-ole-lenku-fired-police-boss-kimaiyo-resigns (accessed April 2016).

Anyanzwa, J. 2014. 'Kenya Revenue Authority Investigating Chinese Companies over Tax Evasion Claims', *The Standard*, 30 May 2014. Available online: http://www.standardmedia.co.ke/business/article/2000122957/kra-investigating-chinese-companies-over-tax-evasion-claims (accessed April 2016).

Appadurai, A. (ed) 1986. *The social life of things: Commodities in cultural perspective*. Cambridge: Cambridge University Press.

Appadurai, A. 1996. *Modernity at Large: Cultural Dimensions of Globalization*. Minneapolis: Minnesota University Press.

Asoka, G. W. N., Thuo, A. D. M. and Bunyasi, M. M. 2013. 'Effects of Population Growth on Urban Infrastructure and Services: A Case of Eastleigh Neighborhood Nairobi, Kenya', *Journal of Anthropology and Archaeology* 1 (1): 41–56.

Bakewell, O. 2007. 'Keeping them in their Place: The Ambivalent Relationship between Migration and Development in Africa', IMI Working Paper Series, 08.

———— 2008. 'Research Beyond the Categories: The Importance of Policy Irrelevant Research into Forced Migration', *Journal of Refugee Studies* 21 (4): 432–53.

———— (ed.). 2012. *Migration and Development*, International Library of Studies on Migration series. Cheltenham: Edward Elgar Publishing.

Bakewell, O. and Jonsson, G. 2011. 'Migration, Mobility and the African City: Synthesis Report on the African Perspectives on Human Mobility Research Programme'. Oxford: International Migration Institute working paper.

Baraka, S. 2013. 'Troubled Kenyan Hustlers in America', *The Standard*, 26 August 2013. Available online: http://www.standardmedia.co.ke/lifestyle/article/2000091848/troubled-kenyan-hustlers-in-america (accessed April 2016).

Barnes, C. 2014. 'Losing Hearts and Minds in Kenya. The Crackdown on Somalis Will Probably Backfire', International Crisis Group. Available online: http://blog.crisisgroup.org/worldwide/2014/04/16/losing-hearts-and-minds-in-kenya/ (accessed April 2016).

Baumann, G. 1996. *Contesting Culture: Discourses of Identity in Multi-ethnic London*. Cambridge: Cambridge University Press.

BIBLIOGRAPHY

Baxter, P. T. W. 1978. 'Ethiopia's Unacknowledged Problem: The Oromo', *African Affairs* 77 (308): 283–96.

Baxter, P. T. W., Hultin, J. and Triulzi, A. 1996. *Being and Becoming Oromo: Historical and Anthropological Enquiries*. Lawrenceville, NJ: Red Sea Press.

BBC. 2014. Kenya Security Bill: MPs Brawl as Measures Approved, 18 December 2014. Available online: http://www.bbc.co.uk/news/world-africa-30530423 (accessed April 2016).

Bernardi, B. 1959. *The Mugwe: A Failing Prophet*. Oxford: Oxford University Press.

Besteman, C. L. 1996. 'Representing Violence and "Othering" Somalia', *Cultural Anthropology* 11 (1): 120–33.

———— 1998. 'Primordialist Blinders: A Reply to I. M. Lewis', *Cultural Anthropology* 13 (1): 109–20.

———— 2016. *Making Refuge: Somali Bantu Refugees and Lewiston, Maine*. Durham, NC: Duke University Press.

Betts, A. 2013. *Survival Migration: Failed Governance and the Crisis of Displacement*. Ithaca, NY: Cornell University Press.

———— 2015. 'Human Migration will be the Defining Issue of this Century. How Best to Cope?' *The Guardian*, 20 September 2015. Available online: http://www.theguardian.com/commentisfree/2015/sep/20/migrants-refugees-asylum-seekers-21st-century-trend (accessed April 2016).

Betts, A., Bloom, L., Kaplan, J. and Omata, N. 2014. 'Refugee Economies: Rethinking Popular Assumptions'. Oxford: Refugee Studies Centre report.

Bhui, K., Craig, T., Warfa, N., Stansfield, S. A., Thornicroft, G., Curtis, S. and McCrone, P. 2006. 'Mental Disorders among Somali Refugees: Developing Culturally Appropriate Measures and Assessing Socio-cultural Risk Factors', *Social Psychiatry and Psychiatric Epidemiology* 41 (5): 400–8.

Bjork, S. R. 2007. 'Modernity Meets Clan: Cultural Intimacy in the Somali Diaspora'. In A. M. Kusow and S. R. Bjork (eds.), *From Mogadishu to Dixon: The Somali Diaspora in a Global Context*. Trenton, NJ: Red Sea Press.

Blessol, G. and Kirk, M. 2013. 'Is Kenya Being Shaped into Africa's Flagship Tax Haven?' Al Jazeera, Available online: http://www.aljazeera.com/indepth/opinion/2013/06/20136461539703262.html (accessed April 2016).

Blixen, K. 1980. *Out of Africa*. London: Folio Society.

———— 1982. *Letters from Africa: 1914–1931*. London: Picador.

Bodomo, A. 2012. *Africans in China: A Sociocultural Study and its Implications for Africa–China Relations*. Amherst, NY: Cambria Press.

Bop, C. 2005. 'Roles and the Position of Women in Sufi Brotherhoods in Senegal', *Journal of the American Academy of Religion* 73 (4): 1099–1119.

Bosire, M. 2006. 'Hybrid Languages: The Case of Sheng'. In O. F. Arasanyin and M. A. Pemberton (eds.), *Selected Proceedings of the 36th Annual Conference on African Linguistics*. Somerville, MA: Cascadilla Proceedings Project.

BIBLIOGRAPHY

Branch, D. 2011. *Kenya: Between Hope and Despair, 1963–2011*. New Haven: Yale University Press.

Bredeloup, S. 2013. 'African Migrations, Work, and New Entrepreneurs: The Construction of African Staging-posts in Asia'. In L. Peilin and L. Roulleau-Berger (eds.), *China's Internal and International Migration*. London: Routledge.

Brettell, C. 2003. *Anthropology and Migration: Essays on Transnationalism, Ethnicity and Identity*. Lanham: Alta Mira Press.

Browne, A. J. 2015. *LAPSSET: The History and Politics of an Eastern African Megaproject*. London: Rift Valley Institute.

Buggenhagen, B. A. 2010. 'Killer Bargain: The Global Networks of Senegalese Muslims and Policing Unofficial Economies in the War on Terror'. In A-M. B. Makhulu, B. A. Buggenhagen and S. Jackson (eds.), *Hard Work, Hard Times: Global Volatilities and African Subjectivities*. Berkeley: University of California Press.

Burbidge, D. 2015. *The Shadow of Kenyan Democracy: Widespread Expectations of Widespread Corruption*. Farnham: Ashgate.

Burton, A. 2005. *African Underclass: Urbanisation, Crime and Colonial Order in Dar es Salaam*. Oxford: James Currey.

Burton, R. F. 1894. *First Footsteps in East Africa or, an Exploration of Harar*. London: Tylston & Edwards.

Campbell, E. H. 2005. 'Formalizing the Informal Economy: Somali Refugee and Migrant Trade Networks in Nairobi', *Global Migration Perspectives* 47, Report for the Global Commission on International Migration. Available online: http://www.migrationdevelopment.org/fileadmin/data/resources/general/research_papers/GMP_No47_01.pdf (accessed April 2016).
———— 2006. 'Urban Refugees in Nairobi: Problems of Protection, Mechanisms of Survival, and Possibilities for Integration', *Journal of Refugee Studies* 19 (3): 396–413.

Campbell, E. H., Crisp, J., and Kiragu, E. 2011. *Navigating Nairobi: A Review of the Implementation of UNHCR's Urban Refugee Policy in Kenya's Capital City*, UNHCR report. Available online: http://www.unhcr.org/4d5511209.pdf (accessed April 2016).

Campbell, J. R. 1999. 'Culture, Social Organisation and Asian Identity: Difference in Urban East Africa'. In J. R. Campbell and A. Rew (eds.), *Identity and Effect: Experiences of Identity in a Globalising World*. London: Pluto Press.

Caplan, P. (ed.). 1997. *Food, Health and Identity: Approaches from the Social Sciences*. London: Routledge.

Carrier, N. C. M. 2005. 'The Need for Speed: Contrasting Timeframes in the Social Life of Kenyan *Miraa*', *Africa* 75 (4): 539–58.
———— 2007. *Kenyan Khat: The Social Life of a Stimulant*. Leiden: Brill.

———— 2014. 'A Respectable Chew? Highs and Lows in the History of Kenyan Khat'. In G. Klantschnig, N. C. M. Carrier, and C. Ambler (eds.), *Drugs in Africa: Histories and Ethnographies of Use, Trade and Control*. Basingstoke: Palgrave Macmillan.

Carrier, N. C. M. and Kochore, H. H. 2014. 'Navigating Ethnicity and Electoral Politics in Northern Kenya: The Case of the 2013 Election', *Journal of Eastern African Studies* 8 (1): 135–52.

Carrier, N. C. M. and Lochery, E. 2013. 'Missing States? Somali Trade Networks and the Eastleigh Transformation', *Journal of Eastern African Studies* 7 (2): 334–52.

Cassanelli, L. V. 2010. 'The Opportunistic Economies of the Kenya–Somali Borderland in Historical Perspective'. In D. Feyissa and M. V. Hoehne (eds.), *Borders and Borderlands as Resources in the Horn of Africa*. Woodbridge: James Currey.

Chalfin, B. 2010. *Neoliberal Frontiers: An Ethnography of Sovereignty in West Africa*. Chicago: University of Chicago Press.

Chhatbar, S. 2012. '43 Ethiopians, Somalis Suffocate in Truck Smuggle', Associated Press. Available online: http://bigstory.ap.org/article/43-ethiopians-somalis-suffocate-truck-smuggle (accessed April 2016).

Cohen, A. 1969. *Custom and Politics in Urban Africa: A Study of Hausa Migrants in Yoruba Towns*. London: Routledge & Kegan Paul.

———— 1971. 'Cultural Strategies in the Organization of Trading Diasporas'. In C. Meillassoux (ed.), *The Development of Indigenous Trade and Markets*. London: Oxford University Press.

Cohen, R. 2008 [1997]. *Global Diasporas: An Introduction*. London: Routledge.

Coleman, S. 2013. 'Anthropology of Religion: The Return of the Repressed?' In J. Carrier and D. Gewertz (eds.), *The Handbook of Sociocultural Anthropology*. London: Bloomsbury.

Cooper, E. and Pratten, D. (eds.). 2015. *Ethnographies of Uncertainty in Africa*. Basingstoke: Palgrave Macmillan.

Crawford, M. 1992. 'The World in a Shopping Mall'. In M. Sorkin (ed.), *Variations on a Theme Park: The New American City and the End of Public Space*. New York: Noonday Press.

Crawley, H. 2010. *Chance or Choice? Understanding Why Asylum Seekers Come to the UK*, report for the Refugee Council. Available online: http://www.refugeecouncil.org.uk/assets/0001/5702/rcchance.pdf (accessed April 2016).

Cross, J. 2014. *Dream Zones: Anticipating Capitalism and Development in India*. London: Pluto Press.

Dahir, A. L. 2010. 'The Nomad's Way of Doing Business: A Guide to Somali Commerce', *Africa Review*, 11 October 2010. Available online: http://www.africareview.com/Special-Reports/Somali-commerce-in-

Kenya/--/979182/1030468/--/ipbe89z/--/index.html (accessed April 2016).

——— 2012. 'Erosion of Trust Hits the Core of Somali Businesses', *Daily Nation*, 7 February 2012. Available online: http://www.nation.co.ke/Features/smartcompany/Erosion+of+trust+hits+the+core+of+Somali+businesses+/-/1226/1321374/-/jpiqmtz/-/index.html (accessed April 2016).

DeHart, M. C. 2010. *Ethnic Entrepreneurs: Identity and Development Politics in Latin America*. Palo Alto: Stanford University Press.

De Soto, H. 1989. *The Other Path*. New York: Harper & Row.

de Wet, C. (ed.). 2005. *Development-induced Displacement: Problems, Policies and People*. Oxford: Berghahn.

Di Nunzio, M. 2012. '"We are Good at Surviving": Street Hustling in Addis Ababa's Inner City', *Urban Forum* 23: 433–47.

Eastleighwood. 2014. Press Release about Radicalization and Extremist Activities in Eastleigh. Available online: http://www.eastleighwood.org/news-and-events/165-eastleighwood-the-press-release-about-radicaliza-tion-and-extremist-activities-in-eastleigh (accessed April 2016).

Eisenberg, A. J. 2012. 'Hip-Hop and Cultural Citizenship on Kenya's "Swahili Coast"', *Africa* 82 (4): 556–78.

Elliott, H. R. 2012. *Refugee Resettlement: The View from Kenya. Findings from Field Research in Nairobi and Kakuma Refugee Camp*, research report for KNOW RESET. Available online: http://www.know-reset.eu/files/texts/00695_20130530121940_carim-knowresetrr-2012–01.pdf (accessed April 2016).

——— 2014. 'Somali Displacements and Shifting Markets: Camel Milk in Nairobi's Eastleigh Estate'. In A. Hamma (ed.), *Displacement Economies: Paradoxes of Crisis and Creativity*. London: Zed Books.

Elliott, H. R. and Lochery, E. 2011. 'Shifting Markets in the Northern Kenyan Borderlands: The Case of Western Donations and Dubai Duty Free', unpublished presentation, British Institute in Eastern Africa Research Day, 19 March, St Hugh's College, Oxford.

Eno, M. A. 2005. 'The Homogeneity of the Somali People: A Study of the Somali Bantu Ethnic Community'. Ph.D. thesis, St Clements University.

Eno, O. A. and Eno, M. A. 2007. 'From Tanzania to Somalia and Back Again: Twice Diaspora Somali Bantus'. In A. M. Kusow and S. R. Bjork (eds.), *From Mogadishu to Dixon: The Somali Diaspora in a Global Context*. Trenton, NJ: Red Sea Press.

Ensminger, J. 2001. 'Reputations, Trust and the Principal Agent Problem'. In K. Cook (ed.), *Trust in Society*. New York: Russell Sage Foundation.

Eriksen, T. H., Laidlaw, J., Mair, J., Martin, K. and Venkatesan, S. 2015. 'The Concept of Neoliberalism has Become an Obstacle to the Anthropological Understanding of the Twenty-first Century', *Journal of the Royal Anthropological Institute* 21 (4): 911–23.

BIBLIOGRAPHY

Escobar, A. 1995. *Encountering Development: The Making and Unmaking of the Third World*. Princeton: Princeton University Press.

Farah, N. 2002. 'Of Tamarind and Cosmopolitanism'. In H. Engdahl (ed.), *Witness Literature: Proceedings of the Nobel Centennial Symposium*. London: World Scientific.

Ferguson, J. 2006. *Global Shadows: Africa in the Neoliberal World Order*. Durham, NC: Duke University Press.

Feyissa, D. and Hoehne, M. V. (eds.). 2010. *Borders and Borderlands as Resources in the Horn of Africa*. Woodbridge: James Currey.

Fourie, E. 2014. 'Model Students: Policy Emulation, Modernization, and Kenya's Vision 2030', *African Affairs* 113 (453): 540–62.

Fratkin, E. 2001. 'East African Pastoralism in Transition: Maasai, Boran, and Rendille Cases', *African Studies Review* 44 (3): 1–25.

Fukuyama, F. 1995. *Trust: The Social Virtues and the Creation of Prosperity*. New York: Free Press.

Gambetta, D. (ed.). 1988. *Trust: Making and Breaking Cooperative Relations*. Oxford: Basil Blackwell.

Gatrell, P. 2013. *The Making of the Modern Refugee*. Oxford: Oxford University Press.

Geertz, C. 1978. 'The Bazaar Economy: Information and Search in Peasant Marketing', *American Economic Review* 68 (2): 28–32.

Gertz, G. 2008. *Kenya's Trade Liberalization of the 1980s and 1990s: Policies, Impacts, and Implications*, Carnegie Endowment for International Peace. Available online: http://carnegieendowment.org/files/kenya_background.pdf (accessed June 2016).

Geschiere, P. 2009. *The Perils of Belonging: Autochthony, Citizenship, and Exclusion in Africa and Europe*. Chicago: University of Chicago Press.

Getachew, K. N. 1996. 'The Displacement and Return of Pastoralists in Southern Ethiopia: A Case Study of the Garri'. In T. Allen (ed.), *In Search of Cool Ground: War, Flight and Homecoming in Northeast Africa*. London: James Currey.

Gitau, P. 2015. 'Building of Kenya–Somalia Wall Begins', *Standard Digital*, 16 April 2015. Available online: http://www.standardmedia.co.ke/article/2000158488/building-of-kenya-somalia-border-wall-begins (accessed April 2016).

Glick Schiller, N. and Caglar, A. 2010. *Locating Migration: Rescaling Cities and Migrants*. Ithaca, NY: Cornell University Press.

Goldsmith, P. 1994. 'Symbiosis and Transformation in Kenya's Meru District'. Ph.D. thesis, University of Florida.

———— 1997. 'The Somali Impact on Kenya, 1990–1993: The View from the Camps'. In H. M. Adam and R. Ford (eds.), *Mending Rips in the Sky: Options for Somali Communities in the 21st Century*. Lawrenceville, NJ: Red Sea Press.

BIBLIOGRAPHY

———— 2008. 'Eastleigh Goes Global', *The East African*, 17 August 2008. Available online: http://www.theeastafrican.co.ke/magazine/-/434746/457396/-/153e07h/-/index.html (accessed April 2016).

Graeber, D. 2011. *Debt: The First 5000 Years*. Brooklyn, NY: Melville House Publishing.

Grant, R. and Nijman, J. 2004. 'Globalization and the Corporate Geography of Cities in the Less-Developed World', *Annals of the Association of American Geographers* 92 (2): 320–40.

Gupta, A. and Ferguson, J. (eds.). 1997. *Anthropological Locations: Boundaries and Grounds of a Field Science*. Berkeley: University of California Press.

Guyer, J. I. 2004. *Marginal Gains: Monetary Transactions in Atlantic Africa*. Chicago: University of Chicago Press.

Hake, A. 1977. *African Metropolis: Nairobi's Self-Help City*. New York: St Martin's Press.

Halliman, D. M. and Morgan, W. T. W. 1967. 'The City of Nairobi'. In W. T. W. Morgan (ed.), *Nairobi: City and Region*. Nairobi: Oxford University Press.

Hammar, A. (ed.) 2014. *Displacement Economies: Paradoxes of Crisis and Creativity*. London: Zed Books.

Hammond, L. 2015. 'Diaspora Returnees to Somaliland: Heroes of Development or Job-stealing Scoundrels?' In L. Akesson and M. Eriksson-Baaz (eds.), *Africa's Return Migrants: The New Developers?* London: Zed Books.

Haneke, G. 2002. 'The Multidimensionality of Oromo Identity'. In G. Schlee (ed.), *Imagined Differences: Hatred and the Construction of Identity*. Hamburg: Lit.

Hanna, W. J. and Hanna, J. L. 1971. *Urban Dynamics in Black Africa*. Chicago: Aldine-Atherton.

Hansen, K. T. 2000. *Salaula: The World of Secondhand Clothing and Zambia*. Chicago: University of Chicago Press.

Hansen, P. 2008. 'Circumcising Migration: Gendering Return Migration among Somalilanders', *Journal of Ethnic and Migration Studies* 34: 1109–25.

———— 2014. 'Diaspora Returnees in Somaliland's Displacement Economy'. In A. Hammar (ed.), *Displacement Economies: Paradoxes of Crisis and Creativity*. London: Zed Books.

Hansen, S. J. 2013. *Al-Shabaab in Somalia: The History and Ideology of a Militant Islamist Group*. London: Hurst.

Harriss, J. 2003. '"Widening the Radius of Trust": Ethnographic Explorations of Trust and Indian Business', *Journal of the Royal Anthropological Institute* 9 (4): 755–73.

Hart, K. 1988. 'Kinship, Contract and Trust: The Economic Organisation of Migrants in an African City Slum'. In D. Gambetta (ed.), *Trust: Making and Breaking Cooperative Relations*. Oxford: Basil Blackwell.

————— 2015. 'How the Informal Economy Took Over the World'. In P. Mörtenböck, H. Mooshammer, T. Cruz and F. Forman (eds.), *Informal Market Worlds: The Architecture of Economic Pressure*. NA1010 Publishers.

Harvey, P. and Knox, H. 2012. 'The Enchantments of Infrastructure', *Mobilities* 7 (4): 521–36.

Hassen, M. 1990. *The Oromo of Ethiopia: A History, 1570–1860*. Cambridge: Cambridge University Press.

————— 2015. *The Oromo and the Christian Kingdom of Ethiopia 1300–1700*. Woodbridge: James Currey.

Haugen, H. O. and Carling, J. 2005. 'On the Edge of the Chinese Diaspora: The Surge of Baihuo Business in an African City', *Ethnic and Racial Studies* 28 (4): 639–62.

Haugerud, A., Stone, P. M. and Little, P. 2000. *Commodities and Globalization: Anthropological Perspectives*. Lanham, MD: Rowman & Littlefield.

Hecht, E. D. 1987. 'Harar and Lamu: A Comparison of Two East African Muslim Societies', *Transafrican Journal of History* 16: 1–23.

Herz, M. 2012. 'Somali Refugees in Eastleigh, Nairobi'. In K. Pinther, L. Förster and C. Hanussek (eds.), *Afropolis: City, Media, Art*. Johannesburg: Jacana Media.

Himbara, D. 1993. 'Myths and Realities of Kenyan Capitalism', *Journal of Modern African Studies* 31 (1): 93–107.

Hoehne, M. V. 2015a. 'Continuities and Changes Regarding Minorities in Somalia', *Ethnic and Racial Studies* 38 (5): 792–807.

————— 2015b. 'Critical Whiteness in Somali Studies and how to Improve Analyses of Somali Affairs', *Sahan Journal*, 30 March 2015. Available online: http://sahanjournal.com/oped-critical-whiteness-somali-studies-improve-analyses-somali-affairs/#.Vrjsm1InNUQ (accessed April 2016).

Horst, C. 2006a. *Transnational Nomads: How Somalis Cope with Refugee Life in the Dadaab Camps of Kenya*. Oxford: Berghahn.

————— 2006b. 'Buufis amongst Somalis in Dadaab: The Transnational and Historical Logics behind Resettlement Dreams', *Journal of Refugee Studies* 19 (2): 143–57.

Horwood, C. 2009. *In Pursuit of the Southern Dream: Victims of Necessity*. Geneva: International Organization for Migration. Available online: http://publications.iom.int/system/files/pdf/iomresearchassessment.pdf/ (accessed April 2016).

Human Rights Watch. 2009a. *Service for Life: State Repression and Indefinite Conscription in Eritrea*. Available online: http://www.hrw.org/reports/2009/04/16/service-life-0 (accessed April 2016).

————— 2009. *Kenya: Stop Recruitment of Somalis in Refugee Camps: Deception Used to Enlist Refugees to Fight in Somalia*. Available online: https://www.hrw.org/news/2009/10/22/kenya-stop-recruitment-somalis-refugee-camps (accessed April 2016).

BIBLIOGRAPHY

————— 2013. *You Are All Terrorists: Kenyan Police Abuse of Refugees in Nairobi.* Available online: http://www.hrw.org/reports/2013/05/29/you-are-all-terrorists-0 (accessed April 2016).

————— 2014a. *Kenya: Plan to Force 50,000 Refugees Into Camps. New Scheme Flouts Court Ruling.* Available online: https://www.hrw.org/news/2014/03/26/kenya-plan-force-50000-refugees-camps (accessed April 2016).

————— 2014b. *Kenya: Security Bill Tramples Basic Rights. Lawmakers should reject amendments.* Available online: https://www.hrw.org/news/2014/12/13/kenya-security-bill-tramples-basic-rights (accessed April 2016).

Hyndman, J. 1999. 'A Post-Cold War Geography of Forced Migration in Kenya and Somalia', *Professional Geographer* 51 (1): 104–14.

Hyndman, J. and Nylund, B. V. 1998. 'UNHCR and the Status of Prima Facie Refugees in Kenya', *International Journal of Refugee Law* 10 (1): 21–48.

Iazzolino, G. 2014. *A Safe Haven for Somalis in Uganda?* Rift Valley Institute briefing paper. Available online: http://riftvalley.net/publication/safe-haven-somalis-uganda#.VxIGpWNGfww (accessed April 2016).

Independent Policing Oversight Authority. 2014. *Monitoring Report on Operation Sanitization Eastleigh Publically Known as Usalama Watch*, 14 July 2014. Available online: http://rckkenya.org/index.php/resources/reports3/item/1183-ipoa-report-on-usalama-watch/1183-ipoa-report-on-usalama-watch (accessed April 2016).

Ingiriis, M. H. and Hoehne, M. V. 2013. 'The Impact of Civil War and State Collapse on the Roles of Somali Women: Blessing in Disguise', *Journal of Eastern African Studies* 7 (2): 314–33.

International Organization for Migration (IOM). 2015. *World Migration Report 2015: Migrants and Cities: New Partnerships to Manage Mobility.* Available online: http://publications.iom.int/system/files/wmr2015_en.pdf (accessed June 2016).

Jacobsen, A. 2011. 'Making Moral Worlds: Individual and Social Processes of Meaning-Making in a Somali Diaspora'. Ph.D. thesis, Washington University in St Louis.

Jacobsen, K. 2005. *The Economic Lives of Refugees.* Bloomfield, CT: Kumarian Press.

Jamah, A. 2009. 'Property Audit Sends Shockwaves in the Market', blog piece published 29 December 2009. Available online: https://wadamxaaro.wordpress.com/property-audit-sends-shockwaves-in-the-market/ (accessed April 2016).

Jerven, M. 2013. *Poor Numbers: How we are Misled by African Development Statistics and What to do about it.* Ithaca NY: Cornell University Press.

Jonsson, G. 2008. *Migration Aspirations and Immobility in a Malian Soninke Village.* Oxford: International Migration Institute Working Paper series.

Jordan, G. 2004. *Somali Elders: Portraits from Wales.* Cardiff: Butetown History and Arts Centre.

Joshi, A., Prichard, W. and Heady, C. 2014. 'Taxing the Informal Economy: The Current State of Knowledge and Agendas for Future Research', *Journal of Development Studies* 50 (10): 1325–47.

Journalists for Justice. 2015. *Black and White: Kenya's Criminal Racket in Somalia*. Available online: http://www.jfjustice.net/userfiles/file/Research/Black%20and%20White%20Kenya's%20Criminal%20Racket%20in%20Somalia.pdf (accessed April 2016).

Jubat, A. 2013. 'How Illicit Trade in Guns, Sugar Thrives along Porous Border', *The Standard*, 1 December 2013. Available online: http://www.standardmedia.co.ke/m/?articleID=2000099083&story_title=How-illicit-trade-in-guns-sugar-thrives-along-porous-border (accessed April 2016).

Kagwanja, P. M. 1998. 'Investing in Asylum: Ethiopian Forced Migrants and the *Matatu* Industry in Nairobi', *Les Cahiers d'Afrique de l'Est* 10: 51–69. Nairobi: Institut Français de Recherche en Afrique.

———— 2000. 'Ethnicity, Gender and Violence in Kenya', *Forced Migration Review* 9: 22–5.

Kantai, P. 2012. 'Eastleigh and the Rise of Somali Capital', published in the *Chimurenga Chronic*, 1 March 2013. Available online: http://chimurenga-chronic.co.za/the-rise-of-somali-capital-2/ (accessed April 2016).

Kapteijns, L. 2004. 'I. M. Lewis and Somali Clanship: A Critique', *Northeast African Studies* 11 (1): 1–23.

———— 2013. *Clan Cleansing in Somalia: The Ruinous Legacy of 1991*. Philadelphia: Pennsylvania University Press.

Kapteijns, L. and Boqor, M. M. 2009. 'Memories of a Mogadishu Childhood, 1940–1964: Maryan Muuse Boqor and the Women who Inspired her', *International Journal of African Historical Studies* 42 (1): 105–16.

Katola, M. T. 1998. 'The Refugees and the Displaced in Africa: A Challenge to Christians', *Africa Journal of Evangelical Theology* 17 (2): 141–51.

Kenya Law. 2014. Case notes of 'Samow Mumin Mohamed & 9 others v Cabinet Secretary, Ministry of Interior Security and Co-ordination and 2 others [2014]'. Available online: http://kenyalaw.org/caselaw/cases/view/99326/ (accessed April 2016).

Kenya Transitional Justice Network. 2013. *Truth, Justice and Reconciliation Commission Report*, Nairobi. Available online: http://www.acordinternational.org/silo/files/kenya-tjrc-summary-report-aug-2013.pdf (accessed April 2016).

Kiberenge, K. 2009 'City Landlords Dump Executives for Cash-hungry Small Traders', *Standard Digital*, 29 September. Available online: http://www.standardmedia.co.ke/mobile/article/1144024993/city-landlords-dump-executives-for-cash-hungry-small-traders?pageNo=2, (accessed April 2016).

Kibreab, G. 2014. 'Forced Migration in the Great Lakes and Horn of Africa'. In E. Fiddian-Qasimeyeh, G. Loescher, K. Long and N. Sigona (eds.), *The Oxford Handbook of Refugee and Forced Migration Studies*. Oxford: Oxford University Press.

Kiminza, S. M. 2010. 'From Shop to Stall: A Study of Exhibition Centres as Retail Outlets in Nairobi's Central Business District'. Unpublished thesis, University of Nairobi.

Kinyanjui, M.N. 2013. 'Women Informal Garment Traders in Taveta Road, Nairobi: From the Margins to the Center', *African Studies Review* 56 (3): 147–64.

————— 2014. *Women and the Informal Economy in Urban Africa: From the Margins to the Centre*. London: Zed Books.

Kirby, C. P. 1968. *East Africa: Kenya, Uganda and Tanzania*. London: Ernest Benn Limited.

Kirkpatrick, N. 2015. 'Kenyan Police Tear Gas Primary School Children Protesting Removal of Playground', *Washington Post*, 20 January 2015. Available online: https://www.washingtonpost.com/news/morning-mix/wp/2015/01/20/kenyan-police-tear-gas-primary-school-children-pro-testing-removal-of-playground/ (accessed April 2016).

Kiyosaki, R. T. 2011. *Rich Dad's Cashflow Quadrant: Guide to Financial Freedom*. Scottsdale, AZ: Plata Publishing.

Kochore, H. Forthcoming. 'The Road to Kenya? The Visions, Expectations and Anxieties around New Infrastructure Development in Kenya', *Journal of Eastern African Studies*.

Kresse, K. 2007. *Philosophising in Mombasa: Knowledge, Islam and Intellectual Practice on the Swahili Coast*. Edinburgh: Edinburgh University Press.

Laakso, L. and Hautaniemi, P. (eds.). 2014. *Diasporas, Development and Peacemaking in the Horn of Africa*. London: Zed Books.

Laguerre, M. S. 1999 *Minoritized Space: An Enquiry on the Order of Things*. Berkeley: University of California Press.

Laitin, D. D. and Samatar, S. S. 1987. *Somalia: Nation in Search of a State*. Boulder, CO: Westview Press.

Lambo, I. 2012. 'In the Shelter of Each Other: Notions of Home and Belonging amongst Somali Refugees in Nairobi', UNHCR Research Paper no. 233. Available online: http://www.unhcr.org/4face3d09.pdf (accessed April 2016).

Latour, B. 1993. *We Have Never Been Modern*. Cambridge, MA: Harvard University Press.

Lee, M. C. 2014. *Africa's World Trade: Informal Economies and Globalization from Below*. London: Zed Books.

Lewis, I. M. 1961. *A Pastoral Democracy: A Study of Pastoralism and Politics among the Northern Somali of the Horn of Africa*. London: Oxford University Press.

BIBLIOGRAPHY

———— 1994. *Blood and Bone: The Call of Kinship in Somali Society*. Lawrenceville, NJ: Red Sea Press.

———— 1998. 'Doing Violence to Ethnography: A Response to Catherine Besteman's "Representing Violence and 'Othering' Somalia"', *Cultural Anthropology* 13 (1): 100–8.

Limo, L. 2012. 'Al Shabab Member Gets 59-year Jail Sentence', *Standard Digital*, 21 September 2012. Available online: http://www.standardmedia.co.ke/?articleID=2000066561&story_title=Al-Shabaab-member-jailed-for-59-years (accessed April 2016).

Lin, Y.-C. 2011. *Fake Stuff: China and the Rise of Counterfeit Goods*. London: Routledge.

Lindley, A. 2009. 'Leaving Mogadishu: The War on Terror and Displacement Dynamics in the Somali Regions', MICROCON research working paper 15. Available online: http://www.microconflict.eu/publications/RWP15_AL.pdf (accessed April 2016).

———— 2010a. *The Early Morning Phone Call: Somali Refugees' Remittances*. Oxford: Berghahn.

———— 2010b. 'Seeking Refuge in an Unrecognized State: Oromos in Somaliland', *Refuge: Canada's Periodical on Refugees* 26 (1): 187–9.

Little, P. 2003. *Somalia: Economy without State*. Oxford: James Currey.

———— 2013. *Economic and Political Reform in Africa: Anthropological Perspectives*. Bloomington: Indiana University Press.

Lochery, E. 2012. 'Rendering Difference Visible: The Kenyan State and its Somali Citizens', *African Affairs* 111 (445): 615–39.

Long, K. and Crisp, J. 2011. 'In Harm's Way: The Irregular Movement of Migrants to Southern Africa from the Horn and Great Lakes Regions', UNHCR Research Paper. Available online: http://www.unhcr.org/4d395af89.html (accessed April 2016).

Lonsdale, J. 2002. 'Town Life in Colonial Kenya'. In A. Burton (ed.), *The Urban Experience in Eastern Africa*. Nairobi: British Institute in Eastern Africa.

Lowe, L. 2015. 'Transnational Conceptions: Displacement, Maternity, and Onward Migration among Somalis in Nairobi, Kenya'. Ph.D. thesis, University of Edinburgh.

MacGaffey, J. and Bazenguissa-Ganga, R. 2000. *Congo–Paris: Transnational Traders in the Margins of the Law*. Oxford: James Currey.

Makovicky, N. (ed.). 2014. *Neoliberalism, Personhood, and Postsocialism: Enterprising Selves in Changing Economies*. Farnham: Ashgate.

Malkki, L. H. 1995. *Purity and Exile: Violence, Memory, and National Cosmology among Hutu Refugees in Tanzania*. Chicago: University of Chicago Press.

Manji, A. 2012. 'The Grabbed State: Lawyers, Politics and Public Land in Kenya', *Journal of Modern African Studies* 50 (3): 467–92.

———— 2015. 'Whose Land is it Anyway? The Failure of Land Law Reform in Kenya', report for Africa Research Institute. Available online: http://www.africaresearchinstitute.org/publications/whose-land-is-it-anyway/ (accessed April 2016).

Manson, K. 2011. 'Money Man Serves the Somali Diaspora', *Financial Times*, 11 May. Available online: http://www.ft.com/cms/s/0/afae0e64–8630–11e0–9e2c-00144feabdc0.html#axzz3AUAt8KYa (accessed March 2015).

Marchal, R. 1996. *Final Report on the Post Civil War Business Class*, report for the European Commission / Somalia Unit.

———— 2002. *A Survey of Mogadishu's Economy*, report for the European Commission / Somalia Unit.

———— 2004. 'Islamic Political Dynamics in the Somali Civil War'. In A. de Waal (ed.), *Islamism and its Enemies in the Horn of Africa*. London: Hurst.

Marcus, G. 1995. 'Ethnography in/of the World System: The Emergence of Multi-Sited Ethnography', *Annual Review of Anthropology* 24: 95–117.

Martin, L. 1998. 'L'émergence d'un marché semi-formel dans le quartier d'Eastleigh', *Les Cahiers d'Afrique de l'Est* 10: 41–50. Nairobi: Institut Français de Recherche en Afrique.

Mathews, G. 2011a. *Ghetto at the Centre of the World: Chungking Mansions, Hong Kong*. Chicago: University of Chicago Press.

———— 2011b. 'Review of: Fake Stuff: China and the Rise of Counterfeit Goods', *Asian Anthropology* 10: 164–6.

Mathews, G., Ribeiro, G. L., and Vega, C. A. 2012. *Globalization from Below: The World's Other Economy*. London: Routledge.

Mathews, G. and Yang, Y. 2012. 'How Africans Pursue Low-End Globalization in Hong Kong and Mainland China', *Journal of Current Chinese Affairs* 41 (2): 95–120.

Mathews, G., Dan Lin, L. and Yang, Y. 2014. 'How to Evade States and Slip Past Borders: Lessons from Traders, Overstayers and Asylum Seekers in Hong Kong and China', *City & Society* 26 (2): 217–38.

Maurer, B. 2005. *Mutual Life, Limited: Islamic Banking, Alternative Currencies, Lateral Reasoning*. Princeton: Princeton University Press.

McCormick, D. 1998. 'Enterprise Clusters in Africa: On the Way to Industrialisation', Institute of Development Studies Discussion Paper 366. Available online: https://www.ids.ac.uk/files/dp366.pdf (accessed April 2016).

Meagher, K. 2010. *Identity Economics: Social Networks and the Informal Economy in Nigeria*. Ibadan: James Currey.

———— 2012. 'Weber Meets Godzilla: Social Networks and the Spirit of Capitalism in East Asia and Africa', *Review of African Political Economy* 39 (132): 261–78.

Meissner, F. and Vertovec, S. 2015. 'Comparing Super-diversity', *Ethnic and Racial Studies* 38 (4): 541–55.

BIBLIOGRAPHY

Menkhaus, K. 2002. 'Political Islam in Somalia', *Middle East Policy* 9 (1): 109–23.

———— 2005. *Kenya–Somalia Border Conflict Analysis*. Nairobi: United States Agency for International Development.

———— 2010. 'The Question of Ethnicity in Somali Studies: The Case of Somali Bantu Identity'. In V. Luling and M. V. Hoehne (eds.), *Milk and Peace, Drought and War: Somali Culture, Society and Politics*. London: Hurst.

Miller, D. (ed.). 2005. *Materiality*. Durham, NC: Duke University Press.

Mintz, S. W. 1986. *Sweetness and Power: The Place of Sugar in Modern History*. London: Penguin.

Misztal, B. A. 1996. *Trust in Modern Societies: The Search for the Bases of Social Order*. Cambridge: Polity Press.

Mkutu, K. A. 2008. *Guns and Governance in the Rift Valley: Pastoralist Conflict and Small Arms*. Oxford: James Currey.

Mogire, E. 2011. *Victims as Security Threats: Refugee Impact on Host State Security in Africa*. Farnham: Ashgate.

Mohamed, A. 2015. 'Not yet Kenyan', documentary for Al Jazeera Available online: http://www.aljazeera.com/programmes/aljazeeracorrespondent/2013/10/Not-Yet-Kenyan-2013102885818441218.html (accessed April 2016).

Mohamed, A. 2015. 'Wajir governor to seek justice for Wagalla massacre victims', *The Star*, 16 February 2015. Available online: http://www.the-star.co.ke/news/2015/02/16/wajir-governor-to-seek-justice-for-wagalla-massacre-victims_c1084925 (accessed June 2016).

Mohamed, D. 2013. 'Gender, Islam and 19th-Century Brava: A Brief Note', *Bildhaan* 12: 106–19.

Morgan, W. T. W. 1967. *Nairobi: City and Region*. London: Oxford University Press.

Morrison, W. M. 2015. 'China's Economic Rise: History, Trends, Challenges, and the Implications for the United States', Congressional Research Service Report. Available online: https://www.fas.org/sgp/crs/row/RL33534.pdf (accessed April 2016).

Muchege, E. M. 2013. 'Refugee Challenges and Coping Mechanisms: Case of Ethiopian Refugees in Eastleigh, Nairobi: 1974–2012'. MA thesis, Department of History and Archaeology, University of Nairobi.

Mung'ou, Titus. 2000. 'Mystery Deepens as Traders are Burnt Out', *Daily Nation*, 19 December 2000.

Muraya, J. 2015. 'Kenya Launches New Foreign and Diaspora Policies', *Capital News*, 20 January 2015. Available online: http://www.capitalfm.co.ke/news/2015/01/kenya-launches-new-foreign-and-diaspora-policies/ (accessed April 2016).

Mureithi, F. 2011. 'Major Swoop to Flush Out Gangs in Eastleigh', *The Star*,

20 October 2011. Available online: http://allafrica.com/stories/2011
10210981.html (accessed June 2016).

Murunga, G. R. 2009. 'Refugees at Home? Coping with Somalia Conflict in
Nairobi, Kenya'. In L. Ben Arous and L. Ki-Zerbo (eds.), *African Studies in
Geography from Below*. Dakar: CODESRIA.

————— 2012. 'The Cosmopolitan Tradition and Fissures in Segregationist
Town Planning in Nairobi, 1915–23', *Journal of Eastern African Studies* 6 (3):
463–86.

Mutongi, K. 2006. 'Thugs or Entrepreneurs? Perceptions of *Matatu*
Operators in Nairobi, 1970 to the Present', *Africa* 76 (4): 549–68.

Mwakio, P. and Ombati, C. 2013. 'Sunday Grenade Attacks in Mombassa,
Nairobi Leave 15 Injured', *Standard Digital*, 10 June 2013. Available online:
http://www.standardmedia.co.ke/article/2000085594/grenade-attacks-
in-mombasa-nairobi-leave-15-injured (accessed April 2016).

Myers, G. A. 2003. *Verandahs of Power: Colonialism and Space in Urban Africa*.
Syracuse: Syracuse University Press.

————— 2011. *African Cities: Alternative Visions of Urban Theory and Practice*.
London: Zed Books.

Nairobi County Government. 2015. 'County Government to Spearhead the
Construction of Eastleigh Market and a Police Station', press release,
11 March 2015. Available online: http://nairobi.go.ke/home/news/
eastleigh-sub-county-police-post-to-be-upgraded-to-a-full-police-station/
(accessed April 2016).

Nairobi Sanitary Commission. 1913. *Nairobi Sanitary Commission, 1913: Report,
Evidence, etc.* Nairobi: Uganda Railway Press.

Neuwirth, R. 2012. *The Stealth of Nations: The Global Rise of the Informal
Economy*. New York: Anchor Books.

Nevanlinna, A. K. 1996. *Interpreting Nairobi: The Cultural Study of Built Forms*.
Helsinki: Finnish Academy of Science and Letters.

Njanja, A. 2015. 'Nakumatt Books Space in Eastleigh's Biggest Mall', *Daily
Nation*, 18 March 2015. Available online: http://www.businessdailyafrica.
com/Corporate-News/Nakumatt-books-space-in-Eastleigh-s-biggest-
mall/-/539550/2658188/-/15uhd4g/-/index.html (accessed April 2016).

Nori, M., Kenyanjui, M. B., Yusuf, M. A. and Mohamed, F. H. 2006. 'Milking
Drylands: The Emergence of Camel Milk Markets in Stateless Somali
Areas', *Nomadic Peoples* 10 (1): 9–28.

Ochiel, H. 2015. 'Kisumu Basks in Glory as Investors Troop In', *The Standard*,
15 April 2015. Available online: http://www.standardmedia.co.ke/
mobile/article/2000158423 (accessed April 2016).

Oded, A. 2000. *Islam and Politics in Kenya*. Boulder, CO: Lynne Rienner.

Omwenga, G. 2014. 'Imam Condemns abuse of Hijab by Commercial Sex
Workers', *Daily Nation*, 23 March 2014. Available online: http://mobile.

nation.co.ke/news/Imam-condemns-abuse-of-Hijab-by-city-commercial-sex-workers/-/1950946/2255228/-/format/xhtml/-/p9pnhqz/-/index.html (accessed April 2016).

O'Neill, E. 2013. 'Lessons from Somali Entrepreneurs', *The Stateless Man*, 16 January 2013. Available online: http://thestatelessman.com/2013/01/16/somalia-2/ (access date).

Oonk, G. 2013. *Settled Strangers: Asian Business Elites in East Africa (1800–2000)*. Delhi: Sage Publications.

Oromo Relief Association. 2011. *Ethiopia Exports More Than Coffee: Oromo Refugees, Fear and Destitution in Kenya*. Report available online: http://www.flickmedia.biz/client/osg/cms/wp-content/themes/osg/pdf/Ethiopia%20exports%20more%20than%20coffee-Oromo%20refugees,%20fear%20and%20destitution%20in%20Kenya.%20December%202010.pdf (accessed April 2016).

Osella, F. and Osella, C. 2009. 'Muslim Entrepreneurs in Public Life between India and the Gulf: Making Good and Doing Good', *Journal of the Royal Anthropological Institute* 15 (S1): 202–21.

Osterfeld, D. 1988. 'The Impact of Corruption on Third World Development', *Economic Affairs* 9 (1): 36–7.

Otiso, K. F. 2005. 'Colonial Urbanization and Urban Management in Kenya'. In S. J. Salm and T. Falola (eds.), *African Urban Spaces in Historical Perspective*. Rochester, NY: University of Rochester Press.

Page, B. and Mercer, C. 2010. 'Diasporas and Development'. In K. Knott and S. McLoughlin (eds.), *Diasporas: Concepts, Intersections, Identities*. London: Zed Books.

Parker, M. 1948. *Political and Social Aspects of the Development of Municipal Government in Kenya, with Special Reference to Nairobi*. London: HMSO.

Parkin, D. 1972. *Palms, Wine and Witnesses: Public Spirit and Private Gain in an African Farming Community*, San Francisco: Chandler.

Patinkin, J. 2014. 'How Kenyan's "War on Terror" Disrupts a Thriving Nairobi District', *Christian Science Monitor*, 17 June 2014. Available online: http://www.csmonitor.com/World/Africa/2014/0617/How-Kenya-s-war-on-terror-disrupts-a-thriving-Nairobi-district (accessed April 2016).

Pavanello, S., Elhawary, S. and Pantuliano, S. 2010. *Hidden and Exposed: Urban Refugees in Nairobi, Kenya*, Humanitarian Policy Group working paper. Available online: http://www.odi.org.uk/sites/odi.org.uk/files/odi-assets/publications-opinion-files/5858.pdf (accessed April 2016).

Paynter, B. 2010. 'Laundered Somali Pirate Money a Boon for Kenyan Arrr-chitecture', *Fast Company*. Available online: http://www.fastcompany.com/1507004/laundered-somali-pirate-money-boon-kenyan-arrr-chitec-ture (accessed April 2016).

Peatrik, A.-M. 1999. *La vie à pas contés: génération, âge et société dans les Hautes Terres du Kenya*. Nanterre: Publications de la Société d'Ethnologie.

BIBLIOGRAPHY

Pérouse de Montclos, M.-A. 1998. 'Nairobi: des étrangers en la ville: quelle assimilation urbaine pour les réfugiés immigrés en Afrique?' *Les Cahiers d'Afrique de l'Est* 10, Institut Français de Recherche en Afrique.

Pérouse de Montclos, M.-A. and Kagwanja, P. M. 2000. 'Refugee Camps or Cities? The Socio-economic Dynamics of the Dadaab and Kakuma Camps in Northern Kenya', *Journal of Refugee Studies* 13 (2): 205–22.

Peter, C. B., Wandera, J. M. and Jansen, W. J. E. (eds.). 2013. *Mapping Eastleigh for Christian–Muslim Relations*. Limuru: Zapf Chancery Publishers.

Pliez, O. 2012. 'Following the New Silk Road between Yiwu and Cairo'. In G. Mathews, G. L. Ribeiro and C. A. Vega (eds.), *Globalization from Below: The World's Other Economy*. London: Routledge.

Portes, A., Castells, M. and Benton, L. A. 1989. *The Informal Economy: Studies in Advanced and Less Developed Countries*. Baltimore: Johns Hopkins Press.

Portes, A. and Zhou, M. 1992. 'Gaining the Upper Hand: Economic Mobility among Immigrant and Domestic Minorities', *Ethnic and Racial Studies* 15: 491–522.

Portes, A. and Sensenbrenner, J. 1993. 'Embeddedness and Immigration: Notes on the Social Determinants of Economic Action', *American Journal of Sociology* 98 (6): 1320–50.

Quarles van Ufford, P. and Zaal, F. 2004. 'The Transfer of Trust: Ethnicities as Economic Institutions in the Livestock Trade of West and East Africa', *Africa* 74 (2): 121–45.

Raghuram, P. 2009. 'Which Migration, What Development? Unsettling the Edifice of Migration and Development', *Population, Space and Place* 15 (2): 103–17.

Refugee Consortium of Kenya. 2008. *Enhancing the Protection of Refugee Women in Nairobi: A Survey on Risk Protection Gaps and Coping Mechanisms of Refugee Women in Urban Areas*, RCK report. Available online: http://www.rckkenya.org/rokdownloads/research/Enhancing%20Protection%20of%20 Refugee%20Women.pdf (accessed April 2016).

Reno, W. 2003. *Somalia and Survival in the Shadow of the Global Economy*, QEH Working Paper Series. Oxford: Queen Elizabeth House.

Ritchie, H. 2014. *Rethinking 'Entrepreneurship' in Fragile Environments: Lessons Learnt in Somali Women's Enterprise, Human Security and Inclusion*, IS Academy on Human Security Occasional Paper #9.

Robertson, C. 1997. *Trouble Showed the Way: Women, Men and Trade in the Nairobi Area, 1890–1990*. Bloomington: Indiana University Press.

Rono, J. K. 2002. 'The Impact of the Structural Adjustment Programmes on Kenyan Society', *Journal of Social Development in Africa* 17 (1): 81–98.

Rosenfeld, M. 2012. 'Mobility and Social Capital among Lebanese and Beninese Entrepreneurs Engaged in Transnational Trade', *International Review of Sociology* 22 (2): 211–28.

BIBLIOGRAPHY

Sachs, W. (ed.). 1992. *The Development Dictionary: A Guide to Knowledge as Power.* London: Zed Books.

Sadouni, S. 2009. 'God is not "Unemployed": Journeys of Somali Refugees in Johannesburg', *African Studies* 68 (2): 235–49.

Samatar, H. M. 2008. 'Experiences of Somali Entrepreneurs in the Twin Cities', *Bildhaan: An International Journal of Somali Studies* 4: 78–91.

Sangira, S. 2012. 'Eastleigh Dual Carriage Tender Finally Advertised', *The Star*, 4 January 2012.

Sassen, S. 2005. 'The Global City: Introducing a Concept', *Brown Journal of World Affairs* 9 (2): 27–43.

Sayer, A. 2001. 'For a Cultural Critical Political Economy', *Antipode* 33: 687–708.

Schlee, G. 1989. *Identities on the Move: Clanship and Pastoralism in Northern Kenya.* Manchester: Manchester University Press.

———— 2007. 'Brothers of the Boran Once Again: On the Fading Popularity of Certain Somali Identities in Northern Kenya', *Journal of Eastern African Studies* 1 (3): 417–35.

Scott, J.C. 1999. *Seeing Like a State: How certain schemes to improve the human condition have failed.* New Haven: Yale University Press.

———— 2012. *Two Cheers for Anarchism: Six Easy Pieces on Autonomy, Dignity, and Meaningful Work and Play.* Princeton: Princeton University Press.

Seal, A. and Bailey, R. 2013. 'The 2011 Famine in Somalia: Lessons Learnt from a Failed Response?' *Conflict and Health* 7 (22): 1–5.

Seierup, S. 2001. 'The *Mkokoteni* in Urban Transport: A Socio-economic Profile'. In P. O. Alila and P. O. Pederson (eds.), *Negotiating Social Space: East African Microenterprises.* Trenton, NJ: Africa World Press.

Seligman, A. B. 1997. *The Problem of Trust.* Princeton: Princeton University Press.

Al-Sharmani, M. 2007. 'Reconstructing the Nation in Diaspora: The Poetics and Practices of Soomaalinimo'. In A. M. Kusow and S. R. Bjork (eds.), *From Mogadishu to Dixon: The Somali Diaspora in a Global Context.* Trenton, NJ: Red Sea Press.

Sheikh, S. A. 2007. *Blood on the Runway: The Wagalla Massacre of 1984.* Nairobi: Northern Publishing House.

Sheikh, S. and Healy, S. 2009. 'Somalia's Missing Million: The Somali Diaspora and its Role in Development', *Somalis in Maine Archive*, Paper 54.

Shipton, P. 1995. 'Luo Entrustment: Foreign Finance and the Soil of the Spirits in Kenya', *Africa* 65 (2): 165–96.

Simone, A. M. 2001. 'On the Worlding of African Cities', *African Studies Review* 44 (2): 15–41.

Simons, A. 1995. *Networks of Dissolution: Somalia Undone.* Boulder, CO: Westview Press.

BIBLIOGRAPHY

Siringi, Simon. 2000. 'Year of Mystery Market Infernos', *Daily Nation*, 30 December.

Smart, A. 1993. 'Gifts, Bribes and Guanxi: A Reconsideration of Bourdieu's Social Capital', *Cultural Anthropology* 8 (3): 388–408.

Smith, D. J. 2008. *A Culture of Corruption: Everyday Deception and Popular Discontent in Nigeria*. Princeton: Princeton University Press.

Smith, J. H. 2008. *Bewitching Development: Witchcraft and the Reinvention of Development in Neoliberal Kenya*. Chicago: University of Chicago Press.

Steinberg, J. 2014. *A Man of Good Hope*. Johannesburg: Jonathan Ball.

Stoller, P. 2001. *Money Has No Smell: The Africanization of New York City*. Chicago: University of Chicago Press.

Sturge, G. 2014. *Migrant and Refugee Integration in Global Cities: The Role of Cities and Businesses, a Case Study from Nairobi, Kenya*, The Hague Process on Refugees and Migration. Available online: http://thehagueprocess.org/migrant-refugee-integration-global-cities-role-cities-businesses/ (accessed April 2016).

Sutton, D. E. (ed.). 2001. *Remembrance of Repasts: An Anthropology of Food and Memory*. Oxford: Berg.

Sztompka, P. 1999. *Trust: A Sociological Theory*. Cambridge: Cambridge University Press.

Tiilikainen, M. 2003. 'Somali Women and Daily Islam in the Diaspora', *Social Compass* 50 (1): 59–69.

——— 2011. 'Failed Diaspora: Experiences of Dhaqan Celis and Mentally Ill Returnees in Somaliland', *Nordic Journal of African Studies* 20 (1): 71–89.

Tiwari, R. C. 1964. 'Nairobi: A Study in Urban Geography'. Ph.D. thesis, University of Reading.

——— 1969. 'An Analysis of the Social Agglomerations among Asians in Nairobi', *Scottish Geographical Magazine* 85 (2): 141–49.

——— 1972. 'Some Aspects of the Social Geography of Nairobi, Kenya', *African Urban Notes* 7 (1): 36–61.

Trillo, R. 1987. *The Rough Guide to Kenya*. London: Routledge.

Trillo, R. 1993. *The Rough Guide to Kenya*. London: Rough Guides.

Tsing, A. L. 2005. *Friction: An Ethnography of Global Connection*. Princeton: Princeton University Press.

Tsuda, T., Tapias, M. and Escandell, X. 2014. 'Locating the Global in Transnational Ethnography', *Journal of Contemporary Ethnography* 43 (2): 123–47.

Turner, S. 2015. '"We Wait for Miracles": Ideas of Hope and Future among Clandestine Burundian Refugees in Nairobi'. In E. Cooper and D. Pratten (eds.), *Ethnographies of Uncertainty in Africa*. Basingstoke: Palgrave Macmillan.

Turton, E. R. 1974. 'The Isaq Somali Diaspora and Poll Tax Agitation in Kenya, 1936–41', *African Affairs* 73 (292): 325–46.

Umbres, R. G. 2014. 'Building on Trust: Open-ended Contracts and the

BIBLIOGRAPHY

Duality of Self-interest in Romanian House Construction'. In N. Makovicky (ed.), *Neoliberalism, Personhood, and Postsocialism: Enterprising Selves in Changing Economies*. Farnham: Ashgate.

United Nations. 2001. *Report of the Office of Internal Oversight Services on the investigation into Allegations of Refugee Smuggling at the Nairobi Branch Office of the Office of the United Nations High Commissioner for Refugees*. Available online: https://oios.un.org/resources/reports/a56_733.pdf (accessed April 2016).

UNHCR. 2009. *UNHCR Policy on Refugee Protection and Solutions in Urban Areas*. Available online: http://www.unhcr.org/4ab356ab6.pdf (accessed April 2016).

———— 2012. *Statistical Summary: Refugees and Asylum Seekers in Kenya*. Available online: http://data.unhcr.org/horn-of-africa/documents_search.php?Page=1&Country=110&Region=&Settlement=0&Category=3 (accessed April 2016).

———— 2014. *Update on the Impact of the Government Directive and Security Operation Usalama Watch on Refugees and Asylum-seekers in Urban Areas of Kenya*, 17 July 2014. Available online: https://www.humanitarianresponse.info/en/system/files/documents/files/Usalama%20Watch%20Update_15%20July_v4%5B1%5D.pdf (accessed April 2016).

———— 2015. *UNHCR Urges Kenyan Government to Rethink on Dadaab Closure Announcement*, 14 April 2015. Available online: http://www.unhcr.org/552d12c49.html (accessed April 2016).

UNHCR and Danish Research Council. 2012. *Living on the Edge: A Livelihood Status Report on Urban Refugees Living in Nairobi, Kenya*. Available online: http://www.refworld.org/pdfid/52401e8f4.pdf (accessed April 2016).

van Dijk, R. 2002. 'Religion, Reciprocity and Restructuring Family Responsibility in the Ghanaian Pentecostal Diaspora'. In D. F. Bryceson and U. Vuorela (eds.), *The Transnational Family: New European Frontiers and Global Networks*. Oxford: Berg.

van Hauwermeiren, R. 2012. 'The Ogaden War: Somali Women's Roles', *Afrika Focus* 25 (2): 9–30. Available online: http://www.afrikafocus.eu/file/9 (accessed April 2016).

Van Hear, N. 1998. *New Diasporas: The Mass Exodus, Dispersal and Regrouping of Migrant Communities*. London: UCL Press.

Vertovec, S. 2007. 'Super-diversity and its Implications', *Ethnic and Racial Studies* 30 (6): 1024–54.

Wachira, M. 2015. 'Heaps of Garbage Choke Nairobi City', *Daily Nation*, 29 December 2015. Available online: http://www.nation.co.ke/counties/nairobi/Garbage-chokes-Nairobi-s-CBD/-/1954174/3013246/-/a2lj30z/-/index.html (accessed April 2016).

Wacquant, L. 1998. 'Inside the Zone: The Social Art of the Hustler in the Black American Ghetto', *Theory, Culture and Society* 15 (2): 1–36.

BIBLIOGRAPHY

Wadhams, N. 2010. 'Somali Pirates Take the Money and Run, to Kenya', National Public Radio Available online: http://www.npr.org/templates/story/story.php?storyId=126510891 (accessed April 2016).

Waldinger, R. 1993. 'The Ethnic Enclave Debate Revisited', *International Journal of Urban and Regional Research* 17 (3): 444–52.

Wambugu, B. 2012. 'Airforce in New Bid to Demolish Sh2bn Property', *Daily Nation* Available online: http://www.businessdailyafrica.com/Air-Force-in-new-bid-to-demolish-Sh2bn-property-/-/539546/1396200/-/cikujwz/-/index.html (accessed April 2016).

Wang, F.-L. and Elliot, E. A. 2014. 'China in Africa: Presence, Perceptions and Prospects', *Journal of Contemporary China* 23 (90): 1012–30.

Warner, G. 2013. 'Fighting Stream of Terrorist Capital, Kenya Cracks Down on Somali Businesses', National Public Radio, 23 February 2013. Available online: http://www.npr.org/2013/02/23/172717056/fighting-stream-of-terrorist-capital-kenya-cracks-down-on-somali-businesses (accessed April 2016).

Weitzberg, K. 2013. 'Producing History from Elisions, Fragments and Silences: Public Testimony, the Asiatic Poll-tax Campaign, and the Isaaq Somali Population of Kenya', *Northeast African Studies* 13 (2): 177–205.

Wells, 2001. 'Construction and Capital Formation in Less Developed Economies: Unravelling the Informal Sector in an African city', *Construction Management and Economics* 19 (3): 267–74.

Weskalnys, G. 2014. 'Anticipating Oil: The Temporal Politics of a Disaster Yet to Come', *Sociological Review* 62 (Issue Supplement S1): 211–35.

White, L. 1990. *The Comforts of Home: Prostitution in Colonial Nairobi*. Chicago: University of Chicago Press.

Whitehouse, B. 2012. *Migrants and Strangers in an African City: Exile, Dignity, Belonging*. Bloomington: Indiana University Press.

Whittaker, H. 2014. *Insurgency and Counterinsurgency in Kenya: A Social History of the Shifta Conflict c. 1963–1968*. Leiden: Brill.

———— 2015. 'A New Model Village? Nairobi Development and the Somali Question in Kenya, c. 1915–1917', *Northeast African Studies* 15 (2): 117–40.

World Bank. 2013. *Pirate Trails: Tracking the Illicit Financial Flows from Pirate Activities off the Horn of Africa*. Washington: The World Bank. Available online: http://documents.worldbank.org/curated/en/2013/01/19226573/pirate-trails-tracking-illicit-financial-flows-pirate-activities-off-horn-africa# (accessed June 2016).

Yurchak, A. 2003. 'Russian Neoliberal: The Entrepreneurial Ethic and the Spirit of "True Careerism"', *Russian Review* 62 (1): 72–90.

Zorc, R. D. and Osman, M. M. 1993. *Somali–English Dictionary with English Index*. Kensington, MD: Dunwoody Press.

INDEX